General Editor: M. Rolf Olsen

TAVISTOCK LIBRARY OF SOCIAL WORK PRACTICE

Family Therapy

Family Therapy

First steps towards a Systemic
Approach

JOHN B. BURNHAM

TAVISTOCK PUBLICATIONS
London and New York

To Lily, John, Alison, Lucy, and Ali

First published in 1986 by
Tavistock Publications Ltd
11 New Fetter Lane, London
EC4P 4EE
Published in the USA by
Tavistock Publications
in association with Methuen, Inc.
29 West 35th Street, New York,
NY 10001

© 1986 John B. Burnham

Phototypeset by Boldface
Typesetters, London
Printed and bound in Great Britain
by Richard Clay, (The Chaucer
Press) Ltd, Bungay, Suffolk

*British Library Cataloguing in
Publication Data*

Burnham, John B.
Family therapy: first steps
towards a systemic approach. –
(Tavistock library of social work
practice)
1. Family social work
2. Family psychotherapy
I. Title
362.8'286   HV697
ISBN 0-422-79100-8
ISBN 0-422-79110-5 Pbk

*Library of Congress Cataloging in
Publication Data*

Burnham, John B.
Family therapy.
(Tavistock library of social
work practice) (Social science
paperbacks; 329)
Bibliography: p.
Includes indexes.
1. Family psychotherapy.
2. Family. I. Title. II. Series.
III. Series: Social science
paperbacks;   329.
RC488.5.B8
1986   616.89'156   86-5887

ISBN 0-422-79100-8
ISBN 0-422-79110-5 (pbk.)

Contents

Terms and concepts used to describe problem situations as
dysfunctional patterns of relationships rather than individual
characteristics.

The genogram as a tool for mapping the development of family
relationships and identifying those transitions associated with
the emergence of problems.

Achieving an interactional perspective of problem situations.
The significance of verbal and non-verbal communicaiton.
Identifying individual symptoms as part of repetitive circuits of
interaction and increasing the options for intervening.

The therapist as an active agent of change. A summary of four

different approaches to family therapy and their implications
for the practitioner.

General editor's foreword

The potential contribution of family dynamics to the problems of individual family members and to collective family misery has long interested social workers and members of allied counselling professions. From its earliest days family and marital therapy has formed a substantial part of social work. This effort has been informed and fashioned by a variety and often competing range of theories occupying the whole spectrum of psychodynamic and behavioural theories. This has spawned fragmented and sometimes highly idiosyncratic therapies which owe more to personal preferences and prejudices rather than to the perspectives which inform them.

The last decade, however, has witnessed the growth of efforts to establish a coherent theory matched by a therapeutic practice which relies upon theoretical concepts rather than individual supposition. This new school has moved away from theories that concentrate attention upon the individual to ideas that view personal difficulties in terms of family interaction. For example, it promotes an understanding of difficult child behaviour not simply from the standpoint of the child, or the mother, or the father, or the sibling(s), but in terms of the patterns and dynamics of family functioning. That is, it looks at problems in terms of the family or collective in which the individual performs and relates. This structured approach has led to the development of a more rational form of family therapy, and to efforts to understand the therapeutic procedures and process. This has resulted in professions from different disciplines uniting in a common effort.

The systemic approach, as described here by John Burnham, not only includes the family in the significant systems that fundamentally govern individual acts or behaviour, but also includes its interaction with the wider systems that influence it, for example, institutions, employment, groups, etc. This book draws on the long experience of the author and his colleagues at the Charles Burns Family Therapy Clinic, Birmingham, to describe vividly the philosophy, theories, practices, and procedures adopted by the clinic. It aims to elaborate the concepts and techniques that have fashioned the clinic's practice not only through a discussion of theory but also by a description of attempts to resolve a series of family problems at the clinic. Throughout there is clear advice together with a series of exercises designed to promote the readers' understanding and to aid and develop their own practice. It should prove an invaluable book to all those who currently work or aspire to work with families.

The Tavistock Library of Social Work Practice series was prompted by the growth and increasing importance of the social services in our society. Until recently there has been a general approbation of social work, reflected in a benedictory increase in manpower and resources, which has led to an unprecedented expansion of the personal social services, a proliferation of the statutory duties placed upon them, and major reorganization. The result has been the emergence of a profession faced with the immense responsibility of promoting individual and social betterment, and bearing a primary responsibility to advocate on behalf of individuals and groups who do not always fulfil or respect normal social expectations of behaviour. In spite of the growth in services these tasks are often carried out with inadequate resources, an uncertain knowledge base, and as yet unresolved difficulties associated with the reorganization of the personal social services in 1970. In recent years these difficulties have been compounded by a level of criticism unprecedented since the Poor Law. The anti-social work critique has fostered some improbable alliances between groups of social administrators, sociologists, doctors, and the media, united in their belief that social work has failed in its general obligation to 'provide services to the people', and in its particular duty to socialize the delinquent, restrain parents who abuse their children, prevent old people from dying alone, and provide a satisfactory level of community care for the sick, the chronically handicapped, and the mentally disabled.

These developments highlight three major issues that deserve particular attention: first, the need to construct a methodology for analysing social and personal situations and prescribing action; second, the necessity to apply techniques that measure the performance of the individual worker and the profession as a whole in meeting stated objectives; third, and outstanding, the requirement to develop a knowledge base against which the needs of clients are understood and decisions about their care are taken. Overall, the volumes in this series make explicit and clarify these issues; contribute to the search for the distinctive knowledge base of social work; increase our understanding of the aetiology and care of personal, familial, and social problems; describe and explore new techniques and practice skills; aim to raise our commitment towards low status groups which suffer public, political, and professional neglect; and promote the enactment of comprehensive and socially just policies. Above all, these volumes aim to promote an understanding which interprets the needs of individuals, groups, and communities in terms of the synthesis between inner needs and the social realities that impinge upon them, and which aspire to develop informed and skilled practice.

M. Rolf Olsen, 1986

Acknowledgements

Many people have contributed directly and indirectly to the creation of this book. I would like to acknowledge the support from staff at the Charles Burns Clinic who encourage the exploration and development of different approaches. I would like to give special thanks to my team colleagues in the Family Clinic, Queenie Harris and Elizabeth Wade Evans with whom, since 1979, I have enjoyed an invigorating partnership. Many of the ideas in this book have emerged from the time we three have shared in extensive theoretical discussion and clinical application of a systemic approach to family therapy. I should also like to give thanks to: Ruth Reay (Newcastle Polytechnic) and Philippa Seligman (the Family Institute, Cardiff) for their valuable comments on draft versions of the manuscript and their encouragement throughout the venture; Rolf Olsen for giving me the opportunity to convert my teaching methods into book form and whose frank criticism on early drafts provided much needed impetus to complete the project; my wife Alison Roper-Hall for her perceptive critiques, tireless patience and proof-reading skills which are an enduring source of support; and to those students and trainees, especially Maureen Gillman, Phil Wolsey, Jill Williams, and Lawrence Moulin whose enthusiastic participation and valuable feedback during training programmes has helped to shape the kind of exercises used in the text.

Finally I should like to thank the following practitioners whose contributions to Part III made the exposition of the ideas more meaningful: Sue Richardson (Cleveland Social Services), Maureen Gillman,

Lyn Boyle and Chris Percival (Newcastle Social Services), David Hutchins, Carol Fernandez, Bob Laws, Sue Anderson and Pete Jackson (Birmingham Social Services) and Jenny Guise, Marion Clarke, Andy Packer, Sheila Davis, Jeanette Whitford, Julie Anderson, and Bernard Jones (Birmingham Divorce Court Welfare Service). However, any errors must remain my responsibility.

John Burnham, 1986

Introduction

The position of family therapy in social work and allied fields

Working with families has always been part of social work. Family therapy, however, is being used increasingly in almost all the helping professions. This approach looks at problems within the system of relationships in which they occur, and aims to promote change by intervening in the broader system rather than in the individual alone. Social work, psychiatry, psychology, and nursing have all embraced the approach to a greater or lesser extent. This in turn has often resulted in professionals from the same or different disciplines working together in *ad hoc* support groups or formalized teams. Although each professional contributes knowledge and skills from his or her own discipline the result is more than multi-disciplinary. The approach that is created and shared is often *trans*-disciplinary since the systemic constructs and working methods do not belong to any of the traditional helping professions and are therefore available to all.

Families of various sizes, configurations, creeds, and cultures are perhaps the most commonly occurring relationship systems with which professions work, and as such they are the focus of this book. However, a systemic approach can be useful when working with and between other systems, such as schools, residential establishments, hospitals, professional networks, and work settings.

2 Family therapy

Key historical developments

Hoffman (1981) and Walrond-Skinner (1981a) point out that in both the UK and USA the conception and early development of family therapy began in the 1950s. The initiatives were often unknown to one another, with projects vigorously 'ploughing their own furrow'. In various venues and through different approaches the utility of family therapy was discovered and theoretical models that conceptualized the family as a system were developed. Theoretical contributions to this movement came from such sources as general system theory, communication theory, and cybernetics. Innovative therapists such as John Bowlby, John Bell, Nathan Ackerman began experimenting with seeing whole families instead of the 'identified patient' alone.

Theoreticians and practitioners alike began to explore the family as a 'system', that is as an entity whose parts interact, co-vary, and evolve with each other in ways which maintain and protect existing patterns of living and adapt to change by creating and promoting new patterns. Within this framework of understanding, symptoms were given a new meaning and led to different therapeutic action. Emphasis shifted from seeing and treating symptoms as expressions of an individual's internal conflict to viewing problems as serving a systemic function in balancing or unbalancing relationship patterns of which the individual is a part.

As this movement gathered momentum it required (and so produced) a language that described situations in terms of interactions, and developed different ways of intervening in these interactions. Therapists began taking on a more active, directive role than previously with the aim of creating a context for change as well as, or in preference to, giving insight into intrapsychic phenomena.

There continue to be many people 'ploughing different furrows' in the development of this field. All seem to share a basic conviction that a systemic understanding of problems is a necessary prerequisite to the initiation of change. The significant differences between schools often emerge on such questions as: What change is necessary? How should change be triggered and promoted? What part should a therapist play in achieving change? These differences have led to a very fertile period in which many novel, creative, and effective ways of working with problems have emerged.

The contribution of this book

This book aims to introduce and elaborate on a collection of concepts and techniques that I have found particularly useful in my work over a period of twelve years. This collection comes from a variety of schools of family therapy, all of which may be thought of as coming under the broad heading of a systemic approach.

Minuchin's 'structural' therapy, the 'strategic' approach of Haley, and the 'brief' therapy model as practised at the Mental Research Institute (Palo Alto) are included as important, formative, and, to varying extents, continuing influences on my thinking and practice. Since 1979 the Milan model (often described synonymously with 'systemic' family therapy) has become the approach that is most influential to the practice and teaching developed by the family therapy team in which I work at Charles Burns Clinic.

The presentation of these ideas and techniques is punctuated by a series of exercises designed to stimulate an interaction between the author and the reader. This style represents the teaching approach I have developed together with various colleagues over a period of ten years in workshops and training programmes. Therefore I intend that readers will be able to use the specific tasks and the general format of the exercises in a variety of training contexts.

The organization of this book

A systemic approach to working with families offers a different view, language, and range of techniques to tackle the problems that face the helping professions.

Part I introduces a framework of systemic concepts and terms with which to analyse, understand, and describe presenting problems. The conceptual notions of relationship types, interactional sequences, the family life cycle, and family tree are outlined as tools that help workers to construct and represent a problem as part of a relationship system of which it is a functional part. The section ends by describing how different schools of family therapy use this framework to initiate the process of systemic change.

Part II describes techniques designed to help workers convene family meetings, prepare and conduct interviews, and devise interventions according to the systemic principles outlined in Part I.

4 Family therapy

Preparation for interviews includes ways of creating a live supervision relationship between co-workers, making systemic hypotheses as a focus for sessions, and developing a repertoire of 'disaster options' to cope with difficulties. Circular questioning, enactment, and sculpting are presented as ways of enabling clients to give a therapist systemic information on which interventions aimed at disrupting problematic patterns of interaction can be based. Direct and indirect interventions are explained in terms of their construction, purpose, and presentation. Failure and impasse are considered as therapeutic challenges and opportunities for learning.

The issue of agency context

Family therapy originated in agencies and professions where 'therapy' is generally accepted as a description of the work done. Often it is the fate of approaches nurtured within specialist agencies and academic institutions to remain peripheral to the work done by 'mainstream' helping agencies. However, there are encouraging signs that the concepts and skills associated with a family therapy approach are being used to good effect in agencies where activity called 'therapy' has often been regarded as interesting but irrelevant to the main tasks of the agencies. Publications such as Bentovim, Gorell Barnes, and Cooklin (1982), Treacher and Carpenter (1984), Berger and Jurkovic (1984), and Campbell and Draper (1985) indicate that a family therapy approach is being usefully and creatively employed across the age spectrum, with a range of problems, by a number of different professions, in a variety of agency contexts.

Practitioners working in agencies which do not currently practise family therapy, especially those in 'non-clinical' settings and those organizations with statutory functions, often recognize the potential of a family therapy approach but wonder how to implement it within their own agency. Part III examines some of the necessary conditions for the successful integration and application of this approach into an existing agency. Emphasis is on: *getting started* by introducing the approach to management, colleagues, and clients; *surviving* through support groups, co-working, and using the approach in ways that best fit the agency and the clients it serves; and *developing* by questioning family therapy 'orthodoxy' through considered experimentation. These conditions are highlighted by detailed reference to the experiences of four

groups of practitioners working in social services and probation departments, and illustrated through case examples.

Presentation of material and how the book should be used

The format of the book is designed to reflect the interactional approach
it sets forth. Ideas are developed through a series of exercises which
invite readers to experiment with systemic concepts and skills by applying them to given situations. After each exercise the text outlines a systemic perspective of the problem which may well be different from that
expressed by the reader. This contrast or 'double description' is
designed to highlight and clarify the issues under discussion. The exercises are arranged in a step-wise fashion, increasing in complexity to
help build the confidence of the reader. This method of analysing and
tackling situations can then be transferred to other situations and
problems in the reader's own agency.

The arrangement of the three parts of this book – concepts, techniques, and agency context – is a personal preference and something
of a literary convention. It is not meant to indicate a 'correct' order of
learning or indeed a 'right' way to practise. Some practitioners 'do'
when they 'understand', while others 'understand' through 'doing'.
The complementary relationship between doing and understanding,
understanding and doing is a circular interaction in which both are
necessary and neither predominates, except through personal preference. Therefore it might be useful for all readers to read through once
and then begin again at the point in the circle which makes most sense
to them.

Theory

Concepts

Family therapy is more than a collection of techniques used by practitioners who work with the whole family as the medium of change. It also provides a different perspective on the problems presented to members of the helping professions. In family therapy, problems are viewed as parts of repetitive sequences of interaction which maintain and are maintained by the problem. Such sequences may be observed in the present or identified as recurring themes throughout a family's history. These repetitive behavioural patterns and enduring beliefs are interconnected into what might be called a family system. Practitioners using a systemic approach aim to identify and change the meaning and function of a presenting problem within the context of such a system. To be useful this perspective requires a descriptive language that informs and guides actions based upon its premises. Part I of this book introduces and illustrates some of the basic conceptual and perceptual tools that systemic therapists use in their work with families.

Chapter 1 presents problems in families in terms of relationships rather than of a single individual. Chapter 2 offers the genogram as a tool for plotting the development of relationship systems over time and as a way of pinpointing transitional stages during which problems often emerge. Chapter 3 proposes that the concept of punctuation facilitates a systemic view of a problematic situation. Such a view expands the range of possible therapeutic interventions. Chapter 4 defines a family therapist as an active agent of systemic change. Several models of family therapy are summarized in terms of their distinctive features. Readers are encouraged to experiment with these concepts through a series of exercises that analyse problem situations in terms of impasses in the relationships surrounding the presenting problem. These exercises are derived from procedures used regularly in my own practice and during training programmes. Therefore readers may find them useful in their own work with families or couples.

Some readers may prefer, and may be able, to use these ideas in their practice 'straight from the package' as it were. For others, it may be necessary to experiment with some of the skills in Part II before these ideas and concepts make coherent sense. There is no correct way. The contents of this book are arranged according to my perception. What is important is that ideas should lead to changes that are useful in practice. As Tomm says (1984c) 'Knowledge is effective action'.

1
Relationships

Introduction

The last decade has witnessed writers such as Jordan (1972) urging social workers to direct their efforts towards changing family interaction rather than focusing on the individual. Many authors, including Pincus and Minahan (1973) and Specht and Vickery (1977), have continued this move to a systemic approach to social work.

Walrond-Skinner (1976) and Skynner (1976) provided the first detailed accounts of how systemic concepts and techniques could be used to focus on family relationships. Surveys by Gorell Barnes in 1980 and Gillman in 1983, and books by Treacher and Carpenter (1984) and Campbell and Draper (1985), indicate that a systems approach to family therapy is applicable across a wide spectrum of social work contexts. This chapter introduces and illustrates some of the terms used regularly by practitioners working from a systemic perspective. These descriptions are intended to be useful in indicating the type of therapeutic interventions introduced in Part II.

The language of relationships: dyads and triads

The way we describe situations reflects our thoughts and influences our actions with respect to those situations. A description of a problem in terms of individuals will lead to our seeking solutions aimed at changing individuals. If we are to take seriously the idea of changing relationships rather than individuals, then we need to be competent in describing human dilemmas in terms of relationships. It is no longer sufficient to assess a family in terms of its members' individual characteristics. For example, saying that the father is a weak, peripheral person and the mother is domineering and controlling describes two individuals rather than their relationship. An interactional description needs to encapsulate the pattern of their relationship, which in this case would be complementary. The basic unit of analysis, description, and then intervention must become the relationship.

Relationship style and the development of rules

During the formative phase of a relationship the participants negotiate, explicitly and implicitly, a style or definition of the relationship. People then relate as if there were certain rules 'governing' the various aspects of their relationship. These rules apply to such issues as who makes the morning tea and to more subtle aspects such as how affection is displayed in social situations. These initial negotiations and the rules that develop will depend on many factors including:

1.   Reasons why people live together, for example: romance, reproduction, necessity, convenience, ethnic custom.
2.   Belief systems of the participants. No relationship starts off with a 'blank sheet'. Each of the participants will bring to the relationship values, standards, and expectations of how life should be lived, how people should behave towards each other, and whose job it is to put the rubbish out. In a study that included over a thousand families, Reiss (1981) shows how partners adopt various aspects of one another's functioning and beliefs, so creating a balance. The effects of contrasting belief systems can be seen most strikingly in interethnic marriages.
3.   Environmental circumstances such as the financial and material constraints within which the people in the relationship exist; size and availability of accommodation; imminence of war; relative availability of work; threat of redundancy; choice of available mates.
4.   Cultural mores. Public opinion and attitudes may influence a couple's choice about a number of factors affecting their relationship, including whether to cohabit or marry, and whether to have children; and if so how many. A couple may be affected by taboos

about a black person living with a white person, or a working-class boy marrying a middle-class girl. According to McGoldrick, Pearce, and Giordano, ethnicity is a 'major determinant of our family patterns and belief systems' (1982:3).

THE PROCESS AND CONTENT OF NEGOTIATION

Through a process of negotiation, relationships establish what Lederer and Jackson (1968) term the quid pro quo. This is an agreement or collection of rules which may be said to constitute the mutual definition of their relationship. In the analysis of relationships it is extremely important to distinguish between the *process* and *content* of negotiation. Process is a term used to describe the patterns of negotiating that develop gradually through trial and error. Content refers to the issue under discussion. An interactional therapist is usually interested in changing the family process rather than the content. Process becomes identifiable as repetitive behavioural sequences based upon a shared belief system. For instance, an observable process in some families may be that whenever the welfare of the children forms the content of discussion, the mother is acknowledged by the other family members as the spokesperson. This rule may be based on the belief that 'mothers know best'.

The development of process and pattern takes place via verbal and non-verbal communication. Some rules about pattern may be consciously and explicitly decided through open discussion. Other patterns of coexistence are implicit and are taken for granted. The content of negotiation may at times be issues which the participants regard as crucial such as: in which partner's home town shall the couple live? which child will give up his or her bedroom when Granny comes to live with the family? and who will that child share with? More often content consists of the ordinary, day-to-day practicalities of living such as housework, baby-sitting arrangements, taking the car for its service, making the meals, and visiting relatives. Through negotiations about major and minor issues the style of a relationship will be formed. Haley (1963) called this 'the struggle to define the relationship'.

In traditional ethnic groups the rules governing ways of living may be universally prescribed and accepted by the members of the culture. In such a society little or no negotiation may be felt necessary. In contrast, in a society where old values and rituals are breaking down, people are freer to be innovative in how they organize their relationships. Examples of this freedom might be: deciding to cohabit rather than marry; deciding not to have children; or choosing to have joint custody of children after a divorce. A consequence of greater freedom is that more negotiation is required to establish each separate relationship. This implies greater potential for the conflict that usually accompanies such bargaining. From an interactional standpoint, people who live together may be said to develop reciprocal patterns of relating which are more or less mutually satisfying. These patterns may be described as conforming to the rules of that relationship.

Relationship patterns

Interactional patterns may be understood in a variety of ways. The search for a satisfactory typology of relationships has always been a major issue in the field of family therapy. Some authorities describe the relationship according to the problem attached to the identified member: hence the alcoholic couple, or the anorectic family. No universally accepted classification has emerged. However, there are some descriptions that are used more frequently than others and which are defined here.

BEHAVIOURAL CONNECTEDNESS

Hoffman (1981) gives the late Don Jackson and his co-authors (Watzlawick, Beavin, and Jackson (1967), Lederer and Jackson (1968) credit for developing Bateson's descriptions of relationships. Three basic modes of interaction are proposed: symmetrical, complementary, and reciprocal, by which he meant a balanced mix of the two. Each type was seen as having the potential for both health and dysfunction.

Complementary relationships

This style of relating follows a sequential exchange based on difference. An example is where one person is cared for and the other is the carer, as with a client and therapist. In another relationship one person may be perceived as being in the teacher or superior position while the other is in the pupil or inferior position; these are referred to as the 'one-up' and 'one-down' positions respectively. Problems occur when a couple become entrenched in the relative positions. A couple in therapy presented a picture of a relationship in which the man was regarded as intelligent, sensitive, and good with children, while his wife was said to be dull, coarse, and neglectful of the children. This could be defined as a rigidly complementary relationship.

Symmetrical relationships

Two people exchanging the same behaviours may be said to relate in a symmetrical fashion. For example exchanging either compliments or insults would each be regarded as symmetrical. The participants compete to be in the 'one-up' position so each attempts to define the relationship on his or her terms.

A husband said that he and his wife had argued every single day since they got married except Christmas Day 1971. The wife responded by claiming that it was on Christmas Day 1972 that they had not argued. 'No,' the husband insisted, 'it was 1971.' This couple displayed a remarkable talent for maintaining a symmetrical relationship.

Reciprocal relationships

A reciprocal relationship contains aspects of symmetry and complementarity. Furthermore, the participants are able, and allowed, to adopt either of the complementary positions. Each partner will have areas in which he or she will be regarded as the expert. Disagreements are permitted and can be contained without irreparable damage to the relationship. The complementary positions can be reversed if the situation demands it. The less ability a relationship has to be reciprocal the more inflexible it becomes and therefore the less able it is to adapt to changing circumstances.

An example of reciprocity failing to operate as required is seen in a couple whose style of interaction has become characterized by rigid complementarity. The man usually makes the decisions and the woman carries them out. If he became ill and could not organize the family affairs, then she would need to be able to take over from him. It may be that the 'rule' of complementarity is so strong that neither is able to accept this reversal of the usual pattern of relating. She may handle things so incompetently that even though he is ill, he still appears in the one-up position. An assessment of this relationship may conclude that it has become 'rule-bound': it has lost the ability to change the rules governing it. In interactional terms it is not so much innate abilities like strength or determination that permit the individuals to do certain things as what the definition of their relationship will allow. At a higher level the relationship operates as if there were a cultural rule saying that men, in order to be men, must always appear to be in charge of families, and women must always behave as if this were true. An interactional view would see them both as the 'victims' of this rule.

The above distinctions are more than new words. They direct the worker to look for and change problem patterns, not problem people. The latter couple described above were referred because their 12-year-old son was failing in school. Viewing this problem as part of the family pattern of failure and success, we were able to see that the relationship rules dictated that: mother was not 'allowed' to help as she was defined as incompetent; father was not allowed to ask for help as he was supposed to be the one who was competent. Thinking in terms of the rules of relationships, instead of personality traits, we aimed to shift patterns of behaviour and beliefs in the family system. We defined the mother as the 'expert in failure' and thus the ideal person to help her son through his difficulties. Thus we conformed to the current family rule whilst simultaneously confronting it. The strict complementarity between the couple was broken. The couple continued with the work and became able to share the success and failure that parents experience.

EMOTIONAL CONNECTEDNESS

Relationships can also be assessed in terms of emotional closeness or distance between the participants. Minuchin (1974) devised the notions of enmeshment and disengagement to describe family patterns and to indicate a therapeutic direction.

Enmeshment

This refers to relationships that are extremely close, often to the exclusion of the outside world. Most relationships go through an enmeshed phase, for example lovers or a mother and newborn child. On a wider scale a group of immigrants may remain enmeshed with one another until they experience their environment as less threatening and can begin to explore it. Therefore enmeshment, like the other terms used so far, is a universal relationship phenomenon and is not in itself an indication of dysfunction. When enmeshment becomes the only way that people relate then problems may occur. Minuchin offers the analogy of 'when someone itches, everybody scratches', as typifying such a style. Those involved in an enmeshed relationship tend to react very quickly to small amounts of distress in their partners. Differences between people seem to be mistrusted and discouraged. A family motto might be 'all for one and one for all'. Emphasis is on loyalty, shared views, and joint activities. Family members may claim to be able to 'read one another's mind'.

During a family interview a 15-year-old boy was asked if he remembered what it was like when his brother lived at home. After a little hesitation he turned to his mother and asked, 'Do I remember that?' Such families often present with difficulties at times of separation and individuation (for example children might refuse to go to school).

Disengagement

This indicates distance and underinvolvement between the people involved in a relationship. There seems to be a tendency not to respond to changes in another part of the family. A high value is often placed on the qualities of independence, individuality, and outside activities. A family motto might be 'stand on your own two feet'. Taken to an extreme, this style of relating may result in such disregard for the distress of other family members that there is no awareness of what other people are doing or feeling. A wife might say to her husband 'You never listen to a word I say', and get the reply 'Pardon?' Such families may present with acting-out type behaviour such as delinquency or attempted suicide.

It is rare that a whole family can be described by a single term. For example, when one relationship becomes enmeshed another looks disengaged. If a father becomes very involved (enmeshed) with his son then he may simultaneously become distant (disengaged) from his daughter. In a family referred to our clinic it was revealed that a paternal grandmother had been very involved with her first set of grandchildren even after her son divorced their mother. As soon as this son had a child with his second wife the grandmother became enmeshed with her new grandchild and disengaged from the first set.

Problems in relationships

All relationships have phases which are characterized by one way of relating more than another. The question is whether the family has sufficient flexibility in its rules. This would enable its structure to adapt to changing circumstances by adopting a different and more workable organization. Family systems that present with relationship problems may be viewed as operating in an outmoded style which prevents them from dealing with certain tasks in the next stage of development.

If participants in a relationship hold tenaciously to their relative positions when change is required, then escalation or 'more of the same' occurs. Neither person seems able to shift from his or her stance. If one of them tries to change the other responds in such a way that the previous definition of the relationship is restored. Haley (1963) calls this phenomenon the first law of relationships. For example, in a symmetrical escalation of insulting behaviour, in which each participant continually disqualifies the other, one of them may attempt to change the pattern by accepting defeat and saying 'Yes, you are probably right, I am a lousy lover', that is taking a complementary (one-down) position. The other may respond, 'That's the least of your faults, it's your cooking that I can't stand'. This is likely to provoke another round of symmetry.

Such chronic escalations may go on for years with only temporary respite to allow the participants to 'get their breath back'; they are often described as the 'game without end'. An excellent example of this is given in an analysis of *Who's Afraid of Virginia Woolf* in *The Pragmatics of Human Communication* (Watzlawick, Jackson, and Beavin 1967:Chapter 5). Complementarity can also become rigidified, as when one person is always seen as the overadequate partner and the other as the underadequate one.

Levels of relationships: overt and covert

Professionals often assess relationships in families that at the overt level appear to be one type but at the covert level are another. We may discover that silence does not represent compliance but is a son's way of fighting his father. Therefore it could be said that the relationship while being overtly complementary is covertly symmetrical. This idea of a two-level relationship is extremely useful in therapy as symptoms can be viewed as one way of taking a fight underground. It often emerges in therapy that manifesting problems is a person's way of fighting back in a relationship struggle, albeit covertly. Conflict that is not overt is more difficult to resolve. An aim of therapy in such a case may therefore be to bring the conflict into the open so that participants need no longer produce symptoms in their attempts to deal with it. For example, an anorexic woman's not eating might be a covert tactic in the fight over independence in an enmeshed family. One aim of therapy might be to enable negotiations about independence to be more open so that such self-destruction is not required.

The descriptions above are essentially bi-polar terms useful when analysing dyadic relationships: individual to individual, family to agency, nation to nation, and so on. They are useful but not sufficient in work with families. The next stage is to look at relationships in terms of triads, and the problems produced in three-party interactions.

Triads

The use of a 'peacemaker' to mediate between two adversaries can be seen throughout history and at many levels of social interaction. ('Blessed are the peacemakers for they shall be the children of God'). However, the peacemaker's role or reward is not always as attractive as it first appears.

Prudent use of the influence of an outsider to assist a relationship can be beneficial. However, the over-involvement of a third person in a dyadic relationship can be problematic. *Triangulation* is the process whereby the conflict between two people is detoured through a third party; this diffuses but does not resolve the original problem. Examples of this are: a child becoming 'caught up' in parental conflict, a mother acting as the 'bridge' between her husband and her children, or a father stepping in between warring children. The 'go between' may perform his or her task in many ways: sometimes openly, e.g. 'I wish you would both stop this constant fighting and be friends'; or this role can be performed in a covert way through symptomatic behaviour.

The following example illustrates this process. Two parents begin to argue (symmetry). As their voices rise and their faces look angrier one of their children may develop a headache or start to cry. Alternatively, two of their children may begin to fight. At this 'signal' from the children, the parents may cease their argument to attend to the child(ren). This is an example of triangulation; it happens in most families. Taken to the extreme, however, e.g. where a child is repeatedly required to use symptomatic behaviour to regulate the distance between the parents, it becomes problematic. The above example might continue thus: after the parents have comforted the child they may begin to blame each other for upsetting it. The conflict thus begins again and so the child has a headache and so the parents stop to comfort the child and so on (more of the same). The term triangulation can be applied to any situation where a third party gets *repetitively* caught up in the disagreements between two others, e.g. a parent between two fighting children, a therapist between two sides of a family in conflict, a worker between a school and family in a disagreement over who is to blame for a child's lack of progress. When such a family seeks help, it is often the 'peacemaker' who is manifesting the problem.

For example a 15-year-old girl presented as seeing ghosts. During the first interview it came to light that the parents, who were separated, never met directly but carried on all their financial and emotional negotiations via this particular daughter. After she began to have these problems she was unable to act as the parents' 'go between' and consequently they began to meet regularly. Byng-Hall has referred to this process in his paper 'The Symptom Bearer as Marital Distance Regulator' (1980). A different example of this phenomenon was seen in a family where three people were always involved in arguments. No matter which dyad began to argue a third party would inevitably intervene. An aim of therapy in such cases is to detriangulate the third party, enabling the dyad to resolve their difficulty and allow the 'go between' to give up their symptom.

PROCESSES IN TRIADS

The following terms are used to describe three-party interactions.

Alliance

This indicates a situation where two parties have made an agreement to share a common interest or project, for example, when two family members join together to share an interest in fishing, cooking, or planning a surprise for another person.

Figure 1 Alliance

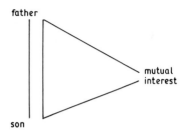

Coalition

This indicates a joining of forces against another. Such coalitions are often arranged covertly. For example, where a mother and child plot together in order to deceive another family member. A mother may know that a child has been in trouble at school and agree not to tell the father if the child does not tell about something that she has done. This example would be noted as crossing hierarchical or generational boundaries.

Hierarchy

This refers to the organization of a family around the notion of executive power in decision-making processes. The power to decide may be related to age, status, knowledge, strength, gender, etc. For example, parents are generally seen as having the power to make decisions for their children and would thus be seen in a hierarchically superior position. An adolescent may be given hierarchical power over younger siblings when parents are absent. Women in a family may traditionally assume a more powerful position than men over issues concerning the emotional welfare of the children.

Some therapeutic schools (Minuchin and Fishman 1974, 1981; Haley 1980) attribute most of the problems that occur in families to the fact that hierarchical boundaries are either too diffuse or too rigid. Hence their therapeutic endeavours are devoted to the restoration and

Figure 2 Coalition

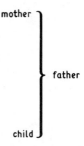

maintenance of an appropriate hierarchy with the parents united and in charge. In the case of the mother–child coalition described above, the therapists might direct their energies towards inducing the parents to make an open alliance for the sake of their child's success, thus breaking the cross-generational coalition. An incestuous relationship between father and daughter would be viewed in hierarchical terms as breaking the appropriate sexual boundary. Work would be directed towards clarifying the intergenerational boundaries and possibly physically separating the father from the family as a first stage in emotional disengagement.

Boundaries

This is a way of circumscribing the spatial, temporal, and emotional territory of relationships. For example, a decision by two adolescents to go on holiday without their parents can be seen as the creation of a boundary. If the rest of the family accept this 'statement' or even help them financially, then the boundary is validated. This concept can be applied to any activity carried out by an individual or group of individuals. The making and breaking of boundaries is a central feature of many therapists' interventions. Enmeshed families are seen as having diffuse boundaries, represented thus: . . . . , while disengaged families tend to have rigid boundaries, represented so: ——————— . Health lies in having clear yet permeable boundaries: – – – – – – . This allows for distance to be established without losing contact, and for contact to be maintained without losing individuality.

Belief systems

The first part of this chapter deals with the behavioural and emotional styles of relationships. These patterns exist within a conceptual framework known as a family's belief system. A belief system is a family's way of knowing and understanding its world. It can be likened to a 'filter' or lens through which events are passed and interpreted. The work of Reiss (1981) shows that families operate within a conceptual and behavioural framework which regulates and maintains family balance. This framework is an amalgam of traditions, myths, legends, shared assumptions, expectations, and prejudices.

The belief system of a family is formed by, and in turn sustains, its patterns of behaviour. For instance, take a family that throughout the generations has maintained its balance during a crisis by calling upon a social work agency to temporarily remove one of its members. This family may well be seen as conforming to a belief that the expulsion of a member is the only solution to a crisis. The more the family believes that expulsion is the only solution, the more it will use expulsion as a solution, the more the family uses expulsion, the more it will believe that expulsion is the only solution, and so on throughout the generations. In such a family the person who is expelled can be regarded as the content and expulsion as the process of crisis resolution.

Some families proclaim their belief system in the form of an official family motto. Beliefs are manifest in catch-phrases. For example, 'Once children reach thirteen they're nothing but trouble', 'Father is always right', 'A house without children is an empty shell'. The catch-phrase of a family whose members constantly argued amongst themselves, and with people at work, school, and in the neighbourhood, was 'If you are a worthwhile person, then you will be right every single time'. Gaining access to these beliefs can help the therapist to understand and change patterns of behaviour. Byng-Hall (1984), building on the transactional analysis concept of an individual's life script, has coined the term 'family script' to describe how the members of a family repeat sequences of behaviour just as actors follow the script of a play.

Family scripts are established and handed down through the generations via family customs. They may be altered according to current circumstances. In an era of great social change it is likely that these scripts will need to be changed or even abandoned in favour of a new version. Work with the family might include re-editing the script so that people can play different parts. This is similar to Whitaker's idea (1984) of helping a family to have a rotating scapegoat instead of one person playing the part all the time. Palazzoli *et al.* (1978) intervened in a particularly rigid family system and likened their interaction to the production of Agatha Christie's *Mousetrap* (a play that had been running for many years) where the actors always played the same part. The way in which behavioural change can be achieved by affecting a system of beliefs will be illustrated in Part II. Earlier models of family therapy tended to concentrate on either the current behavioural patterns of the family or the historical legacies manifested in the form of the family's belief system. Knowledge of the way in which they are intertwined is now thought to offer more options for successful intervention.

MULTIPLE LEVELS OF CONTEXT

The way in which the above ideas can be seen as a series of layers connected through a reflexive, circular process is discussed by Cronen, Johnson and Lannaman (1982) and Cronen and Pearce (1985). The concept of reflexivity emphasizes the mutual and simultaneous effect of the different levels of relationships on one another. *Figure 3* (a simplified and adapted version of Pearce and Cronen's work) shows how the 'expelling' family can be represented diagrammatically. *Figure 3* provides a framework according to which behaviour, to be understood in an interactional sense, must be seen in the context of the episode in which it occurs; the episode must be viewed in the context of the relationship between those involved; the relationship must be understood in the context of the prevailing family script that governs that relationship; and so on in ascending degrees of influence. Each level is influenced by those above. Although Pearce and Cronen consider this influence from higher to lower which they call contextual force to be the strongest, the process is not one-way. They also note the implicative or upward influence from the lower to the higher levels. Behaviour at a lower level can have far-reaching consequences on relationships over time. For example, if a family is helped to resolve a crisis episode without using expulsion as the only viable solution then that episode may in time influence future episodes, relationships, family scripts, and a culture. That is, behaviour at time A can become the context for behaviour at time B.

Figure 3 Multiple levels of context

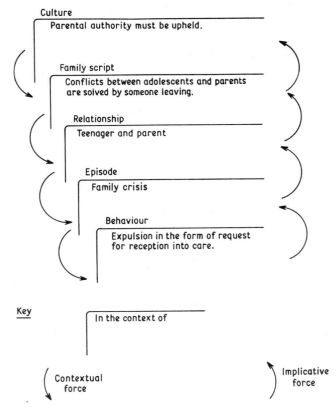

The parents of an 8-year-old boy were asked why he was not allowed out to play unless one of them was with him. They answered that since he had been in a fight with an older boy two years ago, they had not thought it safe to let him out on his own. Not surprisingly this family's script was 'better safe than sorry'. The episode of the attack influenced other levels over time, producing an enmeshed relationship between parents and child, and the child's disengagement from peers. This two-way (though not equal) interchange of influence is known as reflexivity or recursiveness. This conceptual framework can be extremely useful in examining therapeutic failure as will be shown in Chapter 10.

Summary

This chapter inevitably gives a somewhat static picture of relationships. Account has to be taken of fluctuations and variation over time and the family's ability to evolve through developmental stages. The patterns of relating in a family are established over a period of time, through negotiations that are both explicit and implicit. The formation of these patterns will be influenced by the cultural mores of the time and by the particular family's unique process of trial and error. The definition of the relationship will have been reached through the process of bargaining over many content issues. Agreements are reached for a combination of reasons including obligation, necessity, pleasure, and usefulness at any particular time in the family's development. Families tend towards particular behavioural and emotional styles which are based on the definition of the relationships. The repertoire of behaviours will reflect and support a conceptual framework within which the family operates. These many facets of a family's life can be usefully organized schematically as multiple levels of context.

At some future date these patterns will need to be renegotiated either incrementally or transformationally when they are no longer sufficiently functional or emotionally satisfying. Such times of renegotiation are known as transitional stages and are of particular interest and utility to an interactional therapist. The next chapter goes on to look at relationships over time using the ideas of transitional stages and the family tree.

2
Transitions

Information about a family can be organized to reveal relationship patterns and, more importantly, changes in those patterns. By plotting the family relationships on a chart known as a family tree, the effect of the presenting complaint can be analysed by means of the concept of transitional stages.

The family tree (genogram)

Use of a family tree as a relationship chart is a distinctive feature of family therapy. Carter and McGoldrick (1980) give Murray Bowen the credit for developing it in a clinically useful way to gather, organize, and store information. Relationship patterns discussed in the previous chapter can be represented diagrammatically. The therapist can use the genogram as a planning tool, a therapeutic technique in a family session, and as a way of examining an individual's family of origin in a support group. It can be restricted to the family members or can be extended to include other perhaps more significant people, such as friends, neighbours, or professional helpers. The uses are many and varied, and facilitate the shift to an approach that views symptoms in the context of the evolution of family relationships. A major advantage of the genogram is that it shows available information and indicates what else the worker needs to know. Used well, it can highlight patterns and themes which have been occurring in families for generations and may be influencing present interactions. Events that significantly alter the shape of relationships within the

Figure 4 Genogram symbols

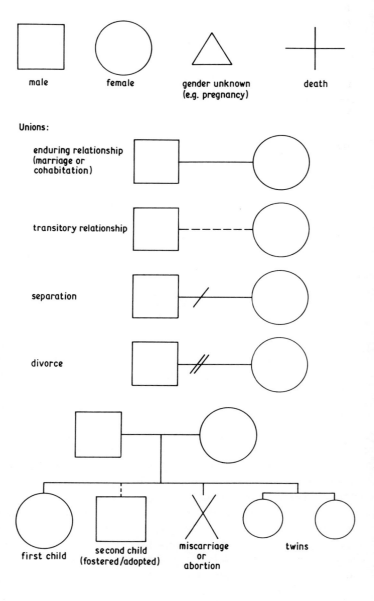

male   female   gender unknown   death
                  (e.g. pregnancy)

Unions:

enduring relationship
(marriage or
cohabitation)

transitory relationship

separation

divorce

first child   second child   miscarriage   twins
               (fostered/adopted)   or
                              abortion

family and between it and its environment, such as births, deaths, meetings, engagements, marriages, separations, divorces, catastrophes, and good fortune, can be recorded by date as concrete information.

Viewed from such a perspective, the problems that individuals or couples present can be seen as parts of a larger framework. This wider view increases the options for therapeutic intervention. For example, a problem regularly occurring for an individual or couple may, when seen in the context of a genogram, be observed to correspond to significant events regularly taking place in other parts of the system. The worker then has the choice of intervening at either one or both levels: the individual and the wider family. That is, the problem in its social context is tackled through analysis and intervention.

THE BASIC FORMAT

A complete genogram should include: 1) names and ages of all family members; 2) exact dates of birth, marriage, separation, divorce, death, and other significant life events; 3) notations, with dates, about occupation, places of residence, illness, and other changes in life course; 4) information on three or more generations. From this basic format and the concepts about relationships plus some ingenuity, it is possible to map out a diagram of most families seen in therapy (see *Figure 4*). Nowadays, divorce, remarriage, fostering, child-minding, and other ways of living together and raising children, make the analysis of some family structures very complex. The genogram can provide an overall view of complex family constellations in an extremely concise and efficient form. An observation and assessment centre found that it could replace several pages of their social history recording with the one-page genogram (O'Brien 1984). Two examples of family information represented in the form of a genogram are given in *Figures 5* and *6*. In the case of a family with young children most practitioners start with the nuclear family. Gradually the grandparents and significant others such as friends, neighbours, or professionals are added.

The family presented in *Figure 5* may be described as an intact family. The spouses, aged 35 and 37, were married in 1978. There have been no separations or divorce. The two children, a girl aged 7 and a boy aged 5, are the biological issue of the parents. The grandparents are all alive. The maternal grandparents live in Edinburgh, while the paternal grandparents live in Birmingham, the same city as

Figure 5

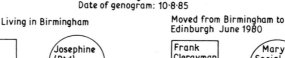

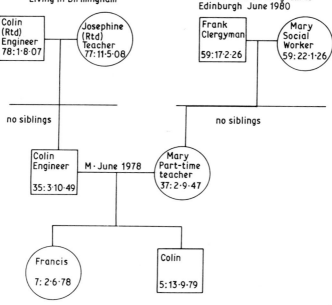

the nuclear family. Even when a lengthy conventional recording format is used, there is more information readily available on the genogram. The families that come to professions are not always as straightforward as this.

Figure 6 shows a more complex picture with symbols to indicate
relationship patterns. This is an example of an intact family who have
fostered a child. Mother and father are aged 35 and 42 respectively.
There are four children: a girl aged 19, a boy aged 18, a boy aged 8,
and the foster son (Sam) also aged 8. Sam was the eldest in his family
of origin but is the joint youngest in the foster family. He was in a local
authority home before being fostered with a view to adoption. He left
his own family after his stepfather battered him and said he was not
wanted. The natural family is closely knit with the strongest relationships between mother and eldest son, and father and youngest. The
daughter is engaged and her boyfriend comes to visit the house frequently. The two 8-year-olds have made friends and have begun to

Figure 6

Name of family: McDonald / Murray
Date of genogram: 10·8·85

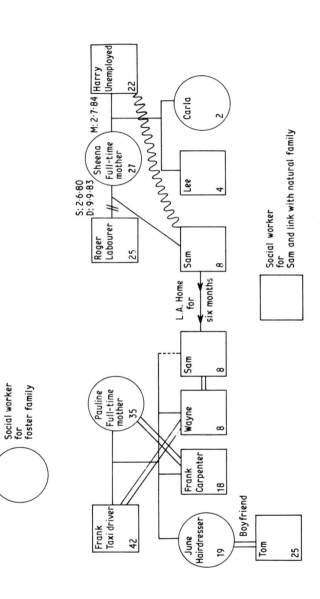

cause the parents some problems. There are two social workers involved, one for the foster child and one for the family.

EXERCISE 2.1
Before continuing with the text interpret the genogram in *Figure 7*, giving description of the family relationships. Indicate some of the information that is missing but would be useful to know.

SUGGESTION
This family formation may be described as 'blended' or 'reconstituted'; stepfamily has been proposed as a better term by the Association for Stepfamilies. It represents a family where there are children from one or both of the spouses' previous relationships. It shows from which unions the children came, when those relationships began and ended, and other relevant information. Looking at the grandparental generation we now see eight people for the children and the parents to relate to. This particular diagram shows that amongst the three children there is one of his, one of hers, and one of theirs. The woman was previously married to a man ten years her senior, and is now married to a man three years her junior. The man's previous marriage was to a wife three years older. The referral stated that Ann (father's daughter) was behaving irresponsibly and causing concern to these parents. Information gained at an assessment interview is shown by symbols indicating conflict between: Ann and her stepmother; and wife and husband since Ann came to live with them. The mother's son is seen as the good child compared to Ann and seems to be in a coalition with his mother against her. We could say that there is a complementarity (good child/bad child) between the two stepsiblings and symmetry between the parents. The father seems triangulated between his wife and his daughter. We do not know the position of the 'natural' child, or how the extended families view the situation. This indicates the need to examine these issues in future sessions, through work with the whole family and its constituent parts.

Thus, the genogram succinctly portrays vast information about family relationships that would take many more lines of text to describe. Of course, different interpretations could be made, and you may take time on them before continuing. The next step is to analyse the way relationships change over time and how symptoms may be linked to transitions in family life. The framework that interactional practitioners use is the family life cycle.

Figure 7

Name of family: Smith/Brown
Date of genogram: 5·10·85

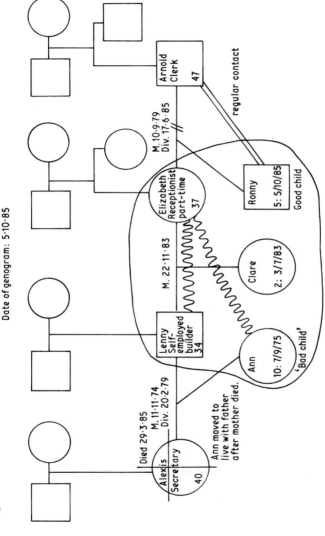

The family life cycle

Authorities such as Erik Erikson (1979) advocate a life span analysis as a model for a therapist or researcher working with individuals. Family theorists have similarly developed a time-related schema for the analysis of family information. Haley (1973) and Dare (1979) outline 'normative' pathways through the family life cycle, while Gorell Barnes (1984) examines common variations such as separation, divorce, single parenthood, and stepfamilies. A thorough exposition of this framework is in *The Family Life Cycle: A Framework for Family Therapy* edited by Carter and McGoldrick (1980).

This model emphasizes the evolution of family relationships over time. Change for an individual is seen as making changes necessary in some relationships and providing the opportunity for change in others. For instance, a girls' transition into adolescence and womanhood is a significant event in her personal development. Simultaneously it may upset prevailing stability and trigger profound readjustments in family relationships.

The mother in a family referred for therapy, described the experience of her daughter's adolescence thus:

'It was as if a belligerent stranger had come to live in our house. Overnight things seemed to change. She used to like to go shopping with me to help her choose her clothes, but then we started to argue a lot. She didn't want my advice anymore, said I was too old fashioned. I didn't know what to do with myself after that. She said that she preferred to be with her friends and told me to ask Dad to go out with me more. I'd never bothered much with friends or my husband, she'd been the centre of my world, I suppose. I suppose I'll have to get used to it. Maybe it's not too late to do something about our marriage.'

The daughter's belligerence and her mother's feeling of isolation may be seen as features of the changing definition of their relationship and signs of the need for changes in other relationships. There is a shift from complementarity to symmetry, and from enmeshment to disengagement. This change could in turn prompt changes in other relationships; the transition, though painful, could be negotiated successfully. The parents may rediscover their relationship with a move from disengagement to closeness or the mother may find new interests. The adolescent and parents may develop a different but still close affinity. Alternatively, as we shall see later in this case, one of the family members may develop symptoms.

Transitional stages in relationships

All family systems experience some difficulties when negotiating a transitional stage. Sometimes at these nodal points in development a family member may develop a problem or symptom that requires professional help. Interactional therapists, such as Haley (1973), Palazzoli *et al.* (1978), and Minuchin (1974), examine the symptom in terms of the impact of transitional stage(s) on family relationships. Minuchin (1974) suggests that the lack of conflict resolution skills disables a family system from successfully negotiating transitions. This deficiency increases the likelihood of symptomatic behaviour being used as an attempted solution to difficulties in transitions.

Take for example the family whose belief system included a firm association between disagreement and tragic consequences. This belief manifested itself in the form of the family rule 'peace at any price' which prohibited disagreement and encouraged a kind of pseudo-harmony. The eldest son married someone whose family enjoyed the stimulation of argument. This difference between the couple increased the potential for disagreement. The husband's attempted solution was to withdraw from any dispute and telephone his mother who would confirm that he was doing the right thing by not arguing, and assure him that all would be well if he went for a walk and allowed his wife to calm down. Meanwhile the wife was convinced that all could be resolved by 'clearing the air' with a good argument. She became increasingly frustrated and argumentative, and eventually took to drinking heavily. This further convinced the husband that arguments must be avoided. The couple thus lacked adequate conflict resolution skills; the symptoms of withdrawal and drinking were their attempted solution to this impasse in the transitional stage of disengaging from their families of origin and forming their own relationship.

Stability and the capacity for change

It has been recognized since Speer's paper (1970) that the tendency towards stability and the capacity for change are both essential characteristics of a functional family system. The tendency towards stability is known as homeostasis and has the function of protecting the family organization from chaos or disintegration. The capacity for change indicates the family's ability to find a new organization more appropriate to changed circumstances.

STABILITY (HOMEOSTASIS)

Between transitional points in the evolution of a family there will appear habitual patterns of interaction that are repetitive, familiar, and predictable. Such processes will be consistent with the belief system and the current definition of relationships. This applies to both pleasurable and problematic patterns; even panics and disasters tend to be predictable. In this way, family members come to know and depend on how others will respond in different situations. This helps them to make sense of their existence and plan their lives.

In this period of stability, there will be a range of acceptable behaviours permitted by a particular pattern. The limits of this range may be narrow and rigid, or wide and flexible. Deviations outside these limitations would usually lead to corrective action to maintain stability. Like the tightrope walker who is constantly adjusting her position in order to remain upright, so the family has to keep changing in order to retain its balance.

The parents of an adolescent girl may tolerate her coming home late, regarding coping with such rebellious behaviour as part and parcel of bringing up teenagers. They find it undesirable but still within the range of acceptability. If, however, she stays out all night without permission, transgressing the limits of their pattern, she may be 'grounded' for two weeks and so made to conform once more. In systems theory this process is known as negative feedback which operates to diminish deviation from the norm and restore homeostasis. The girl's being 'grounded' by her parents has a homeostatic function.

Eventually, however, these limits have to undergo radical changes in order to open the way to a new phase when change can no longer be counteracted by the same relationship rules.

CHANGE (MORPHOGENESIS)

An evolutionary model of the family views change as inevitable. During any transition there is an opportunity for, and a tendency towards, radical experimentation with different ways of behaving and believing. At these times the definitions of relationships may undergo significant changes. Such periods are said to be characterized by positive feedback which encourages deviation from the previous norms. A family enters a period when familiar, secure, and reliable patterns of relating are relinquished, and others are in the process of being formed. The existing balance is disturbed and a new one has to be found.

The balance between stability and change

Loyalties to the past and trepidation about the future make such transitions simultaneously sad and exciting. Family members often differ in attitudes towards change at an affective, pragmatic, and aesthetic level. The greater the dissonance between family members about change, the greater the likelihood of difficulty in the transition. Disagreement and variance are inevitable in human relationships. Intolerance of these differences leads to conflict. When the expression of these conflicts is too great, or is manifested covertly, then the difficulties may worsen and be presented to helping agencies.

Symptom formation

A systemic view would see the symptom as emerging around the time of a transition and serving the homeostatic function of preventing change in the family. For various reasons particular to the constraints of a family's prevailing organizational patterns and belief systems, family members are unable or unwilling to tackle the difficulty overtly. The symptom may often be seen as delaying, reversing, or somehow shaping the redefinitions in relationships that are taking place during the transition. For instance in the case of the adolescent transition cited above, the mother developed symptoms of agoraphobia. This symptom had several effects:

1.   The daughter largely gave up her independence. She stopped seeing her friends in order to be with her mother. She resumed taking her mother to the shops, since she was the only person with whom her mother said she felt safe. Moreover the psychologist who ran the anxiety management group at the hospital involved the daughter in the mother's treatment programme.

2. The parents had begun to resurrect their marriage and were consequently arguing more; but once the mother and daughter were back together this ceased and the father took up his customary disengaged position.
3. The daughter broke off a relationship with a boyfriend which she thought might be getting too serious. She no longer had to worry about whether to sleep with him, what contraception to use, and so on. All these difficult decisions associated with womanhood could be postponed until her mother was better.

This brief example is intended to show how the symptom can be viewed as an attempt to restore the previous relationship definitions or family structure. The homeostatic function serves the whole family, not only the symptom bearer. The pattern reverted to its previous state. However, symptoms as attempted solutions to the difficulties encountered during evolution can only be temporary since change is inevitable. Typically, systemic therapists use a family tree to identify transitional stages. This facilitates a formulation of the problem as an attempted solution to the developmental stage.

Transitional stages

A transitional stage is reached when events make it necessary for family relationship patterns to be renegotiated and redefined. Events can originate inside or outside the system. The stages vary in timing, type, and magnitude according to factors such as ethnic culture, local custom, and family preference.

Rather than taking a judgemental view of the 'normal/abnormal' continuum of changes, one can view transitional stages from three different but interrelated aspects: trigger, timing, and magnitude. Essentially, change may be triggered in a family system by people entering, leaving, or developing. These triggers may occur expectedly or unexpectedly.

TRIGGERS

There are many events or issues that can prompt a family system to change its current patterns of relating. They can be described in many ways. Three basic divisions are as follows:

Formation

Two or more people may decide to commit themselves to a relationship on a regular basis. This process is described in the previous chapter.

Exits

Someone or something is lost, or leaves a relationship, or signals the intention to do so. Leaving may be enforced, voluntary, or by death. In systemic terms leaving not only implies loss and, perhaps, suffering, but also the process of reorganizing and redefining relationships. The memory of those departed plays a significant part in this process. Death, divorce, imprisonment, going into care, working away from home, leaving to get married, going to college, are all examples of exits. Sometimes this may signal the disintegration of a system.

Entry

Someone or something different enters an existing relationship. The pragmatic effect of such an event is that the existing hierarchy and alliances have to be realigned to make way for the newcomer. Whether this is a 'good thing' depends on factors such as the rate at which relationships are expected to adapt in order to assimilate the new information. Stepparents (see *Figure 7*), babies, boyfriends, live-in grandparents are examples of such triggers.

In the flux of family life these divisions are seldom discrete events. For example, someone's leaving may be prompted by another's arrival, or the formation of one relationship may depend upon the collapse of another.

TIMING

These trigger points may be expected or unexpected.

Expected

These are the kind of changes that all families anticipate at particular times in their evolution. People can map these out as part of their future plans. Changes that are prompted by physiological development or prescribed cultural or family patterns come under this heading.

Physiological development: Birth, growth, puberty, and ageing continually prompt the need to redefine relationships by regulating the distance between people. For example, the increase in dexterity that usually accompanies development allows a child independence in tasks that were done by other people, thus changing the relationship between her and them. Carers are freed from these tasks and may turn to other interests or people to fill this 'gap'. Similarly, as a person ages and again becomes more vulnerable, the associated decreasing independence usually prompts a redefinition of the arrangements of living and often leads to increasing dependence on others (family or professional).

Cultural patterns: Socially prescribed events, such as going to school, leaving school, receiving higher education, beginning work, retiring, leaving home, getting married, also prompt changes in relationships. Each child in our culture has to go to school by the age of 5. This custom is supported by law (a cultural rule) and so a change in the relationships between the child and her family is dictated by an outside agency. It significantly alters the closeness/distance between a child and family.

Expected transitions in relationships are more predictable in time and can therefore be planned and even rehearsed. Ethnic groups have specific rituals, like the Jewish bar mitzvah, or the Irish wake, facilitating the transitions of adolescence and death respectively. Major transitions can be rehearsed, as when a parent and young child prepare for separation at primary school through incremental separations at play-school and in the company of other adults. Spouses who spend time maintaining their marital relationship during the parenting phase are more likely to adapt successfully when their children leave home. This type of preparation demonstrates a family system's flexibility and ability to reduce the confusion and distress that are commonly experienced at a time of transition.

Such events signal cultural-specific rules, i.e. that children should become autonomous from their parents. If a family rule is at variance with this, e.g. the child should spend all its time with the parents or vice versa, then such transitions are more likely to be difficult.

Family scripts: Families have idiosyncratic rules and rituals that govern transitions in the life cycle of relationships. These family scripts may be explicit or implicit. For example a family may have a rule handed down through the generations that the daughter who does not marry is expected to give up her personal plans and devote herself to looking after the aged parents.

These levels of biology, culture, and family system are not exclusive and there is an interplay between them. The greater the congruence between the levels the more smoothly will transitions go and vice versa.

Unexpected

These stages are triggered by events that are not in the family's schedule of anticipated events. Their timing cannot be predicted and adjustments cannot therefore be planned. Examples of such events include: the discovery of an incestuous relationship; job loss; a premature or accidental death; a miscarriage; or an unwanted pregnancy. An unexpected transition is also triggered when there is a surprise variation in the way that an expected event occurs, as when an adolescent declares himself gay, or a handicapped child is born. There may be no pool of knowledge in the family or community to offer advice. There will probably be no rituals to guide and support people through the experience. These deficiencies increase the risk of isolation which is already present as friends and relatives may not know how to approach those undergoing such changes. In many ways these events test the flexibility of a system's response to change more than the expected stages.
    Another example of such a stage would be divorce. This would throw the family relationships into turmoil and confusion. A systemic practitioner would look at the ways relationships were reorganized, and the associated suffering of the individuals. Some alliances are severed, coalitions may be formed, other relationships become more distant. When children are involved the adults have to negotiate the end of the marriage but maintain the parental relationship. An excellent example of how a modern ritual, the divorce ceremony, was created to facilitate this process is outlined in Part III by a Birmingham divorce conciliation team.

MAGNITUDE OF CHANGE

This refers not to the size of the triggering event but to the degree to which a family needs to alter its beliefs and behaviours in order to accommodate the event.

First-order change

This is a change that can be incorporated into the existing pattern or definition of relationships. A couple who decide to increase the number of evenings they see each other from three to four while still defining the relationship as platonic are making a first-order change.

Second-order change

Bateson (1979) refers to this level of change as a 'difference that makes a difference'. It denotes a change in the definition of relationships, which profoundly changes the system. This kind of change requires a fundamental reorganization of relationships, not merely an adjustment based on the prevailing beliefs and behavioural repertoires. A 22-year-old woman living at home begins to spend less time with her parents and more time with her boyfriend. This is seen by the family members as part of the continuing process towards her independence from them. It is within the pattern that has existed for some time. Therefore they do not feel it is out of the ordinary, and there are no homeostatic 'alarm bells' ringing. It is news of a difference that does not make a difference. Suppose instead that one evening the young woman comes home and says 'I've packed in my boyfriend because I think I'm gay. I'm going to live with a woman, please don't try and stop me, it's something I've got to do.' This would be out of the ordinary for the family. It would be news of a 'difference that made a difference' at the level of behaviour and beliefs, and thus one that significantly changes the patterns of relationships and the previously held views about those relationships.

Difficulties can turn into problems when first-order solutions are applied to second-order problems. An example of this would be if the parents said to their daughter, 'Don't be ridiculous, go to your room and don't come down until you are ready to say you are sorry.' This is using a solution that was appropriate at an earlier stage, when the definition of their relationship was a complementary one of parent and child, not the current person-to-person symmetry.

The implications of second-order change are often more significant to a family as they can devastate current routines, beliefs, and emotional ties. It usually takes place when someone is entering or leaving the family system. There is a need to find a new pattern or 'map' to fit the new system. From the point of view of therapy, first-order difficulties are more likely to respond to a direct, educative approach. Second-order problems usually require more challenging or strategic approaches. Different therapeutic models are considered in Chapter 4.

The next exercise could best be accomplished on a blackboard or large sheet of paper.

EXERCISE 2.2
Before continuing to read the following information and complete the exercises.

THE ZANUSSI FAMILY   Date 13/11/84

Family members:

Mother (35 years)   secretary } separated November 1983
Father (42 years)   builder   }

Sharon (14 years) Acorn Green School

Andrew (10 years) Red Lane Juniors

Would you please see the above family for possible family therapy? Mrs Zanussi came into our office last week asking if we would take her youngest child Andy into care as she feels he is beyond her control. According to the mother the problems started about a year ago, after the father left home. Apparently there is very little contact with the father now and no hope of a reconciliation. Andy is said to have been very close to his dad and to have missed him a lot. His behaviour includes not coming in on time, wandering the streets, refusing to go to bed when asked, and fighting with his sister who the mother says is no problem. The family are of West Indian extraction and have been in this country for thirty years. Mrs Zanussi's father returned to Jamaica two years ago. Her mother lives nearby and does try to help but without success. The family agreed to come for help before making any further decision about care.

42   Family therapy

1.   Construct a genogram from the above information.
2.   Identify potential triggers for transitional stages.
3.   Imagine how the relationships might be realigned during these transitions.
4.   Hypothesize how the symptom might have a homeostatic effect.

SUGGESTIONS
1.   The above information represented on a genogram would look something like *Figure 8*.

Figure 8

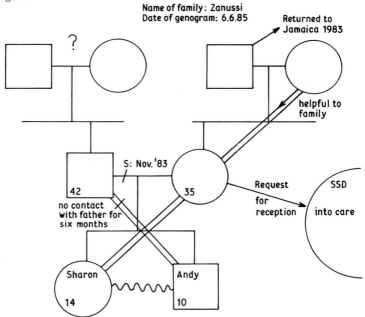

There are several ways of interpreting the information. The following are some suggestions.

2.   Transitional triggers:
     a)   Parents' separation one year ago.
     b)   Grandfather's departure for Jamaica two years ago.
     c)   Adolescence of eldest child.
     d)   Mother's beginning work after father left home.

3. Possible rearrangement of relationships (all assumptions made during this stage need to be verified in the assessment phase):

    a) If Andy was close to his father then it may be that since he left Andy has been trying to get closer to his mother and/or vice versa. This may well have disturbed the relationship between mother and daughter.

    b) Maternal grandmother (MGM) may be lonely since her husband returned to Jamaica and may be trying to take the place of the absent father, thus coming into closer proximity with the children. Andy may be triangulated between the differing standards of mother and MGM.

    c) As Sharon matures, she may be promoted in the authority hierarchy to the position of parental child while mother is out at work. This could spark off conflict between the siblings.

    d) Mother may be exhausted emotionally since the separation and physically since going back to work. She may have become more disengaged from both the children. Alternatively work may be stimulating her and she may be preoccupied with new friends and interests, thus distancing herself from the children in a different way.

    e) An interesting intergenerational pattern seems to be that a solution to relationship problems is for men to leave the household: grandfather, father, and now Andy?

These ideas are not mutually discrete and if they are valid will probably be interlinked. They are only divided in this fashion for clarity. It may transpire after closer scrutiny that none of them is useful and they need to be revised or discarded, and available information considered again. Their function at this stage is to orientate the worker towards the waxing and waning of relationships.

4. Homeostatic function of the symptom:

    a) If the father hears that his favourite son is having trouble, he could come back on to the scene. Andy may go and live with his father if he cannot be controlled at home.

    b) These problems may regulate the distance between grandmother and this family. They may draw her in or keep her out.

    c) It may result in the demotion of Sharon or the expulsion of Andy.

d)   These problems may be the children's 'anti-depressant' for the mother. Each time she becomes sad then the sibling symmetry provokes her into action.

These suggestions are designed to help the reader to make connections between the symptoms and the system. They show the way that problems manifested by an individual may be seen as an attempt to resolve a problem in the family system. You may have generated different ideas that are equally valid at this stage in the work.

Summary

This chapter has described ways of representing complex family information in the clear graphic form of the genogram. It has examined the concept of evolution of family relationships over time and how this evolution is punctuated by transitional stages. These transitions necessitate fundamental changes in relationships which may give rise to symptomatic behaviour and dysfunctional patterns. These symptoms may be viewed as an attempt to maintain the prevailing homeostatic balance of family relationships. The next chapter explains ways of organizing information presented in interview. It introduces the concept of punctuation to analyse dysfunctional relationships in current family interaction.

EXERCISE 2.3
Readers might now find it useful to draw their own family tree. If this is done in a group then members could elicit necessary information to construct one another's genogram. This would provide an opportunity to practise using the genogram as an interviewing technique. Points of interest might be illustrated by looking at: 1) the family tree at three different developmental stages or ages; 2) changes that occurred in the important relationships; 3) the negotiation of transitions.

3

Punctuation

'It is the theory that determines what we observe'

(Albert Einstein)

The genogram has been presented as a way of organizing information systemically by mapping relationships, tracing intergenerational patterns, and identifying the transitions through which they evolve. It can, as Exercise 2.2 demonstrated, help the workers to organize their thoughts before and between sessions. Used during a session, it can also serve the useful purpose of eliciting information about family relationships in a way that is helpful to the worker and interesting to the family. Adults and children alike have spontaneously said that constructing their genogram had provoked powerful thoughts and feelings about past, current, and future relationships.

This chapter focuses on the concept of punctuation as it is used to organize the patterns of family communication during an interview. The aim of punctuation is to identify the circuit or circuits of interaction in which the problem is embedded and so enable the worker to intervene at the level of the pattern rather than of the individual. This approach increases the number of ways an episode can be analysed and therefore expands the possible therapeutic options available.

Levels of communication

Watzlawick, Jackson, and Beavin (1967) distinguishes between two levels of communication.

1. Digital communication. This is simply the *content* of the spoken or written word, such as a statement, 'I went to see my mother

today', or a note saying 'Would you please write to me as soon as you can'.

2.   Analogic communication. This is the *manner* by which the digital message is conveyed. It includes every other way of communicating that qualifies the digital statement. In speech it is the tone and inflexion of voice, the sequence, rhythm, and cadence of the words themselves, that expand their content. This is more difficult to convey in writing but could be presented as follows: 'She *said* she was happy and she certainly *sounded* like she was'. Non-verbally, it includes facial expressions, gestures, body posture and movements, and so on.

Compare these two samples of prose:

'As soon as I walked into the room, she *smiled*, *ran* over towards me, gave me a great big *hug* and *giggled* as she *said*, ''How delighted I am to see you''.'

'As soon as I walked into the room, she *frowned* at me, *turned* away, *shrugged* her shoulders and said in a *sarcastic* voice, ''How delighted I am to see you''.'

The same spoken words may take on an entirely different meaning when qualified by different analogic messages. The ability to distinguish between two levels of communication is extremely useful in family therapy.

From this perspective, it becomes impossible *not* to communicate since all behaviour, even silence and not listening, can be viewed as messages at the analogic level. Analogic communication is considered to reflect the relationship between the participants. It is more difficult to disguise than digital messages and so may be regarded as more reliable and therefore more useful to the therapist. For instance, a family may talk very little but cannot avoid signalling their thoughts and feelings by glances, nervous coughs, and other such analogic cues and clues.

In the analysis of communication the terms digital and verbal are often used interchangeably (though this is not strictly correct), as are analogic and non-verbal. The terms verbal and non-verbal will be used throughout the text to describe communication because they are better known and understood, and because the difference between them is self-explanatory.

PROBLEMS IN COMMUNICATION

Incongruency

A therapist checks to see if the message at the verbal level and the message at the non-verbal level are congruent, as in the first sample on p.48 or incongruent as in the second. Incongruency tends to produce confusion and is generally regarded as something to be clarified and changed during the course of therapy. Attempts to clarify ambiguous messages aim to increase the degree of congruence by helping people to 'say what they mean and mean what they say'. An exception to this rule is the incongruency evident in a humorous exchange, as when a parent says 'I'm going to pull your arm right off' but simultaneously smiles to indicate that this is mock anger.

Disconfirmation

Disconfirmation occurs when a person does or says something but is treated as if nothing had happened. Ignoring, replying with *non sequiturs*, and repeatedly talking across someone are evidence of disconfirmation. The persons thus disqualified may begin to feel as if they do not exist. The father of a girl who had made a serious suicide attempt said it was unlikely that any of his children would disagree with him; if they did, it would mean that they had not thought about the subject properly. After enough 'proper' thought, they would surely see things his way. Thus, a disconfirmation does more than disagree with another's viewpoint; it has the practical and emotional effect of disqualifying a person, not his or her statements.

SYMPTOMS AS A COMMUNICATION

In this framework symptomatic behaviour may be viewed as a communication within the context of a relationship. Sadness may be seen as a message, 'comfort me'. Irritation as a communication to 'leave me alone'. More seriously, attempted suicide may be an appeal to be recognized and confirmed. Chapter 1 in Haley (1963) remains one of the best expositions on symptoms as 'tactics' in relationships. For a fuller exploration of communication theory the reader is referred to the seminal work of Watzlawick, Jackson, and Beavin, *Pragmatics of Human Communication* (1967).

The following is an edited transcript of a conversation between the members of the Zanussi family discussed at the end of Chapter 3. It includes examples of both verbal and non-verbal communication to enable the reader to make a fuller assessment. Please read through it and then complete the exercise which follows

Scenario: A single mother (35 years) with her daughter Sharon (14 years) and son Andrew (10 years) are sitting in a room (see *Figure 9*) in conversation:

Figure 9 Seating positions

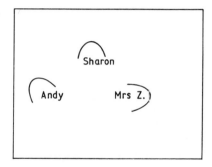

MUM [*to A.*] Now, Andrew what were you telling me about the races at school today?

ANDREW [*very quietly*]. I came first in the running.

MUM [*smiling*]. What did you get then?

ANDREW. Chocolate.

SHARON. That wasn't a prize.

MUM [*to S.*]. That's nice anyway, they didn't have to give a prize. [*To A.*] Didn't you get anything for just running?

[*Andrew mumbles something inaudible.*]

MUM. Open your mouth and talk to me.

ANDREW [*still mumbling*]. I came second in the bean bag races and first in the sack race.

MUM. Well, don't they have normal sprinting? Didn't you run at all?

SHARON. Yeah . . . he won that. . . .

MUM [*to S.*]. No! Who told you that?

SHARON [*to M.*]. He just told you.

MUM [*to S.*] No he didn't, he said he came first in the bag race.

MUM [*to A.*]. How many did you enter? [*Andrew mumbles inaudibly and begins to count on his fingers.*]

MUM [*to A., more insistently*]. How many races did you enter?

SHARON [*to M.*]. He doesn't understand 'enter' Mummy. [*S. turns to A.*]

SHARON [*to A.*]. How much races did you do? [*Smirks at M.*]

MUM [*smiles to A.*]. How many did you do then?

ANDREW. Three.

SHARON [*to A.*] Was it three?

MUM [*to A.*]. Well you can't [*to S.*] if he entered three. . . .

SHARON [*to M.*]. He won three.

MUM. But how could he win three and come second in one?

[*Sharon and Mum laugh.*]

SHARON [*to A.*]. How much running did you win man?

[*Andrew gets up and walks away, looking very unhappy. Sharon and Mum laugh again.*]

MUM [*to A., smiling, but in a firm, sharp voice*]. Andrew come over here and stop being silly. Why are you acting like that?

[*Andrew comes back and sits down but continues to look away.*]

SHARON [*to A.*]. How much running did you do?

ANDREW. Two.

SHARON. Did you win both of them?

ANDREW. Yes, I won the . . . [*trails off into an inaudible mumble*].

SHARON [*to M.*]. Oh don't bother askin' him nothin'.

MUM [*to S.*]. But I want to ask him.

SHARON [*to A. with renewed vigour*] Did you win all the races you went into?

ANDREW. Yes.

SHARON. Well how come you told me you came second in one?

MUM [*to A.*] Come here Andrew. [*A. walks across and M. tries to take his coat off.*] Take your coat off if you're warm.

[*A. struggles, M. stops trying to remove the coat and asks in a softer, gentler voice*] How many races did you enter?

ANDREW. Three.

SHARON [*leaning across between M. and A.*] I thought he said four.

MUM [*to A.*] Show me them on your fingers. [*A. holds up three.*] And how many did you win?

ANDREW. Four times and I lost one.

SHARON [*to M.*]. He said that in the first place!

MUM [*to S.*]. Be *quiet*. I'm not talking to you. [*To A.*] So how many chocolates did you get then?

SHARON. One.

MUM [*to S.*]. Sharon, *be quiet*, I said, I'm talking to Andrew. [*To A.*] How many chocolates did you get?

ANDREW. One.

MUM [*to A.*]. Why did you only get one if you came. . . .

ANDREW. Everybody got one.

MUM. Oh . . . you mean the whole school? Oh that was nice.

[*Sharon mumbles something.*]

MUM [*to S.*]. Can't you be quiet for a minute!

[*Andrew slouches in his chair looking very miserable. Mother and Sharon continue to argue. Therapist enters and sits down.*]

MUM [*to A.*]. Why are you sulking? [*To therapist.*] He's getting all upset about his races. . . .

EXERCISE 3.1

Using the concepts and terms that are familiar in their current practice the reader(s) is invited to take fifteen minutes or so to record:

1.   The feelings and opinions generated by the scenario portayed in the transcript.
2.   An assessment of how the situation came to the conclusion 'He's getting all upset about his races'.
3.   An indication of how the reader(s) might intervene in the family.

Of course the reader would like more information, especially at the non-verbal level. A new skill or idea is more efficiently assimilated if the process is initially broken into small parts.

Refer to the text again if necessary. Of course, some readers may prefer to read on.

SUGGESTIONS

Observers of the above piece of interaction often make the following type of comments: 'The boy is being scapegoated.' 'The mother's attitude is punitive.' 'Does it really matter how many races he won?' 'The sister keeps interfering.' 'They (mother and sister) are making a mountain out of a molehill.' 'The mother must be working out or projecting her own problems onto the boy.' 'It's obvious she (mother) doesn't love him.' 'There's a rule in this family about not liking men.' 'That poor boy, no wonder he is disturbed.'

Perhaps you have made the same or similar comments in your assessment of the transcript. Quite often the feelings and comments expressed by observers focus on how badly the mother, and to a certain extent the daughter, handle the boy. The boy is seen as the victim of his mother and sister. Any assessment that divides family members into victims and victimizers is likely to lead a worker to pursue a line of enquiry and intervention that aims to rescue the victims and blame those perceived as the victimizers. Such interventions tend to be rejected by the family members, including the so-called victims.

John Bell, one of the 'founders' of the family therapy approach, describes one of his first experiences in the 1950s of working with whole families instead of individuals:

'I had accepted the idea that the girl about whom the referral originated was the problem. I heard mother and father, particularly mother, who was one of those women, to quote Saki, who would have been "enormously improved by death" tell about the difficulties she and the family were having with this girl. The parents always spoke with firmness and often with rancor. Somewhat nonplussed by their attack, I would try to put myself in the place of the girl, to think about how it must feel to hear herself talked about in this way. I tried to see her father, mother and brother's world through her eyes, to uncover the past so I could answer the question how she became the problem she is, and to engage her in a relationship through which I could understand and help her. I was full of good will . . . so I began to increase my concentration on her. Theoretically this was fine. Practically it did not work.   (Bell 1967)

What happened? Bell writes that the brother became restless and left, the parents offered elaborations of her problems in detail, and, perhaps more surprisingly to Bell, 'the problem girl did not seem to welcome my help nearly as much as I thought she should'. Bell goes on to explain that it was not until he began to think in terms of the context (including the problem girl) being the problem (in this case the family) that he began to cease experiencing and creating the problems he describes. Bell and other family theorists and therapists, such as Walrond-Skinner (1976), Barker (1981), and Gorell Barnes (1984) emphasize the importance of moving away from what Hoffman (1981) describes as the 'blame frame', in which causality is attributed to one part of the family. This essentially linear approach is based on a monadic cause-and-effect theory of problem formation. In contrast a family therapy approach uses 'circular' thinking and is based upon theories of systems and communication which view problems in their context. Assuming that readers are operating more on the monadic model, it is likely that their ideas have been expressed in linear terms as in the list of comments. These ideas seem inevitable given that workers often, at an emotional level, feel drawn to empathize with the person who is, apparently, in the one-down position, especially when that person is a child. However, as Bell points out, 'practically it did not work'. For therapy to be effective, a circular view of the problematic pattern, including the contribution of the 'underdog', needs to be obtained.

How then can the shift be made from a linear view to a more holistic, circular way of seeing, understanding, and talking about the type of event portrayed in the transcript? Neat terms such as complementarity, symmetry, and triangulation seem to desert a therapist when faced with a live family. Emotions can run high and the session may seem to be out of control. The whole may be obscured by the prominence of the parts. It is in just such a situation that the tool of punctuation is useful as it helps to connect the parts into discernible circular wholes as we shall see.

Wholes and parts

'The whole is greater than the sum of the parts' (von Bertalanffy 1968). This concept is fundamental to a systemic view. Consequently it is impossible to 'sum up' a family as the aggregate of the 'personality traits' of its individual members. Cooklin (1979) likens such an attempt to define a family by summation to listening to the individual members of an orchestra playing their particular 'piece' and then trying to imagine the symphony. It cannot be done, since when they play together they produce music which supsersedes their individual contributions. Bateson (1979) calls this holistic view 'the pattern which connects'. This concept is represented figuratively in *Figure 10*. In this well-known figure, one can see two faces or a vase, but not both simultaneously. A therapist with an interactional perspective alternates between the perceptions but will concentrate mainly on seeing the vase. The vase represents the process between the people, the pattern which

Figure 10 The vase and the faces

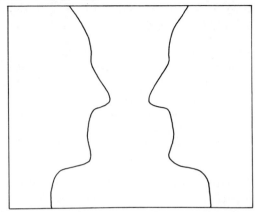

connects them. The development of a systemic view is facilitated if the therapist is able to understand the individual as part of the whole pattern, not in isolation. Koestler coined the term 'holon' for such an entity, which Minuchin and Fishman describe thus: 'Part and whole contain each other in a continuing, current and on-going process of communication and inter-relationship' (1981:13).

How does one begin to 'see' wholes rather than only parts? A useful way of beginning to see the 'vase' instead of only faces is to develop the ritual of punctuation.

Punctuation

The transcript of the conversation between Sharon, Andrew and their mother could be considered in terms of the verbal and non-verbal communication of the individuals; then the motivation or emotion governing their behaviour could be inferred. People observing this example of interaction often select a particular participant's point of view. A debate usually ensues to establish the 'real' or 'true' explanation. The discussion might include the following: 'The mother interrogates the boy – no wonder he wouldn't talk to her!' (i.e. mother is domineering), 'The way that the boy mumbled, I'm not surprised that the mother spoke sharply to him!' (i.e. the boy is rebellious), 'Every time that the boy and his mother start talking, the girl interferes and they end up having a fight' (i.e. the girl is jealous).

From an interactional stance, however, each observation is taken as one of several ways to make sense of what happened. Each opinion is a particular *punctuation* of the *interactional sequence*. As Bateson puts it:

'In the punctuation of human interaction, adjectives which purport to describe individual character are really not strictly applicable to the individual but rather describe transactions between the individual and his material and human environment. No man is "resourceful" or "dependent" or "fatalistic" in a vacuum. His characteristic, whatever it be, is not his but is rather a characteristic of what goes on between him and something (or somebody) else.'

(1979: 269)

Observers of the quoted transaction, like each participant in the episode, tend to select the most 'blameworthy' punctuation. They will make a case for one person being responsible for starting and maintaining the argument. They search for verbal and non-verbal evidence to support their 'truth' and usually within a sequence are able to find some. Some observers may point to the *incongruence* of mother's communication: 'The mother says she's pleased but look at her scowling face and listen to her disapproving voice, she's obviously confusing the boy.' Alternatively, but far less often, the boy's behaviour is seen as a *disconfirmation* of his mother: 'The boy is disrespectful, every time his mother talks to him he mumbles and looks in the other direction, no wonder she's angry.' Andrew's mumbling and withdrawal are judged as a *symptomatic communication* to 'leave me alone, or don't persecute me'. Whichever punctuation is selected it is likely that there will also be evidence that supports that perception.

Each observer will perceive the episode through the lens of his or her theoretical and personal framework. Groups of professionals will often debate vigorously from the position that there is one correct interpretation of the event. A systemic view would see each view as an arc of a circular sequence or a *partial explanation* of the event. Watzlawick and Beavin (1977) state:

'Man tends to pattern the stream of communicational events into an order which to him is familiar and predictable. . . . Discrepancies in the punctuation of jointly experienced events are, in fact, at the root of many conflicts in most areas of human interaction, and the ever present blindness for the other's punctuation, coupled with the naive conviction that reality is the way I see (punctuate) these events, almost inevitably leads to the mutual charges of badness or madness.' (Watzlawick and Beavin 1977: 65)

Each punctuation of a particular sequence of events is but a different side of a coin, or a different arc of a circle. To the observer who accepts and utilizes the idea of punctuation, sequences of behaviour can appear more circular or interactional in nature. Developing the ritual of punctuating family interactions enables the worker to avoid being 'trapped' in a linear, uni-directional explanation. Initially this ritual is done by rote, until it becomes part of one's view or framework. It is probably one of the most important first steps towards a systemic approach.

THE MOTHER – SON DYAD

If the transcript is punctuated from the point of view of Andrew's behaviour the ritual might be expressed as in *Figure 11*.

Figure 11 The mother–son dyad (i)

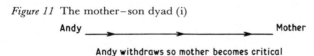

Punctuation from the point of view of mother's behaviour gives the pattern presented in *Figure 12*.

Figure 12 The mother–son dyad (ii)

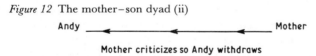

If we accept each of these views as punctuations rather than truths or 'the reality of the situation' then we can begin to see them as parts of a circular whole, as in *Figure 13*.

Figure 13 The mother–son dyad (iii)

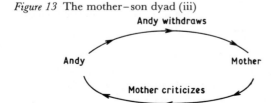

Statements about the behaviour of two individuals give way to two different ways of punctuating how a complementary relationship escalates. This escalation continues past the point where contact can be maintained; communication breaks down to the mutual frustration and disappointment of the parties involved. Instead of Andrew being seen as a quiet boy and his mother as a noisy adult, both behaviours are seen as forming a complementary pattern based on the exchange of different behaviours. This makes the *connection* between two people rather than seeking internal causes in one or both participants. To arrive at this interactional view, first punctuate the sequence from one position and then reverse that punctuation. The description becomes one of escalation or, as Watzlawick, Weakland, and Fisch (1974) have termed it, 'more of the same'. This refers to a process of repetitive sequences of behaviours manifested between two or more people and which go 'round in circles' in a game without end.

Looking over the whole transcript it can be seen that the more Andrew mumbles or walks away, the more critical, insistent, and nagging the mother becomes, the more Andrew mumbles, the more the mother nags, the more Andrew mumbles, and so on. Viewed in this way the focus of the observer is on the repetitive patterns of behaviour which occur between the participants in the transaction. Minuchin and Fishman (1981) call this 'the family's dance'.

THE SISTER–BROTHER DYAD

This dyad exhibits essentially the same escalation of a complementary pattern as the mother–son dyad, with the exchange of nagging and withdrawal. An example of symmetry is shown in the mother–daughter dyad.

THE MOTHER–DAUGHTER DYAD

Exchanges in the mother–daughter dyad show a symmetrical escalation as the following segment of the transcript shows:

MUM [*to A*.]. How many races did you enter?
ANDREW. Three.
MUM [*to A*.]. Show me them on your fingers. [*A. holds up three.*]
  And how many did you win?

ANDREW. Four times and I lost one.

SHARON [*to M*.] He said that in the first place!

MUM [*to S*.]. Be *quiet*. I'm not talking to you. [*To A*.] So how many chocolates did you get then?

SHARON [*to M*.]. One

MUM. Sharon, *be quiet*, I said. I'm talking to Andrew.

Mother and daughter may be described as competing to be the person who can talk to and understand Andrew. The transcript shows several examples of mother and daughter taking it in turns to question Andrew about the content issue of the races and then disputing who has the better understanding. This can be described as a symmetrical relationship in this context. The more the mother claims that she understands what Andrew means, the more Sharon claims that she has a better understanding, and so on.

THE MOTHER–DAUGHTER–SON TRIAD

The analysis becomes more complex and more useful when the interaction is examined triadically. A fine example of the concept of triangulation is displayed by the triad involved in the episode. Consider the following sequence:

MUM [*to A*.] How many did you enter?

[*Andrew mumbles inaudibly and begins to count on his fingers*.]

MUM [*to A., more insistently*]. How many races did you enter?

SHARON [*to M*.] He doesn't understand 'enter' Mummy. [*S. turns to A*.]

SHARON [*to A*.] How much races did you do? [*Smirks*.]

MUM [*smiles to A*.] How many races did you do then?

Including Sharon in a linear analysis could lead to the conclusion that the problem is not the boy or his mother. Instead it is the way that the girl persistently butts into their conversation. It could be said that Andrew and his mother do not resolve their difficulties because Sharon interferes or interprets for them (in this and other sequences). If the observer repunctuates, then equally it could be said that Mother and Andrew always turn to Sharon when they cannot resolve their difficulties. That is, Sharon may be described as pushing in or as being pulled in.

This analysis can be taken a stage further by connecting these two punctuations in a circular or spiralling fashion, as in the sequence between Andrew and mother. The following description could apply: The more Andrew and his mother seem not to understand each other, the more Sharon offers/is required to interpret for them, the more she interprets for them, the more they seem not to understand each other, and so on.

Figure 14 A three-person sequence

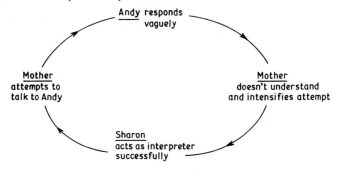

Some readers may be able to transfer this type of interactional analysis from the sequences within a family to those that frequently occur between a family and helping agencies. The more helpfully an agency behaves, the more helplessly a family behaves, and so the more the agency endeavours to help, and so on. Both in the case of a family sequence and a family–agency sequence the act of punctuation shifts the emphasis from looking to see which particular element needs to be changed to proposing a change in the process between the elements. The case study in Part 3 from Cleveland Social Services demonstrates that including the agency response in a systemic analysis of problem maintenance can lead to more productive interventions.

Each interpretation of a sequence is a valid punctuation of the same event and neither one can be regarded as the 'true' or the 'real' way of viewing it. Tomm (1982) quotes a member of the Milan Associates, Luigi Boscolo, as stating '[the higher level of truth is that] there is no truth, there is only punctuation'.

Difficulties in punctuation

Punctuating a behavioural episode requires acceptance that each of the participants has at least a partial responsibility for what happens.

It questions many of the concepts in traditional views of behaviour which tend to search for a culprit. This may make the reader feel uncomfortable, or have doubts about such a view. Particular difficulty can be experienced in situations where the repunctuation of an event makes workers feel that they are transgressing their personal ethics or moral code. It may be difficult for the worker to think or say something like the more the baby cries, the more the mother batters, the more the mother batters her, the more the baby cries, and so on.

Any transition or departure from commonly accepted views leads to initial feelings of uncertainty. There is often a temptation to dismiss a new approach and revert to the familiar one. Some readers may immediately doubt the concept of punctuation and choose to stay with their current belief system. Others may suspend judgement until they have used the ideas and have seen whether they prove useful.

Those who elect to use the concept of punctuation will probably find it one of the most useful first steps towards a systemic view. Individual behaviour can be understood as part of the context in which it occurs. Punctuation is not only useful for viewing the behaviour of families but also other human situations. Readers may decide to wait until they interview a family before trying the 'exercise of punctuating', or they could start by looking at the interaction between themselves and a client or colleague, boss, etc. As Bateson says: 'The polarization of opinion then will not be simply between practitioners of individual therapy and practitioners of family therapy, but between those who think in terms of systems and those who think in terms of lineal sequences of cause and effect' (1971: 243). Multiple punctuations enable workers to achieve a meta view or overview of a family situation, thus expanding the frame in which the problem is seen and facilitating the use of a class of interventions known as positive reframing. This will be examined in detail in Part 2, Chapter 9, but here is a brief example from the case described in this chapter. One intervention drew attention to Sharon's involvement in the mother – son dyad which was seen as helping to maintain the problem. Instead of the negative interpretation, her behaviour was positively reframed as *helping* her mother and brother to communicate. The worker pointed out to Sharon that as long as she accepted this work from the other two, she was depriving herself of the enjoyment of all the other things she might be doing. This reframed her involvement and pointed to potential benefits to her if she ceased to perform this function. This positive reframing justified the therapist's next move which was to get Andrew and Sharon to change seats so that she was not caught between her mother and brother. Andrew and Mother were then given the task of talking to one another to clarify the issue of the races. This intervention was thought to be partly responsible for successfully detriangulating Sharon from the dyad in a way that was seen as beneficial for her as well as for her mother and brother.

Summary

Part I of this book has so far illustrated the concepts and terms used to analyse problem formation from a systemic perspective. It is by no means comprehensive but offers the basic conceptual tools needed to begin this kind of work. The behaviour of individuals can be defined in terms of a relationship. Relationship problems may be viewed as functioning within transitions in the broader patterns of family life. Current behaviour can be punctuated from the aspect of each participant involved in an interactional sequence. This collection of ideas leads to ways of intervening in families so as to change the patterns of behaviour, systems of beliefs, and the affective experiences of the family members.

It is in problem resolution that family therapy offers the broadest range of options. There are many theories of family change which govern the approaches used by family therapists in their practice. This will be the subject of the next and final chapter in the theoretical section.

4
Models of therapy

Introduction

Part I of this book is concerned with providing a conceptual map for observing the problems that occur in families. This map associates problems manifested by individuals with the traditional and current organization of their family patterns. Commensurate with this systemic view of problem formation is a different approach to achieving change and problem resolution. Practitioners are regarded as active agents of change. As Fisch, Weakland, and Segal put it: 'For practice, this view proposes that the therapist's task is not just to understand the family system and the place of the problem within it but also to take action to change the malfunctioning system in order to resolve the problem' (1982: 9).

Most schools of family therapy seem to share this view, though they may carry out this activity in different ways. Newcomers to the field are lucky in the sense that there is a range of schools, methods, and techniques from which to choose one that suits them, their agency, and their clients. This chapter examines some theories of systemic change espoused by different practitioners and outlines the implications for the reader's practice.

Analysing problems in terms of interactional patterns means that the target of change is patterns, of behaviour and of beliefs. The divergences between the different models of therapy emerge at the stage of problem resolution. They differ in relation to the target of change, the worker's goal, and the part that the therapist plays in achieving change.

The reader's preferences will inevitably shape their selection of family therapy model (a model is a pattern of working). For those who decide to be eclectic or integrative, it will influence what is chosen from the wide selection of therapeutic 'software' now available.

Available models

It has been said that there are as many ways of practising family therapy as there are workers in the field. There have been various attempts to categorize and discriminate between different approaches (Beels and Ferber 1969; Foley 1974; Guerin 1976, Madanes and Haley 1977; Ritterman 1977; Bentovim 1979; Hudson 1980; Hoffman 1981; Grunebaum and Chasin 1982; Speed 1984). It is beyond the scope of this chapter to examine these descriptions in detail. The different approaches towards achieving change will be outlined so that the reader may be better able to make a choice between them. For the sake of clarity the approaches are organized into four categories based on the protagonists' view and organization of the process of therapy. These categories are not mutually exclusive: maverick models; method models; team model; agency model.

MAVERICK MODELS

This refers to those practitioners who have not sought to be, and indeed actively resist being, defined in a particular form or school. They have often been, like Virginia Satir (1964), Nathan Ackerman (1958, 1966) and Don Jackson (1967), pioneers in new and often difficult areas of work. They shun the notion of routine implicit in any method, including their own, and emphasize creativity, intuition, and unpredictability. They often display an irreverence towards orthodoxy. Carl Whitaker resists theorizing or writing too much about his work as he considers it 'hinders therapy' (1976). Observers often describe these people as artists whose work cannot be replicated.

A common feature of the work of mavericks, such as Carl Whitaker's 'Therapy of the Absurd' (Hoffman 1981: 228–31), Milton Erikson's 'Uncommon Therapy' (Haley 1973), or Brian Cade and Phillipa Seligman's 'Marx Brothers Approach' (1982), is that they are unteachable in a precise, concrete sense, although much can be learnt from them at an abstract, creative level. They nevertheless have a pattern, established by trial and error, which provides a firm foundation to the therapists' often seemingly curious and unusual actions. However, it is not always apparent to the uninitiated observer. Rigorous descriptions and analysis of their way of working have usually been undertaken and sometimes accomplished by their followers. For example, Haley (1973) describes the framework of Erickson's approach, while Napier (1978) tries to capture the essence of Whitaker's style.

Whitaker's work has recently been unveiled in the UK at a series of conferences. His work, as described by Hoffman, seems to be 'calculated to shock, amaze, enchant and confuse' (1981: 228–31), and specializes in pushing the 'unthinkable to the edge of the unimaginable'. When observing his work in a consultation interview at the Family Institute, Cardiff, I was struck by the following example of this. He asked a 13-year-old boy who was presenting with 'nervous' behaviour since the death of his father, to 'go over and sit on your dead father's lap. He's sitting right over there. Yes, I think I can see the dent that his backside is making in the chair.'

Whitaker says: 'My tactic has become a kind of tongue-in-cheek, put-on, an induced chaos now called a positive feedback – that is, we augment the pathology until the symptoms self destruct.' In the example of the father's ghost it might be said that Whitaker expanded the boy's fantasy by making it ordinary and therefore no longer bizarre. Once the idea became ordinary it was no longer frightening and the beliefs that surrounded it disappeared. In highlighting the characteristics that make such approaches unique it is not intended to give the impression that the above practitioners are uncaring or cynical. My observations have confirmed for me that their work, while unusual and often amusing, is done in an empathic, healing way.

Much can be learnt from the maverick practitioners and their irreverence for orthodoxy. Emphasis is on the worker using his or her personal qualities to bring about change. Whitaker describes this as retaining 'personhood' (1984). No one would question that a therapist's personal attributes are important but are they sufficient to effect the necessary change? There may be a tendency for personal value systems to intrude unnoticed into the therapeutic process in an unhelpful way. Maverick models provide the very necessary inspiration to begin a journey and also give variety and novelty on the way. However, it is perhaps from the frameworks provided by the method models that the beginner can derive the rigour that is necessary to sustain a family therapy approach.

METHOD MODELS

This category includes those practitioners or groups of practitioners who have formulated their theory of change, and therefore their approach to therapy, in such a way that its principles and practice can be taught to and by others in a systematic way. Often these practitioners are just as charismatic and inventive in their work as the mavericks. However, for present purposes the focus will be on the clear methods of practice they have devised which enable beginners to acquire specific skills and develop competence. From such a base practitioners are better able to use their personal qualities selectively and effectively. Of all these schools the four chosen here are those which have been most influential in the development of my own practice. The choice is therefore based on the grounds of familiarity and is not intended as an indication of superiority. The methods are: a) Minuchin's structural family therapy; b) Haley's strategic therapy; c) the Mental Research Institute brief therapy; d) the Milan Associates systemic therapy.

Each of these methods of family therapy has been documented, demonstrated (live and on videotape), and is the subject of many training courses available in this country. (See Appendix I family therapy training resources which includes details on the availability of videotape libraries, training courses, seminars, workshops in the UK.) Therefore they are available to the practitioner who chooses to follow a particular method. While the maverick concept emphasizes personal idiosyncrasy, a method approach requires conformity to a structure at least until the procedures of the model are mastered. Thereafter individual adaptations according to choice and necessity are possible and desirable. To reap the benefits of any method it seems necessary for workers to accept a temporary sacrifice of their individual inclinations. Once the basic techniques and concepts are mastered, then the worker may feel able to be spontaneous and to take risks from a position of relative competence. Below is a table that outlines the main stated aims of each model with respect to: theory of change; therapeutic goals; the function of the therapist; and the main advantages and disadvantages of each model.

Minuchin's structural family therapy

Minuchin is one of the great pioneers in family therapy. His model was developed with *The Families of the Slums* (Minuchin *et al.* 1967) and refined with *Psychosomatic Families* (Minuchin, Rosman, and Baker 1978). *Families and Family Therapy* (Minuchin 1974) is a classic in the family therapy literature and exemplifies this approach.

Theory of change: 'Patients move for three reasons. First, they are challenged in their perception of reality. Second they are given alternative possibilities that make sense to them, and third, once they have tried out the alternative transactional patterns, new relationships appear that are self reinforcing' (Minuchin 1974: 119).

Goal: To create a structure that is appropriate to the normative developmental stage of the family. Minuchin provides a clear 'blueprint' for an effectively functioning family in terms of clearly defined, permeable boundaries around the different subsystems (spouse/parent/child, etc.). For example, Minuchin uses the enactment of a family meal to enable an anorectic girl and her parents to fight openly about the issue of independence without the need for a symptom. In this way he challenges the family's perception that their daughter is sick and reframes not eating as an act of independence in an overinvolved family. Work is focused on helping the parents to unite around the issue of making the girl eat and dissolve the coalition between one of the parents and the girl. Hence the boundary around the parental subsystem is clarified. The girl is encouraged to find other ways of communicating her independence.

Therapist function: A structural therapist initially *joins* with a family and then *challenges* 'how things are done' (Minuchin and Fishman 1981: 143) and then *restructures* the family by offering alternative, more functional ways of perceiving and behaving. The therapist uses verbal and non-verbal techniques to achieve her aims. Minuchin likens himself to a distant relative of the family. He uses an educative style to good effect with some families.

Advantages: It presents a clear model for therapy; targets and goals are clearly stated; techniques are given to recognize and describe process. Techniques for change are tried and tested. Research validates this method as effective (Minuchin, Rosman, and Baker 1978). Although the therapist profile of this model is said not to fit the stereotypical reserved character of the British therapist, it has been successfully employed in many British agencies.

Disadvantages: It appears deceptively simple. Beginners can make the error of restructuring too early, before they have a sufficient grasp of the family rules. The application of too rigid a blueprint of family functioning can have the effect of imposing the therapist's solution on the family.

Haley's strategic therapy

Haley has zigzagged his way through the field of family therapy and is associated with major theoretical discoveries and therapeutic innovations. His early theoretical ideas were formulated in collaboration with Bateson, Jackson, and Weakland (1956). He gained enduring inspiration for his clinical practice from the techniques of Milton Erickson (Haley 1973). Erickson's strategic approach was viewed by Haley as 'a logical extension of hypnotic technique' (p.19) inducing change through metaphor, persuasion, and indirect influence. His later involvement was with the structural approach of Minuchin at the Philadelphia Child Guidance Clinic. His approach is therefore a unique blend of the subtleties of hypnosis and the clarity of structure. He is a prolific author who writes clearly about his approach to a wide variety of problems. *Problem Solving Therapy* (1976) provides an excellent introduction to Haley's 'cook book' methods of working.

Theory of change: Hoffman (1981: 280) differentiates Haley's theory of change from those with which he has himself been associated in the following way: 'Haley thinks of therapy in terms of a step-by-step change in the way that the family is organized, so that it goes from one type of abnormal organization to another type before a more normal organization is finally achieved. By then, presumably, the symptom is no longer necessary.'

Goal: To remove the power that the symptom has in defining relationships; to restore an appropriate 'power' hierarchy in the family; to design an intervention that fits the problem, without overt reference to any normative state. For example, a 6-year-old boy was referred because his fear of dogs was restricting his social development. This fear has not responded to individual treatment. Haley's strategy included asking the boy to find a puppy that was afraid of humans and cure it. The overinvolved mother was asked to allow the previously peripheral postman father to help his son with this task since his job qualified him as the expert in doghandling. This strategically reversed the problem situation and achieved a structural change in the organization of the family.

Therapist function: To help families overcome the particular problem which is preventing them from getting to the next developmental stage in the family life cycle. Therapists are discouraged from explicitly teaching families about a 'correct' way of living. This approach spans the divide between structural methods already described above and brief methods, to be described next. It utilizes both direct and indirect strategies.

Advantages: A wonderfully clear outline of his therapeutic process and theoretical position is provided (e.g. Haley 1963, 1976, 1984). It gives easy-to-follow instructions for a first interview and the subsequent stages of therapy.

Disadvantages: Haley claims that in order to be effective the therapist needs to have control over issues such as medication and admission or discharge. Therefore his method is of limited use in situations where the therapist does not have this control.

The Mental Research Institute brief therapy method

This is most clearly illustrated in *Change* (Watzlawick, Weakland, and Fisch 1974) and *The Tactics of Change* (Fisch, Weakland, and Segal 1982). It has also moved into the neglected area of elderly people (see *Counselling Elders and their Families* (Herr and Weakland 1979). This multidisciplinary group of practitioners base their work on the theoretical brilliance of Watzlawick, Jackson, and Beavin (1967). They give credit to the therapeutic genius of Milton Erickson (Fisch, Weakland, and Segal 1982: x) for the development of the practical aspects of their method.

Theory of change: 'If problem formation and maintenance are seen as parts of a vicious-circle process, in which well-intended ''solution'' behaviours maintain the problem, then alteration of these behaviours (or beliefs) should interrupt the cycle and initiate the resolution of the problem (Fisch, Weakland, and Segal 1982: 19).

Goal: To interrupt the vicious circle through reframing and tasks that are often paradoxical or contrary to common sense. For instance, take the case of parents who are increasingly frustrated by the rebellious behaviour of their teenage offspring. The parents' complaints only seem to exacerbate the problem and lead to a deterioration in relationships. The Mental Research Institute (MRI) therapist might suggest the strategy of 'benevolent sabotage'. This may involve something like asking the parents to take a one-down position, by frankly admitting to their children that they are unable to control them. The mother might be asked to continue acceding to her son's demands, for example to make his bed, but to be sure to sprinkle toast crumbs on the bottom sheet. On discovery of her 'mistake' she is to adopt an apologetic manner and promise to do better next time. The adolescent soon finds that he is defying thin air as his parents sidestep his assertiveness with similar one-down manoeuvres.

Therapist function: The therapist could be described as a 'salesman' selling interventions that offer new perspectives and unusual solutions to the 'customer' (client). Therapists do not aim to teach people to be a better husband/wife/family, etc. They aim for minimal involvement in order to get the customer moving and then terminate therapy to avoid enmeshment and possible hindrance to other changes occurring in the wider system.

Advantages: A clear model is presented of how to elicit information about the attempted solutions and construct an intervention to resolve the problem. Ingenious interventions and ways of motivating people to change that can be applied to many situations are suggested. Strategies are also provided for working with individuals, couples, or families; this is useful when a whole family cannot be convened.

Disadvantages: Problems illustrated are not usually in the serious range encountered by many social workers. The method is deceptively simple, implying that no knowledge of systems theory is required. But Hoffman (1981) says, 'they know it by heart'. The method is often criticized for being manipulative.

Milan Associates systemic therapy

This was developed by a team of four Italian psychiatrists, Selvini

Palazzoli, Boscolo, Cecchin, and Prata, who had been influenced by Watzlawick, Beavin, and Jackson (1967) from the MRI. It appears to be the method that most closely adheres to the systemic ideas of Bateson (1973). It was initially used with families containing a member designated as either anorectic or schizophrenic, but is now applied to many types of problems (see Campbell and Draper 1985), especially those declared as chronic. The method is described in *Paradox and Counterparadox* (Palazzoli *et al.* 1978) and *Hypothesizing – Circularity – Neutrality* (Palazzoli *et al.* 1980a). Other publications illustrate various techniques within the method.

Theory of change: 'Since the symptomatic behaviour is part of the transactional pattern peculiar to the system in which it occurs, the way to eliminate the symptom is to change the rules' (Palazzoli *et al.* 1978: 4).

Goal: To discover the current systemic rules and traditional myths which sustain the present dysfunctional patterns of relating; to use the assumed resistance of the family towards outside help as a provocation to change. Change is achieved by clarifying the ambiguity in relationships that occurs at a nodal point in the family's evolution. The Milan group professes to have no clear blueprint of how an ideal family should function.

Therapist function: The neutrality of the therapist is emphasized. Information is gathered and discussed by the team before any intervention. Systemic interventions put a positive connotation on the apparently negative relationships between family members and paradoxically prescribe their continuance until some future time when the family will be ready to change. The rationale given is often unacceptable to the family who rebel and thus change in the process. For instance in one family the women (who covertly hated being put down by their menfolk) were commended for always letting the men (who despised the women for their subservience) have the last word so that they would feel like real men. They were asked to continue to sacrifice themselves in this manner until the men convinced them that they could be masculine without dominating the women.

Advantages: The method frees the therapist from the stereotype of an ideal family structure and reduces the risk of value judgements. It provides a clear systemic interviewing format and ingenious systemic interventions and analysis of traps in therapy. It expands the systemic analysis to include professionals and institutions, thereby increasing options for change.

Disadvantages :   It developed in the treatment of chronic problems and may be unnecessarily elaborate in cases where a simpler, more direct approach would suffice. Teamwork is regarded as essential, so the lone worker may find the method difficult to use. Maintaining therapist neutrality can be problematic when a case involves statutory duties.

Advantages of following a particular method

Guidelines, aims, and objectives are all clearly defined. Familiarity engenders competence. Proficiency and ability to apply the method across the board are developed. Ability to understand and evaluate other models is facilitated by a base of competence in one. The confusion engendered in therapist and clients by 'method hopping' is avoided.

Disadvantages of following a particular method

If a set of principles is applied as a matter of routine, the approach may become too rigid. This may result in staleness, leading to lack of imagination and invention. The therapist may suffer from loss of 'self', and become robotic.

The methods of family therapy mentioned so far readily acknowledge that the therapist takes an active role in seeking to influence change in family systems. This position often attracts the criticism that family therapies are manipulative. In general family therapists confirm that such accusations are correct. The argument, so eloquently expressed by Watzlawick (1978: 9–10), is that it is impossible not to influence others, just as it is impossible not to communicate. The issue becomes not how to avoid manipulation but how to use influence in the most beneficial way for those whom the worker is trying to help.

   The development of any of these methods can be difficult for a lone therapist and it is increasingly recommended that workers practise from the security, support, and inspiration of a group or team of like-minded people. Such a group or team should have at least two aims: a) to develop a common method likely to enhance the cohesion and effectiveness of the group; b) to develop and adapt the chosen method within the working context, and to meet the requirements of the agency in which the group works. A detailed examination of these two issues forms the rest of this chapter.

Team model

A striking feature of the exponents of the above family therapy models has been their willingness to expose their practice to peers and trainees. This has been made possible by the use of one-way screens, video and audiotape recordings, and the process known as live supervision. The latter process can be achieved with or without the use of technical aids. It involves two or more workers sharing the work with a family. It breaks with the traditional mode of supervision by verbal report alone (which has the drawbacks of the worker's selectivity of information, memory loss, and the time-lag between the work and supervision). Elsewhere (Burnham and Harris 1985), I have described more fully the theoretical aspects of live supervision; here I will refer to the most important aspects for the uninitiated. So-called 'live supervision' is arranged along the following lines:

a)   Two or more people in the same or neighbouring agencies agree to work together on a family therapy approach and gain the approval of management to do so.

b)   They agree on frequency, duration, and venue of meetings.

c)   They select a particular method of working (in pairs if there is no one-way screen), and agree to read the relevant literature and apply it in their work together. In this way they are usually able to develop a common language and communication is facilitated.

d)   They discuss cases so as to become acquainted with one another's styles and use of systemic concepts such as the genogram.

e)   They select families to work with from current caseloads or new referral (factors governing selection are discussed in a later chapter).

f)   They negotiate the live supervision relationship. Smith and Kingston (1980, 1982) give a detailed account of the issues that need to be clarified during this continuing process. These points are elaborated in Part II of this book.

Live supervision involves at least two workers (in the same room or linked via a one-way screen or close-circuit video). One worker engages directly in interviewing the family while the supervisor sits outside the circle. If videotape facilities are not available then an audiotape recorder is certainly useful at first. The supervisor's function is to observe the session and to offer suggestions to the therapist during the interview or during a break from the session. Most workers and families soon find that the benefits of this approach outweigh their early doubts and feelings of being deskilled. Workers take turns in being the therapist or supervisor with different families so that they can maintain reciprocity. The success of this relationship is crucial to the success of therapy and so must be constantly discussed and evaluated.

Speed (1984), among others, has observed that much of family therapy in this country seems to have developed within the context of teamwork. Teams may vary in size from two to five members. They may function as a formal unit offering live supervision on a regular basis or as an informal but regular support group. This system could result from the often complex and sometimes chronic nature of the problems that family therapists are asked to deal with. The advantages for the worker of having a team include the following:

a)   A supportive environment in which a new method can be learned through discussion, role play, and tape reviews can help to avoid the phenomenon of staff 'burn-out' as a result of the disillusionment that is often experienced by the lone worker in stressful areas of work.

b)   The supervisor is able to attain a meta position to the interview and through timely interventions can reduce the likelihood of the interviewer's becoming enmeshed with the family system and consequently a part of the problem instead of part of the solution.

c)   Optimism in difficult cases is more easily created and maintained.

d)   The number of punctuations that can be made in each case is increased; this reduces the likelihood of acting upon value judgements and increases the therapeutic options.

Team preparation for interviews is examined in Chapter 8. A team can be a potent agent of change, enhancing the work of its members and improving the service to clients. However, in my experience of consulting to such teams in social service and probation departments, they can be seen as élitist groups who have adopted a fanciful technique and only work with 'easy' cases. Rivalry for resources with other groups in the agency can develop. A team must always remember that it will only survive if it is seen to be fulfilling the tasks of that agency in some way. If this factor is ignored the team or group may be starved of referrals or less subtly disbanded. This point leads to the next way of approaching change.

THE AGENCY MODEL

While the principle of adopting a method and sticking to it is a good one, there are several practical reservations that must be expressed. None of the methods outlined above, and indeed none of the major family therapy approaches, originated in the UK. Nor have they been developed in public service agencies such as those in which the majority of readers are likely to work. Therefore each of these models must undergo a transitional stage in which it adapts to the constraints and imperatives of the agency in which it is to be used. Otherwise the models are unlikely to be useful and will not survive. It is perhaps in this area – the adaptation of a family therapy approach to the functions of public service agencies – that British therapists have made the most significant and original contributions. Haley (1975), from the American context, wrote that it was not possible to use family therapy alongside other methods of working. However, in this country practitioners have indeed been required to do just that since private practice is not as widespread as it is in the USA. Treacher and Carpenter's book *Using Family Therapy* (1984) represents a benchmark in the literature on family therapy. The edited collection shows how the members of a family therapy co-operative have adapted a family therapy approach to the problems which face agencies involved in work with the elderly, psychiatric patients, and children in care.

A group that decides to adopt a family therapy approach can choose to be known by the name of the method it uses, such as the 'brief therapy project', or more simply as the 'family therapy support group'. That is, it can identify itself by its method of working in a general or specific way. Recently there has been a trend for teams to focus on particular areas of their agency's work, using whatever model or method best facilitates it. In doing so they are promoting not a method of family therapy, but family therapy as a solution to a particular problem with which the agency is faced. Family therapy is thus seen as a useful commodity without its cellophane packaging. Voluntary agencies such as the Rochdale Special Unit of the National Society for the Prevention of Cruelty to Children (NSPCC) have adapted a family therapy approach to the problem of child abuse (Dale *et al.* 1985, 1986). O'Hagan (1984) describes a family approach to crisis intervention in local authority social services. In the National Health Service, Great Ormond Street Hospital has established a family approach to the sexual abuse of children. Scott and Starr (1981) use family interviews in the community to help prevent admitting adults to psychiatric hospitals. Each has tackled difficult problems in the contexts in which they occur: the families, the courts, and institutional bureaucracy. In all of these examples the emphasis is on adapting family therapy to the agency's problems so that the agency can be adapted to a family therapy approach. The influence is therefore reflexive or two-way. The beginner may not wish to embark immediately on such difficulties. These examples are included here to illustrate that family therapy can be more than a fringe method for use with that rarity, the 'motivated' family. Taken seriously, a family therapy approach can increase job satisfaction, tackle some of management's biggest problems, and above all help severely disabled and disabling families. Particular examples of this process in the social services and the probation service are examined in Part III.

Summary

This chapter has attempted to clarify some of the different approaches to family therapy and the implications for the reader's practice in the context of their personal preferences, co-working, and the agency in which they work. It recommends that a worker's individual strengths can best be used within the framework of a structured method. A family therapy approach is more likely to be successful in the context of a supportive group or team of colleagues. Any model must be adapted to fit the constraints of the worker's agency if it is to survive as a useful entity.

Part II introduces a selection of skills associated with the concepts presented in Part I that practitioners need in order to facilitate systemic change.

Practice

Skills and techniques

Part I introduced and illustrated some of the basic ideas that might be regarded as essential in the development of a systemic approach to family therapy. Part II is concerned with the application of these ideas in practice. It is important to emphasize that the order in which these ideas and this practice are presented does not imply a 'rule' governing how a new therapist must proceed. Many of the 'great originals' of family therapy (Haley, Minuchin, Ackerman, etc.) applied family therapy and later found a theory which offered a plausible explanation for their observations of families' behaviour and their therapeutic work based on those observations. There is no correct order in which to begin – a beginner should read the theory and practice simultaneously in order to make each aspect meaningful in relation to the other.

This part does not claim to present an encyclopaedic coverage of skills and techniques. Rather it outlines and illustrates some of the basic skills and techniques that can be useful at various stages of the therapy process. It offers advice and encouragement as to how to start putting these skills into practice, that is how to combine thinking and doing. The step from reading or observing to doing is perhaps the most difficult one to take. There always seems to be a good reason to wait for a better opportunity or a more suitable family, for example. This part offers direct advice on making the step less difficult. The main areas covered in Part II are: convening a session – getting families to come and begin work; preparing for a session – deciding how to structure and plan an interview; conducting an interview – techniques for eliciting systemic information; intervening – initiating change; failure – recognizing and overcoming impasse and failure.

5
Convening

Introduction

September, 1978 saw the beginning of the Family Clinic in Birmingham as a specialist unit within the Charles Burns Clinic. On this particular Friday morning everything had been arranged: a one-way screen, a video recorder, and a group of very interested and enthusiastic professionals eager to try out this new and exciting way of working. As if this were not enough, Dr Karl Tomm, an experienced family therapist from Calgary, Canada, was behind the screen to give us the benefit of his advice. How could we fail? What could go wrong? The family did not attend! Technology, skills, and enthusiasm, all is in vain if the family does not arrive or is not at home when you visit.

The essential prerequisite of convening a family session is largely ignored in the literature. This contrasts with the host of articles written about successful case studies, skill development, and outcome studies. Perhaps this neglect reflects the lack of apparent significance of successful convening: you got the family to come – so what? It may be that those who write about family therapy are working either with families who are highly 'motivated' or in prestigious agencies which can attract families by their reputation. Although both these suppositions may be true, there are other factors involved. You may work in an agency that does not have the prestige of others; indeed you may work in an agency that is not usually associated with therapy at all. While you may be at such disadvantages, there are ways and means of increasing the attraction of what you offer and therefore the likelihood of families attending sessions. This is the skill of convening.

The importance of convening a family session

Is it important to convene the whole family? Napier and Whitaker (1978) refer to the convening process as 'the battle for structure' and suggest that the convening of family members is a necessary prerequisite for successful family treatment. Other schools of thought, such as the Brief Therapy Centre at the Mental Research Institute in California, believe that family systems can be changed by working with the 'customer', i.e. the person who most wants to effect change. The results of their work show that this is possible with their client population. However, Stanton and Todd (1981) suggest that the more severe the problem the more important it is to work with the whole family.

While change may be achieved through work with only part of a family, wherever possible it is best to convene the whole family and any significant others for the following reasons:

a)   It is easier to comprehend the systemic nature of the problematic behaviour.
b)   It is generally more difficult to get people to attend later in therapy if they have not done so from the beginning.
c)   It emphasizes to the family the interactional nature of the problem and its solution.
d)   The therapist is less likely to be swayed by the views of the participating members against the absentees.

Persistence in convening the whole family

While it is recommended that therapists should aim to convene the whole family in order to achieve the best assessment and outcome, the time and energy that any therapist is willing to devote to this aim cannot be dictated. The decision will be made on the basis of several factors including the therapist's philosophy about the task and the function of the agency in which she works. At a recent conference in Cardiff, Professor Selvini Palazzoli, who practises family therapy at her own private centre in Milan, stated that if a family does not wish to come to her centre to engage in therapy that is entirely up to them. She will make certain attempts to recruit absent members by letter, but she avoids being seen as 'chasing' the family, however serious the problem. She states: 'If they wish to go on living as they do then that is entirely up to them.' This view is consistent with Professor Palazzoli's philosophy of therapy and agency setting. However, Stanton and Todd (1981), in their government-sponsored prevention of drug abuse programme, do not adopt Palazzoli's approach. The nature of their agency dictates that drug abusers must be worked with if they come to the centre. However, their therapeutic philosophy (supported by research) is that a treatment programme for drug abuse which includes family therapy results in a much higher success rate than a programme which does not. It is not surprising to learn that Stanton and Todd advocate a much higher rate of persistence in attempts to convene the whole family than does Professor Palazzoli: 'It needs to be emphasised that these addicted young men die or become imprisoned at rates that are many times higher than for similar men in their age range . . . in this context a sense of ''mission'' was hardly inappropriate' (Stanton and Todd 1981:261).

Between these two extremes there will be various intermediate positions. Only individuals can decide which to adopt in their particular agency. The degree of persistence rests on such factors as: hierarchical position in the agency, amount of support received from peers and management, relation of agency to statutory system, and so on. Later in this chapter convening strategies ranging from simple to complex are considered and readers can decide on their own level of persistence. First, issues that facilitate convening are outlined.

Pre-convening preparation

However humble or elaborate the service offered to a family, it should generally be presented in a confident, clear manner indicating that the therapist values it. Otherwise the recipient is unlikely to value the service. Before inviting a family to a session it is useful to be clear in your own mind just what you are asking a family to participate in. This includes who, where, when, for how long, and how often. 'An indecisive stance tends to create a vacuum that is filled by a client who will dictate convention composition' (Teismann 1980: 394).

WHO TO INVITE

As a general rule you should invite all the family members living in the household. However, in specific cases others significant to the problem should also be convened, for example, members of the extended family, school staff, neighbours, etc. The composition should be determined by who is significant to the problem, or as Skynner (1976) describes it, the 'minimum sufficient network'.

WHERE TO MEET

There is often a great debate about the best place to hold family meetings – the family's home or therapist's clinic/agency. There are different advantages to both venues.

If meetings are held at the agency: 1) it saves worker time; 2) there may be access to video tape, etc.; 3) workers are on their own territory; 4) the way families organize themselves to come to the agency can provide useful information to the therapist and a useful exercise for the family; 5) families often feel that the work is somehow more special or worth while if it is done at a centre rather than in their home; 6) the family has more choice as to whether to take up the offer of therapy than if the therapist comes to their home; 7) interviews are easier to control than when conducted in the family's home, e.g. individuals are less likely to pop out to 'make a cup of tea', neighbours to pop in, etc.

Advocates of home visits (e.g. Lindsey 1979) state that therapy done in the family's home either as a one-off visit or as a regular way of working offers: 1) a powerful engaging move – showing the family how motivated the therapists are to help; 2) a valuable insight into how the family lives – room size, seating positions, etc. – which could not be gained in a clinic setting; 3) a better chance of convening the whole family – especially a potentially 'reluctant'/non-attending member; 4) a chance to see who is in the 'network' (neighbours, etc.); 5) a start to change in the place where things happen, the home.

Given the choice, I interview in an agency setting. When interviews are held in the home, they should be conducted as if in an office. The following type of statement sets the ground rules: 'Of course, I realize that this is your home, but I would find it easier to help you if I could work as I do at my office. I'd like all the family to sit in this room for the next three-quarters of an hour or so while we discuss things (your problem). I would like the chairs arranged so we can all see each other.' The format of the session then approximates to an office interview.

WHEN TO CONDUCT SESSIONS

The issue of time is extremely important. Negotiating a time when all the family can be present at the same time as the worker can often be a stumbling-block during therapy as well as in the convening phase. There should be some flexibility in the time of day offered in order to accommodate family members' working patterns, etc. However, making *ad hoc* arrangements means time-consuming negotiations each session. It can also give an impression of indecisiveness or poor organization. For example, the therapist might have to say as she flicks through the pages of her diary: 'Well, I think I can fit you in between admitting an old lady to part III accommodation and . . . oh no, sorry, I've got a team meeting straight after that. Perhaps Wednesday 3rd? Oh, you can't make that, well let's look at the next week shall we?'

The system used at the Charles Burns Family Clinic and by other family therapy groups (including those in some social services departments) is fixed sessions. One or more workers allocate set times to family therapy, e.g. Monday 2.00 till 8.00 p.m., Wednesday 9.00 a.m. to 12.30 p.m. The time is divided into hour-long appointments thus: Monday 2.00 p.m.; 3.00 p.m.; 4.00 p.m., etc. In this way a particular family can be offered a vacant slot or choice of a day or evening appointment. This introduces structure and organization while retaining some flexibility. In general most agencies that used fixed sessions find an improvement in the number of first interviews attended. If therapists negotiate with their agency to have this 'protected' time, they increase the impression of commitment to the activity; this may open the way to other concessions from the agency. Setting aside a fixed time also facilitates research projects and the formation of a team. The frequency, duration, and total number of sessions are also important issues and potentially powerful tactics during therapy; these will be discussed in Chapter 10 'Failure'. However, if a family asks questions about these matters at the convening stage, it is important to be able to give an answer, however general. For example:

CLIENT. 'How long will all this take then?'

THERAPIST. 'To make a comprehensive/thorough assessment we need to meet for an hour to begin with, then I/we shall be able to give you a more complete/accurate answer.'

CLIENT. 'How many times will we have to come/you visit?'

THERAPIST. 'Each family is different but we generally propose/try to keep the number of sessions to a minimum/as few as it takes.'

Where a more definite answer is called for, you may say something like: 'What we have found most helpful is to meet for two (three) (four) sessions and then review progress at that stage.' The language that is used will vary from family to family but this type of answer has an element of concreteness (the worker's conviction/confidence) while still maintaining flexibility.

Referring agencies

It may be advantageous to relay basic information to agencies who are likely to refer families. If influential referring agencies suggest that the whole family be asked to attend as a matter of routine, then this can considerably ease the convening process. Referrers should be encouraged to adopt the same non-blaming stance as the therapist and should be discouraged from giving detailed information about the therapeutic arrangements such as the number of workers and whether one-way screens, video or audiotapes should be used. This is best explained when family meetings begin rather than at referral, though opinions vary. The fantasies family members develop about such things can become more formidable than the actual experience. This issue is thus examined in the section on conducting a session.

Summary

Some of the important pre-convening issues that need to be considered are outlined above. In all situations therapists should be clear as to who to include in sessions and where and when meetings take place. Any offer to a family is then made with conviction by the therapist. This instils confidence in the family. It can also indicate that this offer of help is different from others that the family may have had in the past.

Convening a first family session

Convening a family session can be easy. It can also be the most difficult stage in the whole therapeutic process. Stanton and Todd (1980), in work with drug abusers and their families, anticipated that the main problem would be keeping families in treatment. However, they found that 94 per cent of the families who attended a first interview completed therapy. Their main problems arose in the convening stage: 'What we did not foresee was the inordinate amount of difficulty we would have in simply getting the family members in for the initial family evaluation programme' and that 'engagement of resistant families requires a rethinking or reframing of the therapeutic enterprise.'

SUCCESSFUL CONVENING

Agency intake procedure, therapist skills, family factors, and the type of problem are all important variables in successful convening. The interplay between these factors determines whether convening is a relatively simple or complex task.

Example 1

A family experiencing difficulties with one of their young children goes to an agency seeking help. This problem has arisen quite recently, and is the first one that has necessitated their seeking outside help. The agency's intake procedure is to ask the whole family to attend the initial interview. The invitation is made by an experienced family therapist.

In these circumstances, an invitation, issued by letter (see *Appendix II*) or by personal contact, is likely to result in the family attending the first session.

Convening can be significantly more complex (but still achievable).

Example 2

Consider a family where an adult member is experiencing long-standing problems, possibly involving the law or a life-threatening syndrome. There is a long history of failed treatments with a variety of agencies. The individual concerned has left home and is currently in a residential establishment (jail/hospital/hostel) whose policy is to view the family as either irrelevant or as victimizing the individual in their care. The institution has been pursuing an individually orientated treatment programme.

A junior member of staff (keen to try family therapy, but inexperienced) suggests to the identified patient that a meeting should be held with the whole family to discuss the ways they sabotage the institution's treatment plan through their involvement or lack of co-operation.

It is likely that there would be problems in getting this family to attend the first session.

DEGREES OF DIFFICULTY

There are many occasions when family members openly express enthusiasm about coming as a family, even when the problem is severe and long-standing. 'Oh yes – we saw a programme about that on television (*Man Alive* documentary – Dr C. Dare, 1979) and it seems like a really good idea.' However, there are some families who are initially very suspicious, frightened, and nervous of being blamed for the predicament of the identified patient. Thus, degrees of difficulty are involved in getting a family to an interview and solutions will need to vary correspondingly from simple to complex. The remainder of this chapter suggests strategies along this continuum.

ROUTINE RECRUITMENT OF FAMILIES

If therapists have attended to pre-convening preparation and invite a family such as that in example 1, then the recruitment should be easy and therapy can commence. It seems that the more practitioners and other agency staff such as receptionists and secretaries expect convening to be routine, and convey this attitude to the family, the more compliant families become. Likewise, the more compliant they become, the more we expect them to be so.

Often the first hurdle encountered in recruiting the whole family is the question: 'But why do you need all of us? There's nothing wrong with her brothers or sisters, we're a normal family apart from her.'

EXERCISE 5.1
What would your answer be? Before reading on take a few minutes to record some possible responses to this type of question.

Common responses include: 'This may well be a family problem', 'Perhaps this is to do with how your family is functioning'. Usually this type of response is an error, as it appears to blame the family for the problem (whether or not that is the intention of the therapist).

The underlying message of any reply should be based on a no-blame stance. It is mostly futile and often fatal to the convening process to attempt, at this stage, to shift the blame from the identified patient to the rest of the family. The kind of response that is often useful is: 'We do our best/most effective work this way. This way we harness the strengths of the family to deal with the problem.' 'We find that problems such as these are solved more quickly when the whole family is involved.' 'The family are the people with the information that we need to make a thorough assessment so that we know how best to help you.' 'At this stage, we would appreciate the views of everyone in your family.'

This policy of no blame is useful at all stages during the therapy and helps both the family and the therapist to avoid taking a linear cause-and-effect view of the problems. So, when asked 'why a family session?', give a response that attributes no blame and emphasizes how helpful you (and your colleagues) have found this way of working. This often has the effect of reducing the family's anxiety about being blamed and increases the likelihood of their attending the first session. There is an increasing trend for practitioners in 'non-therapeutic' agencies to avoid the term 'family *therapy*'. Sessions are referred to as assessment, discussion, and feedback. Alternatively, family meetings are declared to be necessary in order to fulfil the agency task, social enquiry report, psychological assessment, and so on (see Chapter 4 and Part III).

Often the next difficulty comes when the therapist is told prior to the session by a 'willing' family member (often the person who initiated the referral) that another member of the family is reluctant to attend. Or it might be that one or more family members fail to attend the first or subsequent sessions. Various reasons are offered – work schedules, she/he isn't really involved with (or doesn't know about) the problem or doesn't see the point in coming.

EXERCISE 5.2
Take some time before reading on to record the solutions that you would use to tackle these problems.

An important decision at this stage is whether the recruitment of the reluctant person should be the therapist's task or the family's task.

THE FAMILY'S TASK

Reluctance

If the choice is to make a willing member of the family responsible, then the following procedure may be adopted:

a) Listen to the initiator's story.
b) Re-emphasize how valuable it is to have all the family members present in order to assess how you can be most helpful to them.
c) Say you need to know how this problem affects the rest of the family (not vice versa).
d) Reschedule the appointment to accommodate the work schedules of family members.
e) Coach the willing family members in how to recruit 'unwilling' members to the sessions.

If the family achieves this task of convening itself, then it may be the '*pièce de résistance* of successful therapy' (Teismann 1980). For example, the mother of a family rang to say that the father could not keep the appointment. She asked if she should come with the children. The above format was followed and the whole family came. During the initial session the husband said that this was the first time that he had felt that his wife really valued his opinion on matters concerning the children.

Absence

When a family arrives without one or more members for the first session the situation is more difficult because the therapist will be reluctant to turn willing members away. It is tempting to hear from them why 'so and so' hasn't come to the session. To refuse to see the attenders at all, merely offering another appointment, would probably, at this stage of therapy, cause the family to drop out. To go ahead could give the message (to attenders and non-attenders alike) that all your talk about the importance of everybody attending for the first session was meaningless. Therefore, it is advisable that the attending members are seen and the following type of strategy is used:

a) The session begins by focusing on who decided that the absent person should not come – did he or she decline the invitation or were they not invited at all?

b) Useful information can be gained through asking who among the 'attenders' is most likely to be able to persuade the 'non-attenders' to come to a session.

c) Questions may then be asked around how the 'attenders' are going to recruit the 'non-attenders' and setting them the task of doing so for the next interview.

A strategy might be to limit this session to 30–40 minutes and call it information gathering rather than a first session to emphasize that the real sessions begin when the whole family has been convened. The family may then be asked to contact the therapist in order to confirm that the whole family will attend the rescheduled appointment.

THE THERAPIST'S TASK

For various reasons the therapist will not or cannot accept refusal to attend, and recruitment becomes the therapist's task. It may be that the family fails to convene itself; then the therapist, enthusiastic to try a new method of work, decides to take on the task of convening. Other reasons may relate to the agency context – there may be statutory responsibilities on the therapist to take action. The identified patient may be in some form of residential care, the family does not convene itself, and rehabilitation cannot proceed without its participation.

EXERCISE 5.3

Before reading on take some time to record how you would embark on the task of recruiting reluctant/absent family member(s), bearing in mind the agency in which you work.

SUGGESTIONS

Common replies include: 'Tell him or her that the problem concerns everybody', 'He or she must be made to see that it is their duty to attend', 'It's impossible to recruit these peripheral fathers'. Whether the family's resistance to convening efforts is actual or anticipated, the therapist must be careful to embark on convening in a way that implies that the family is not to blame and that it will actually benefit in some way from attending. 'The therapist must approach the family with a rationale for treatment that is non-pejorative, non-judgemental, and in no way blames them for the problem' (Stanton and Todd 1981).

This attitude is especially important in recruitment of 'resistant' families since their reluctance may be a signal that:

a) the symptoms/problems are or are becoming chronic, dangerous, and disturbing;
b) the 'non-attenders' feel (or perhaps have been told previously) that they are to blame for the problem;
c) the family members fear that other facets of their lives will be revealed to their discredit and embarrassment;
d) their experience of other professional involvement has been of failure to change.

Once the therapist has decided to take on this task, there are various methods that can be used. These include contact by letter, telephone, personal contact, or through a third person. All these methods bypass the willing family members to reach the unwilling.

By letter

Letters may be straightforward requests to the reluctant or absent member saying how you would 'appreciate their views on the situation since you have already heard what the rest of the family has had to say'. Palazzoli and her colleagues suggest positively connoting the absence as follows:

'Dear Mr . . .
At this time for some good reason, you have decided to help your family with their concerns by not attending the interviews. Since no father wants to hurt his family or add to the existing pain, I sense that you are trying to tell your family something that is difficult to share in words and can only be told by your actions. I will try to help them understand your good intentions and the difficulty in which you find yourself with them.'   (Palazzoli *et al.* 1978)

The letter may be written during a session and given to a family member to deliver or sent by post. This message conveys the sense of 'no blame' but may also provoke the absentee to attend since he or she may not wish to be talked about without being present. It also gives an implicit message that the absentee cannot halt the therapy by his or her absence.

By telephone

Telephoning provides an opportunity to engage the reluctant member in conversation and so deal with his or her objections. Ringing at the point of intake or during the first session makes it less likely that the therapist's message to this person will be altered by comments from the attending members or messages relayed through them. Stanton and Todd recognized a cardinal principle in the convening process: 'Do not expect the index patient to bring in the family on his own' (1981: 267).

The procedure for telephone contact might be as follows:

a)   Listen to what the attending member(s) have to say about the problem.
b)   Obtain their permission to make direct contact with the non-attender(s).
c)   Telephone immediately, or certainly before the attender(s) have a chance to meet them and discuss the issues, translating your request in a way that may not be successful.

The kind of things to say on the telephone will vary but the following examples may help to illustrate the general pattern:

THERAPIST. Hello, Mr Smith, I'm John Burnham from the Charles Burns Clinic. I've just been talking to your wife about the problems that your daughter, Sheila, has been having for the past few months. Did your wife tell you she was coming to the Clinic?

FATHER. She mentioned something about it.

THERAPIST. Well, I'm calling you to see if you would join us in an effort to overcome the problems, which I'm sure must worry you too. I've heard your wife's side of the story so far but I always find it very useful to hear the father's viewpoint too – you know because nobody else can know just what you think or feel and I usually find that fathers have some good ideas when I actually get to meet them.

FATHER. Well, I'm not sure. . . .

THERAPIST. Well, I just thought I ought to give you an opportunity to find out what's going on . . . because once things start to change with your wife and children, I think it's only fair to you to know what's going on. I wouldn't want you to be caught by surprise.

FATHER. What changes?

THERAPIST. Well I don't know exactly what changes, but there will probably be some and I think you have a right to be part of them so you don't lose out. You should be able to share the benefits too.

FATHER. Well maybe.

THERAPIST. OK. I'll look forward to seeing you at the first appointment on . . . [or] OK well listen, take some time to think it over and if you decide to come in to help me out I'll be glad to see you.

Some of the essential ingredients in the phone call are: (a) validation of the father's point of view; (b) arousing his curiosity about 'changes' taking place; (c) offering choice as to whether or not to attend the sessions (no coercion); (d) increasing the attractiveness of attending the session for the father (he will benefit too).

Obviously the content of a telephone call will vary but these are useful principles on which to structure such conversations. The same kind of approach may be adapted with other members.

Personal contact

As an expression of empathy, the therapist may make personal contact at the reluctant member's home, or some neutral place such as a café, bar, or park. In addition to the non-blaming attitude that the therapist should adopt, it is often useful to tailor the goals of therapy to include those of the reluctant member: accept the phrases of this person such as 'I want to get him [the identified patient] straightened out' and include them in the overall therapeutic aims – 'Yes that's one of my aims too – but I really need your help to do it'.

In an 'extreme' case of personal contact, Stanton and Todd (1981) cite a therapist who made 28 contacts (4 with the patient and 24 with the family) in 30 days. This literally 'wore them down' and they came into therapy.

Enforcing strategies

The tactics of convening hitherto cited may be said to come under the heading of 'enabling' (Teismann 1980), the therapist being willing to be extremely adaptable so as to encourage the family members to join in therapy. When enabling has not worked, the more vital the therapist and agency consider it to have family participation, the more likely it is that 'enforcing' strategies will be utilized. The decision to use such strategies is undoubtedly a difficult one and is probably taken most often by therapists working on such problems as residential care, child abuse, addiction, etc.

DELAYING OR DENYING TREATMENT HELP

It seems that very few therapists are actually willing or able to utilize the denial of treatment as a convening strategy but delaying treatment may be useful. For example, if the family are depending on the therapist's agency for some service (e.g. in-patient or residential care, court report), then this may be a powerful tool in getting the family to the first session. 'Enabling' methods may then be used. Agencies such as the Department of Psychological Medicine, The Hospital for Sick Children, Great Ormond Street, London (Hildebrand *et al.* 1980) make it a contractual stipulation of in-patient care that the family undertake to attend family sessions. Where practically possible, a similar contract could be established in other residential facilities. The NSPCC Special Unit (Rochdale) (Davies *et al.* 1985) advocate the use of a 'non negotiable contract' in cases of severe child abuse. In situations where children have been removed from home their parents are required to give a written undertaking to attend a centre for family sessions. Only on completion of these sessions is a decision taken either to begin a process of reuniting the family or to seek alternative care for the children. Enforcing may also include 'mobilising the referring and linking networks to exert pressure on the family to convene itself while permitting the therapist to remain relatively supportive' (Teismann 1980). Juvenile courts, conciliation services, lawyers, and judges may all be useful allies in convening particularly difficult families. 'The enforcing may range from threat of prosecution, hospitalisation, discharge, or expulsion, to the network person's gentle encouragement, depending upon the family, the agent and the seriousness of the situation' (Stanton and Todd 1981: 278).

By now some readers will be horrified at the use of words such as 'enforcing' in the same context as 'therapy'. Others will be delighted to have permission to use these strategies to help them to engage families who are difficult to convene. In this way solutions may be found to problems which seemed intractable when treatment was aimed at the identified patient only. Whatever strategies are utilized, think of convening as the first potentially therapeutic intervention, rather than as something that takes place before therapy begins. 'The whole recruitment process then is an intervention that shifts responsibility for the problem to the total system of intimate others. These people are told that they are important if not in generating the problem, then in helping to alleviate it' (Stanton and Todd 1981).

Summary

This chapter proposes that the issue of convening a family for therapy should be taken seriously. Motivating a family to begin therapy is the first and most crucial intervention to initiating systemic change. Attention should be paid to who is convened, where therapy takes place, and how people are invited to participate. A non-blaming stance on the part of the therapist towards family members is recommended as essential to facilitate their involvement. A range of convening strategies is offered that ranges from enabling to enforcing. Readers are urged to consider their agency context, legal mandate, and the severity of the problem as important factors in making a choice of strategy.

An additional source of ideas on the issues explored in this chapter can be found in Carpenter and Treacher (1983).

6
Preparation

Most family therapy models subscribe to the view that preparation for interviews is necessary (for example, Palazzoli *et al.* 1978, 1980; Minuchin and Fishman 1981; de Shazer 1982). This chapter introduces some preparation procedures and suggests useful tools and rituals. It is important to remember that preparation is an important 'ritual' to be observed before each session.

Introduction

Planning makes interviews more productive: it reduces confusion and gives the therapist the initiative in the session. Routine preparation establishes sets of regular plans which need only minor revision from session to session. Fundamental procedures should be periodically questioned and amended as necessary. This ensures that practice does not become rigidified. The suggestion that therapists plan a session sometimes meets with objections: that planning is controlling, diminishes therapist spontaneity, ignores the client's position, and may cause important issues to be overlooked. These comments do point to some disadvantages of rigorous planning. However, the advantages of being prepared for a family session far outweigh these disadvantages, especially for a beginning therapist. Family systems present a wealth of information on many levels. If workers are confused, their chances of helping a family are greatly reduced. For these reasons most therapists do some preparation before each session. Preparation can give the worker a clear framework that allows them to take the initiative

and conduct the interview in a productive way. The following basic
requirements are necessary.

Preparation ritual: LAST TO DO

A preparation ritual may be ordered into the following format: Think
of the ritual as the LAST things TO DO before you see a family.

L live supervision: rules of the relationship
A agency constraints: in this particular case
S single workers: need to plan for themselves too
T technical details: video/audio/room/seats/toys/etc.
T therapeutic hypotheses
O options for the interview: techniques to test hypotheses
D disaster options: contingency plans
O overview: of the session for the therapist

The above are not ordered in priority but are presented in a way that
might be easier to remember. LAST concerns preparation of the therapist system while TO DO is concerned with preparing for the family
system.

Live supervision

The theoretical basis for this procedure was discussed in Chapter 5.
Here I will outline the practical aspects. Live supervision involves at
least two professionals working with a family. The worker designated
as therapist conducts the interviews while the supervisor sits out of the
circle (behind a one-way screen or in the same room) and supervises
by periodically interrupting the session to make suggestions to the
therapist. These interventions may be made in the presence of a family
and/or in discussions between therapist and supervisor outside the
room. This method is potentially extremely powerful. For its promise
to be realized, the rules of the live supervision relationship must be
clearly defined in several important areas. Basic guidelines for development are divided into first- and second-stage negotiations.

FIRST-STAGE NEGOTIATIONS

It is vital to identify and clarify how the following issues can be dealt
with for a working relationship to be formed successfully: a) hierarchy

between team members; b) rules for resolution of disagreements; c) advice or commands? status of supervisor's interruptions; d) model choice: which model to adopt and when?

EXERCISE 6.1
Take a break and consider these topics. Single workers may contemplate these matters in anticipation of live supervision. Co-workers may attempt to debate and resolve these issues in terms of their working relationship.

Hierarchy

Differences in status and/or discipline must be openly discussed and the ramifications clarified. For example under what circumstances would these differences matter? When this is clearly defined then the situations in which the workers may operate as peers are revealed. For example, a social work team leader may feel obliged to act as a manager in a case of child abuse. A member of a multidisciplinary team may observe a problem that needs investigating at a biological, intellectual, or material level. The issue of clinical or administrative responsibility in teams can be tricky and needs to be dealt with openly as it arises. In this way trust may become established and maintained.

Disagreements

All workers have different points of view based on gender, age, colour, creed, or profession and which may result in disagreement. This is a healthy condition and has the advantage of illuminating different punctuations of the same situation. What needs to be established is:

i)   who has the final decision if there is a difference that cannot be reconciled during a session. Usually in the case of peer supervision the therapist decides, while a student would be expected to defer to a tutor.
ii) an agreement to work on disagreements so that they are resolved before the next session.

Advice or commands

This concerns the status of the supervisor's interventions. Peers usually offer advice to each other. When there is a supervisor/student relationship a supervisor carries ultimate responsibility for the case and so commands may be used. These are best kept to a minimum and clearly spelt out, or the student will be operating in a straitjacket.

Model choice

The difficulties posed when practitioners working together are using different models are particularly acute in live supervision. Ideally, therapists should agree to use the same model. However, practitioners working together may be attracted to different models on the basis of personal preference. Agreement must be reached on ways to handle these differences. A solution may be to work on a particular model for an agreed period of time or type of problem until a review.

SECOND-STAGE NEGOTIATIONS

Practical issues are a) introductions to the family; b) therapist tasks; c) supervisor tasks; d) communication during the session; e) time out protocol.

Introductions

An introduction should inform a family how a session is conducted and should include a positive rationale of the method chosen. Issues that need to be included in an introduction are: who you are; the method of and reason for live supervision; technical equipment; time out; why you have invited the people there. Some groundwork may have been done in the process of convening.

EXERCISE 6.2
Compose an introduction along these lines that fits your agency setting and function before you proceed. A suggested introduction will be given in the following chapter on interviewing.

Therapist tasks

A therapist's task during the interview is primarily to engage the family and conduct the interview according to a pre-session plan. (See

Options p.104.) The degree of therapist autonomy is an important area. The therapist's initial feelings of being manipulated by the supervisor must be weighed against the benefits of having someone with a meta view. Experienced team co-workers promote therapist spontaneity within a team framework.

Supervisor tasks

A supervisor's task is to achieve a meta view of therapy by gathering information about the interactions within the family and between the family and the therapist. Supervisors behind a one-way screen are free from the family's gaze and so can easily remain relatively detached. Supervisors in the room must use other devices to ensure that they are not drawn into the interview process by the family members. Avoiding eye contact and taking notes are two useful ways of staying external to the interview. Practice enables supervisors to gather different information from the therapist's by observing the non-verbal responses of other family members to issues being discussed with one particular person.

Communication during the sessions

The communication between supervisor, therapist, and family during sessions depends on decisions about the timing and frequency of interruptions. Eagerness to share the meta view with the therapist may lead the supervisor to interrupt too soon or too often. This may unbalance the rapport between therapist and family. Generally, allow fifteen to twenty minutes before interrupting and interrupt not more than four times during a session. Address comments directly to the therapist and phrase them in such a way that the therapist can act upon them; for example: 'It would be a good idea if you asked the family members, in turn, how they are going to reorganize when Frank comes home from the hospital', rather than 'You've been talking to Mr Jones too long. Could you talk to someone else now.' In the event of a therapist consistently disagreeing with the supervisor's proposals, then time out should be taken for clarification.

Time out protocol

The protocol for taking time out is usually at the discretion of either supervisor or therapist. It can be announced as follows: 'We'd like to take a break now and discuss what you have told us so far/collect our thoughts/consult with my colleagues.' There should be at least one and not more than three times out during a session. For the final break in which the intervention is decided, arrange for the family to be able to sit elsewhere or to have some refreshments in some way.

An effective live supervision relationship emerges through trial and error. Suggestions from a supervisor come to mean more than simply the content of the words spoken. Establishing simple ground rules and ensuring periodic evaluation increase the likelihood of a successful partnership. Other useful preparation includes discussing cases, attending workshops together, and comparing the similarities and differences in the co-worker's responses to emerging issues.

Agency constraints

Therapy always takes place in the context of a particular work setting. Practitioners who ignore this fact are likely to be ineffective. Procedures that are appropriate in one agency are not necessarily effective in another. In the planning stage, therefore, the institutional constraints within which a therapist operates must be considered. Imaginative workers have turned agency constraints to therapeutic advantage. An excellent illustration is the situation where parents arrive at social services departments demanding that their child be received into care. They are not usually asking for family therapy. Dungworth and Reimers (1984: 76) recommend that in such cases a worker's initial stance should be: 'Yes I do receive children into care, but first of all the law requires me to assess whether it is in your child's best interests that I do this.' Family meetings are held to establish whether the statutory requirements for reception into care are being met in accordance with the Child Care Act (1980), Section 2. Dungworth and Reimers conclude that the multiple roles of a social worker may actually give them more flexibility than those operating in a clinical setting. Integrating a family therapy approach into non-clinical settings is examined more fully in Chapter 11.

Single workers

Preparation is even more important for the lone worker if some order is to be maintained in the session. A written plan of the session is extremely useful. Haley (1976: Chapter 1) provides an adaptable blueprint for a structured interview. A lone practitioner can find it valuable to take time out during an interview. Develop a ritual based on time elapsed, topics covered, or an impasse in the session. Time out can be introduced thus: 'I usually take a break at this stage so that I can consider what you have told me so far and get one or two things clearer in my own mind.' The family may be set a task while the therapist is out of the room or they may be left to their own devices. It is surprising how much work some families achieve during these intervals. I was working alone with an extended family in dispute over where a 12-year-old boy should live. The grandmother was determined that he should live with her and had the support of the aunt and uncle; the mother and stepfather demanded that he should go into care. My attempts to help them resolve this issue were profoundly unsuccessful; the harder I tried the more entrenched the quarrel became. I left the room in order to gather my thoughts and develop a different approach. On my return some ten minutes later the family had decided that the boy would go to live with the grandmother for a trial period of three months and then they would review the position.

During a break you might refer to the pre-session plan, or ask yourself a series of set questions such as those suggested by Sebastian Kramer (1981) 'Why worry?' 'What for?' 'Why now?' and – one that I find useful – 'Why me (my agency)?'. If you remain single and cannot find a like-minded person in your agency with whom to discuss cases contact someone in a similar position from another agency. The local branch of the Association for Family Therapy is usually a good contact place (see Appendix I for details of AFT). Better still, start a support group in your own agency.

Technical facilities

These include such items as: recording equipment; play materials; seating arrangements; and blackboards.

RECORDING INTERVIEWS

It is now generally possible to have a facility such as an audiotape recorder for as little as £20 or a video camera, monitor, and recording deck for £1,000. Focused analysis of recorded interviews is recommended as one of the quickest and most effective ways of improving practice. After any initial embarrassment has been overcome, the advantages soon become apparent. Before recording interviews you must: i) give a verbal explanation to the family of why you are making the recording; ii) obtain a written consent form that explains how you intend to use the tape and what safeguards you are taking to protect the confidentiality of the material (contained in Appendix IV).

PLAY MATERIALS

Unless play is intended to be a major part of the session then only a few, quiet toys such as drawing material, plasticine, and a set of family dolls should be provided. If sexual abuse is being discussed then it can be useful to have anatomically correct dolls.

SEATING ARRANGEMENTS

Seating positions are a valuable source of information about family relationships. Where possible have at least one more seat than there are people in the interview so family members can choose not to sit next to each other. A therapist chooses the seat with the best view of the family. A home visit is different but there it is often still possible to get people to sit approximately in a circle. During home visits, televisions should be switched off, cups of tea politely refused until the work is done. Attention to these details can make for a more profitable interview. Permission to use their home as if it were your office for the duration of the interview is usually granted.

BLACKBOARDS

Blackboards or large sheets of paper are useful to draw genograms with the family as a therapeutic exercise and as a prompt for the therapist in asking questions during the session.

Preparation has so far been considered in general. Organization for a particular family involves constructing therapeutic hypotheses, choosing options for conducting the interview, anticipating disasters, and overviewing the whole preparation process.

Therapeutic hypotheses

A systemic hypothesis is developed through studying a genogram, identifying transitional stages, and formulating ideas that link the function of the problem to the family life cycle. A systemic hypothesis is a crucially important part of a systemic interview. Interviewing techniques can then be chosen to enquire about patterns of behaviour, emotions, and beliefs that may elaborate or refute a hypothesis. A validated hypothesis provides the basis for an intervention designed to initiate change. It is likely that workers will modify a hypothesis several times as new information is gathered and the family responds to interventions made.

The following exercise addresses the task of constructing some hypotheses for a first interview with a family referred to our centre.

EXERCISE 6.3

Using the referral data given below attempt to construct at least one hypothesis for the session. Data were obtained from a referrer.

> Dear xxxx
> Would you please see Pat and let me know your opinion. Pat is 10 years old and lives with her unmarried mother Miss Jones. The problem is basically Pat's violent temper tantrums over the last few months, culminating in an attack by Pat on her mother with a knife. Pat is becoming increasingly dependent on her mother and needs her to do every little thing for her. She is doing well at school and they are pleased with her progress. Miss Jones has a boyfriend Terry, whom Pat is said to dislike coming round. I saw Pat on her own on several occasions but just as I thought I was getting somewhere she decided to stop coming.

An appointment letter to the family is accompanied by a questionnaire which asks for information about family transitions and about their view of the problem. The response from Miss Jones indicated that she and Pat had recently moved into their own home after living with the maternal grandparents for many years.

Use the information to:

a)   draw a genogram showing information given and missing;
b)   identify transitional stages;
c)   formulate hypotheses about the homeostatic function of the problem;

d)   indicate areas to be investigated to test each hypothesis.

Some readers may need to refer back to Part I pp.25 – 44 to refresh their memory about the concepts and the terms used to express these ideas when constructing systemic hypotheses.

SUGGESTIONS

Some ideas offered about this referral are: the girl is obviously missing her grandparents; Pat is jealous of Terry; Mother has probably never had to be a mother before and doesn't know how. Mother probably has less freedom now and so the girl is rebelling. This is obviously attention-seeking behaviour.

Systemically these ideas can be regarded as speculative punctuations from which to start. To make a hypothesis systemic a worker must think in terms of the process between *at least* three people, or two people and an idea/event. For example, statements such as 'this is attention-seeking behaviour by Pat to Mother' should be followed by a question which makes a connection to someone or something outside the dyad, for example 'in competition with whom?', 'since when?'. Thus a series of triadic hypotheses may be developed. Beginners often identify events in isolation and therefore interview in a way that produces startling but disconnected facts (births, deaths, ages, illness, entries, exits, violence, hospitalization, etc.) about a family's life. Such information becomes systemically meaningful when connected to the problem in a circular way.

The hypotheses our team arrived at in the pre-session discussion were as follows:

a) Genogram (see *Figure 15*)

b) and c) Transitions (T) in relationships and functions (F) of the problem: Transitions can be punctuated from the perspective of each person by asking the question 'How might this problem be useful for each person in the system at this transitional stage?' This is another way to propose a systemic hypothesis. The symptoms manifested by an individual may then be hypothesized as serving a covert homeostatic purpose or purposes, for the system. The transitional stages that we identified and the possible function of the symptoms in regulating these stages were:

i)   (T) The move by Pat and her mother from the grandparents to

Figure 15

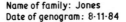

Name of family: Jones
Date of genogram: 8·11·84

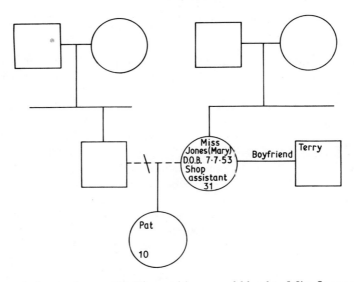

their own home. (F) The problems could lead to Miss Jones and Pat returning to the grandparents.

ii) (T) The development of the relationship between the mother and a boyfriend could threaten the relationship between mother and daughter. (F) The symptoms may regulate the closeness/distance of this relationship.

iii) (T) The freedom of the mother and child may present the opportunity for the return of Pat's father. (F) The problems could be influential in this decision.

Each hypothesis is linked to a transitional stage where relationships will need to be redefined, and includes at least three people. They are phrased so that no single individual is given the total responsibility/blame. The ideas are not mutually exclusive and are separated only for the sake of clarity, which facilitates investigation. Attempting this exercise the first few times, groups often make the error of arguing about which hypothesis is 'true'. At the pre-session stage all hypotheses represent valid starting-points which need testing in the session.

Futile arguments can be avoided by listing all the hypotheses and ordering them on the basis of plausibility. Devote energies to devising various options for the therapist to test these ideas out during the session.

d) Areas for investigation: Generally speaking it is unprofitable to investigate a hypothesis directly. Therapists who ask or suggest straightforwardly 'Is Pat playing up because you've got a new boyfriend then?' are likely to be met with responses such as 'No, she's always been a problem', thus limiting the scope of the interview. Family members become reluctant to talk and suspect (perhaps rightly) that the worker is out to identify someone or something as *the* cause of the problem. Workers are advised to contemplate which areas of everyday family process are likely to be most affected by a transition. When they lived at the grandparents who did Pat ask to help her with homework? Did the grandparents approve of the mother's boyfriends? How often did Pat and her mother go out together? Where did they go? What did they like doing? How did they spend their evenings together? Did mother ask Pat to choose food, clothes, house decorations, and so on. How has the fact of mother having a boyfriend influenced these patterns? It is often in the simple, unspectacular events of a family's life that a hypothesis can best be tested. The definition of a relationship is manifest in the humdrum organization of family life. Redefinitions of relationships will also be evident by their effect on ordinary routines.

Workers may begin to recognize family patterns associated with the type of problems referred to their agency. For example, where a young child is out of control there is often disagreement between the parents over discipline. Where there is dispute over custody or access to children after divorce a frequent hypothesis is that the couple have not divorced at the emotional level. When a young adult is behaving in peculiar ways there are often problems surrounding the separation stage in the family life cycle (Haley 1980). Minuchin and Fishman (1981) identify nine types of family patterns illustrating the inherent strengths and tendency for dysfunction in each. Therapists and teams develop metaphors that economically portray 'favourite' hypotheses, for example 'vertical marriage' symbolizes a family pattern in which there is a cross-generational relationship which is stronger than, and perhaps a substitute for, a marital union. Such shorthand is useful but workers must always beware of stereotyping families in such a way that they, the therapists, become complacent.

Options for the session

There is a range of systemic interviewing techniques that may be used to evaluate systemic hypotheses. Selection from this range tends to be specific and deliberate rather than intuitive, especially in the initial stages of practice. Planning continues to be a feature of good practice though experience enables workers to use techniques in a more spontaneous and effective way. Systemic interviewing skills may be divided broadly into verbal skills and action skills, and are elaborated in the next two chapters. In this preparatory stage workers must decide on the techniques they will use to evaluate their hypotheses. Most of these techniques involve a departure from traditional ways of enquiring into family problems. Therefore workers must familiarize themselves with these techniques through reading and rehearsal. A worker may need consciously to dismiss previously preferred techniques while developing new ones.

Disaster options (contingency plans)

Anxieties about using techniques of family therapy are usually expressed in the form of the question: 'what should I do if . . . happens?' Taking risks is a necessary part of any helping process. The risk becomes worrying when a worker lacks contingency plans for difficult circumstances. The more contingency plans available, the more confidently risks can be taken. Common concerns are the following.

DIFFICULT QUESTIONS

These are questions that put the worker on the spot. Such questions should always be answered at some stage. Giving an immediate answer may force the worker to lose neutrality or commit him or herself to doing something impossible. Time can be bought in a variety of ways, for example, 'I would like to consider that question properly and give it the thought it deserves. I will come back to you later in the session/ after discussion with my colleague/at the next session.' It may become possible to recognize such questions as parts of a pattern in the session. For instance each time you ask about the behaviour of the good child the father asks your opinion about the bad child. Identifying questions as part of a pattern helps a worker to know how to change future enquiry. Utilizing questions to ask further questions may be done as follows:

Question: 'Just what do *you* think we should do when he insults our guests?'

Answer: 'Before I answer, let me ask what do you think your husband/ mother-in-law/elder sister would tell you to do?' Or: 'That certainly is a difficult issue, who in your family deals with it most successfully at the moment?'

If the family pushes you to give an immediate answer then it is often useful to give multiple answers, like 'Well it's different for each family. There is view *x* which says *y*, and view *o* which says *p*. Which do you think would be most likely to work best for your family?'

DIFFICULT BEHAVIOUR

Trainees who worry about not feeling calm in difficult situations are often told 'You don't have to feel calm, you only have to look calm. In fact if you are too relaxed you will not do a good interview.' The knowledge that it is acceptable, desirable even, that they should feel nervous somehow makes them feel calmer. Even when a therapist has prepared well, difficult behaviours such as crying, refusal to talk, or walking out, or disruptive children, make the mind go blank. Sitting still, saying nothing, and watching are the best responses but the hardest to master. The first temptation to overcome is to comfort the distressed person, control the disruptive child, or bring an absconder back into the room. Therapists may sense the family is waiting for them to say or do something about the problem. Begin a session with a family with young children by saying to the parents, 'if the children do anything you don't want them to during the interview please feel free to handle them in the way you usually do.' If someone cries or explodes angrily, or a child becomes disruptive, this constitutes an opportunity to observe a spontaneous enactment of the family's patterns. Therapists can capitalize on or even request these opportunities. Such enactments may illustrate a problematic pattern which needs to change or demonstrate an area of the family's competence on which they can be congratulated. Therapists might use the following pattern in difficult situations:

i)   Observe the responses of the family members to the event: who comforts or controls, how they do it. What is the reaction of the person being comforted, how does the rest of the family behave when this is happening?

ii) Enquire 'When X gets upset like this what usually happens, who is the first person to comfort her?' If there is an angry exchange between two people, do not get drawn into being the umpire! Sit, observe, then ask another person 'Do you see your two brothers fighting very often? Who usually separates them, your mother or your grandmother?'

iii) Request that someone in the family attempt to resolve the problem and see who responds first, how they act, what the others do. For example, 'Could someone organize the children to play quietly while we talk?' In these ways it is possible to gain valuable information about the family's patterns through simply 'doing nothing'. The live supervision model proposed allows time out when necessary. It is remarkable how often something different springs to mind once you are out of the presence of the family. Do not take risks unless it is safe to do so. If the children begin to wreck the room, or people damage one another in a way that is completely unacceptable to you, then at that moment do what you think is appropriate. A retrospective examination of how the episode occurred will help you plan to work differently in future. Do not be dispirited about making mistakes; learn from them so that you do not repeat them. Through the analysis of errors therapists build a repertoire of what works for them in their agency.

Overview

Immediately before a session it is helpful for a therapist to go through a checklist of what he or she intends to do. Procedures become second nature. Adaptations are necessary for new or unusual situations. It takes time before the format, techniques, and way of questioning become familiar and easy to remember. Until then take a written account of the introduction, plan, and questions (even as reassurance) into the session with you.

Summary

This chapter has suggested that preparation and planning are important throughout the process of a family therapy.

Regarding general preparation, single workers need to pay attention to planning and endeavour to initiate or join a supportive group of like-minded individuals. The relationship between co-workers needs to be clearly defined initially and periodically examined. Disagreements and worries need to be openly admitted and resolved to facilitate the development of a successful partnership. Practice must always relate to agency tasks and constraints which sometimes can be turned to therapeutic advantage. Technical equipment aids the rapid acquisition of skills and techniques and are within the reach of most agencies' budgets.

The specific questions and techniques chosen to assess and intervene in a family's problem must be linked to one or more systemic hypotheses which connect the problems to a transitional stage in the family's development. Investigation of the systemic function of the problem should include the emotional, behavioural, and ideational levels of meaning. Therapist competence is enhanced when their repertoire of skills includes contingency plans for potential 'disasters' in interviews. Taking a written plan into a session facilitates clarity and increases confidence, especially while a worker is becoming familiar with an interview format that requires new skills.

The next chapter examines how therapeutic plans are put into practice during interviews, beginning with the Jones family discussed in this chapter. The therapist is my colleague Dr Elizabeth Wade-Evans. The team behind the screen is Dr Queenie Harris and myself.

7
Interviewing I

The evaluation of systemic hypotheses requires systemic interviewing techniques. This chapter introduces and illustrates circular questioning, a technique devised by the Milan group (Palazzoli *et al*. 1980a), which primarily elicits information through verbal enquiry. The next chapter looks at enactment and sculpting as two of the main action techniques which 'make patterns visible' (Gorrell Barnes 1984).

EXERCISE 7.1
Please refer to the introduction that you drafted during the last chapter and compare it to the one that follows:

'Hello, as I said in reception my name is X. To start with I would like to explain the way in which we work [pause]. I work as part of a team, and my colleagues are sitting behind this [gesturing], which is a one-way screen. They watch the way in which I work in order to help me to help you. From time to time they may knock on the door to call me out of the room, so that we can share our opinions. I may also choose to go out [pause]. We make a videotape-recording of the session, using those two cameras that you can see [gesturing]. This is so that I don't need to take notes and can pay full attention to what you have to say. I look through the tape in between sessions to work out what is the best way to proceed [pause].

We have a consent form which explains your safeguards about the confidentiality of the information on the videotape. I'll give you the form later in the session. I'd like you to read through it and sign it if you are in agreement. [See Appendix IV.] Are there any questions right now? [pause] No? OK. Before I ask you to tell me what the problem is, perhaps you could introduce yourselves to me.'

This is our standard introduction and can be adapted to many settings. Beginnings influence how the rest of the interview unfolds and should be rehearsed as a skill. A therapist should endeavour to look at everyone and no one in particular while delivering it. A family should gain the impression from the therapist that this way of working is routine. Subsequent interviews may begin in a variety of ways: 'How are things'? 'Could someone bring me up to date?' 'Did you manage to do the task I set you last time?' 'Susan [an identified patient], who was most helpful in getting you to do your part of the "task"?' 'Which couple had most discussion about what we said to your family at the end of last session?' A beginning that stimulates interactional information is desirable.

Family introductions

An open invitation to the family to introduce themselves allows a worker to view the response as a clue about family relationships in terms of the pre-session hypotheses. A therapist looks at seating positions and body postures. Do people introduce themselves? Who takes charge? Who is given responsibility? At this early stage it is important to observe, but unwise to challenge, the family organization. Often one person acts as the family 'gatekeeper' and the therapist may wait until this spokesperson has introduced everyone before proceeding to make contact with each person directly. Therapist neutrality should be aimed at by gaining an appreciation of each family member's point of view.

During this period, referred to by Haley (1976) as the social stage, a therapist can enquire about parental occupations and any changes (actual or anticipated) in these patterns. Children may be asked about their age, schooling, and interests. In this way a worker can attempt to engage each family member through non-threatening areas.

A family member may express eagerness to proceed to the problem stage by pointing at the referred person and announcing, 'It's him, he's the cause of all this, ask him, go on ask him what he did last week.'

Such interruptions may be dealt with by saying such things as: 'I'd like to get an idea of who is here first before I hear about the problem. Could you hold on to what you were saying and I'll give it my full attention in a moment.' A therapist should aim to create an atmosphere of purposeful interest rather than social chitchat.

Circular questioning

This technique represents an original contribution to the ways in which systemic hypotheses may be evaluated using the verbal mode. The theme is to gather information by asking questions in terms of differences and hence relationships. In addition to the usual direct questions, family members are asked, in turn, to comment on the thoughts, behaviour, and dyadic relationships of the other members of the family. For example, the therapist might say to the father, 'Since your mother-in-law came to live with your family has the relationship between your son and his mother been better or worse?'

A therapist is able to perceive simultaneously the verbal answer to a question and the non-verbal responses of the family members to that answer. The triadic information gained is more useful in the evaluation of a triadic hypothesis. The range of questions is inexhaustible but must always be linked to a hypothesis if it is to be useful. Family therapists who have been taught that each family member should speak for him or herself may disapprove of this method. To maintain this rule of therapy, triadic questions should be prefaced with phrases such as 'in your opinion', 'from your point of view', or 'from your position'. For example, 'Susan, in your opinion how do your mother and younger sister get on since your father died?' The novelty of this mode of enquiry seems to make people stop and think rather than give stereotypical answers. It is common to observe the quizzical and eager anticipation of family members as they wait to hear how another person perceives their relationship. Triadic questioning may be used even when important members are absent or even dead. For example, 'Suppose that your father were alive today what do you think his opinion would be about this problem?' It is extremely advantageous with families who are initially reluctant to answer direct questions about relationships. It only needs one family member to 'drop their guard' and reveal an important piece of information for a cumulative effect to develop; soon everyone is willing to talk. Those family members who do not respond verbally cannot help but betray their non-verbal message since it is impossible not to communicate on this level.

There are six main categories of question.

Sequential questions

These enquire into specific interactive behaviour in specific circumstances (not in terms of feelings or interpretations).

The question, 'How did you feel when your son told you that he felt that life wasn't worth living?' focuses attention on an individual's internal state. A series of sequential questions would put this event into a circular context:

THERAPIST [to Mother]. When your son [Frank] says that life isn't worth living, what does your husband do?

MOTHER. He talks to him, tells him to pull himself together.

THERAPIST [to Brother]. When your father tells your brother to pull himself together what does your mother do?

BROTHER. She gets furious and tells Dad to lay off, Dad and Mom usually end up having a furious row about whether Frank is putting it on or not.

THERAPIST. What does Frank do then?

BROTHER. He goes up to his room and locks himself in and won't come down.

THERAPIST [to Father]. What does your wife do when Frank goes to his room?

FATHER. She tells me that if I don't stop getting on at him I might as well go back to long-distance lorry driving.

These questions have elicited a pattern in which an individual's distress is embedded. It begins to show how the symptoms may be connected to the transitional stage prompted by the father's change in work routine.

Action questions

These enquire into differences as indicated by behaviour rather than descriptions of individual characteristics.

Avoid accepting descriptions such as 'he's absolutely impossible', 'she does nothing at all', or 'he's such a nice child compared to his sister'. Always enquire what a person does that earns that description.

THERAPIST. What did your mother-in-law do when your husband got admitted to hospital to dry out from alcohol?

WIFE. Nothing, absolutely nothing, she's pathetic.

THERAPIST. What does she do or say that makes you say she is pathetic?

WIFE. Well she visited him and spoiled him. Says he can't help it. Can't help it my eye!

This reveals the different attitudes between mother-in-law and daughter-in-law towards the son/husband's alcohol problem. It prompts a therapist to think in terms of a vertical marriage between son and mother, the triangulation of the husband's mother into this marriage, and the symmetry between the two 'wives'.

Classification questions

These allow the ranking of responses by family members to specific behaviour or specific interactions.

Open out the scope of enquiry by finding out the differential responses (pleasure, anger, suspicion, etc.) or beliefs (optimism/pessimism, doubt, etc.) of all family members towards, for example, a transition, a problem, or an attempted solution.

A TRANSITION

THERAPIST [to Husband]. When your wife said that she was fed up with being at home and was thinking about getting a job, which of the three children, in your opinion, showed most enthusiasm towards the idea?

HUSBAND. I think it was Fred, then Susie, and then Raymond. Come to think of it Ray was pretty upset about the idea when it was first mentioned.

THERAPIST [to Fred]. Who do you think was most keen for Mommy to get a job, including Daddy?

A PROBLEM

THERAPIST [to child]. When your sister stays out all night who in the family do you see getting most annoyed?

CHILD. Oh it's Granny. She always comes round first thing in the morning, 'cos she only lives across the road, and she gets really mad.

THERAPIST. Who does she get most mad at?

[*Child remains silent but looks across to Father.*]

THERAPIST [*to Sister*]. Who do you think your Gran gets most mad at, you or your parents?

SISTER. Well she says it's not my fault really, 'cos I don't get proper guidance from Dad, I mean stepdad.

AN ATTEMPTED SOLUTION

THERAPIST [*open question*]. Who most believes that putting Ronny in care will solve the problems?

FATHER. It's me really. I think that a few months away from home will make him see what he is missing.

THERAPIST [*to Father*]. Out of everybody else who do you think agrees with you the most?

FATHER. I'm not sure really.

THERAPIST. Take a guess.

FATHER. Well I hope my wife does but I'm not too sure to tell the truth.

THERAPIST [*to Mother*]. Do you agree with your husband's view that if Ronny goes into care that things will get better?

MOTHER. No, I think that he [*Father*] should spend more time with him, I think that would help. . . .

THERAPIST [*to Sister*]. Whose view do you agree with most, your mother's or your father's?

SISTER. Well, I think Ronny does want to be closer to Dad but I'm not sure about Dad what he feels about Ronny.

These examples show: i) beginnings of a hypothesis that reveals the function of Ray's problems in keeping mother at home; ii) enmeshment of a grandparent with her granddaughter resulting in an intergenerational coalition against the stepfather; iii) the bringing into the open of a covert disagreement between parents about the removal of a child to care, and the emergence of a different solution.

Diachronic questions

These investigate changes in behaviour that indicate a change in relationships at two different points in time, i.e. before and after a specific event. This type of question elicits behavioural manifestations of the redefinition of relationships prompted by a transitional stage.

BROTHER. Greg and Mommy are very close to each other.

THERAPIST. Yes, I understand that but did they get close to each other before or after your father died?

BROTHER. I think it was afterwards, they got close because Greg was really upset when Daddy died, 'cos they always did lots of things together.

THERAPIST. Before Greg got to be so close to Mommy who was closest to her then?

BROTHER. I don't. . . . Well perhaps it was Jean, then me and then Greg.

THERAPIST. And who is Jean close to now?

BROTHER. No one.

THERAPIST. How about outside the family?

BROTHER. I think she talks to her social worker, but Mommy doesn't like her.

A shift in relationships, triggered by an unexpected transition, shows how a professional can become part of a family system by replacing a 'missing' member.

Hypothetical questions

These look into differences of opinion with respect to imagined situations (past/current/future). Such questions release people from the concreteness of 'factual' answers and reveal hopes, fears, and aspirations.

THERAPIST [to Daughter]. Let's just suppose that you were able to concentrate at school, you passed exams, got a place at university, and move away from home. Which of your parents do you think would suffer the most?

DAUGHTER. How do you mean suffer?

THERAPIST [to Daughter]. Well they are both close to you and when somebody special leaves, they are missed. Who would miss you the most if you went?

DAUGHTER. I think my father would.

THERAPIST [to Mother]. If your daughter left home who do you think would be able to take her place for your husband?

MOTHER. Well certainly not me, I've always come second best to her.

THERAPIST [*to Mother*]. If your daughter leaves do you think your husband would be more likely to stay or leave?

MOTHER. I'm not sure about that at all.

THERAPIST. What do you imagine that your husband would say if he were here today?

DAUGHTER [*interrupts*]. I once overheard him say I was the only reason that he stayed.

This example shows the 'catastrophic expectations' inherent in an impending transition. The daughter might be seen as triangulated in the parents' marriage. If she successfully individuates then she anticipates that her parents may end their marriage. She can only succeed in helping her parents by failing at school.

Mind-reading questions

This type of question examines the quality of communication in a family, showing the extent to which members are aware of each other's thoughts and feelings. It also reveals differences of opinion between family members over important issues.

THERAPIST [*to Mother*]. If your mother were still alive today, what do you think her opinion would be about the problems you are having with the children?

MOTHER [*long silence*]. She, she would say it was inevitable, she said I'd never make a good mother.

THERAPIST [*to Mother*]. In a moment I'm going to ask your husband if he agrees or disagrees with your mother's opinion. What do you think his answer will be?

MOTHER [*looks quizzically at the therapist, then across to husband*]. That's a funny question.

THERAPIST. Yes, most people find them a bit strange to begin with but they're very useful to me. What do you think he will say?

MOTHER. I'm not sure, not sure at all. I hope he would disagree.

THERAPIST [*to eldest son, 19 years old*]. What do you think your father will say?

SON. I think he would agree. I don't think he backs Mum up enough. . . .

FATHER [*interrupts*]. What do you mean? I think your mother does a good job. . . .

MOTHER. Well that's a surprise to hear you say that. . . .

FATHER. Just because I don't say it doesn't mean I don't think it.

THERAPIST [*to Father*]. I'm going to ask your wife what she thinks of how you handle the children. What do you think she will say?

Such enquiries often provoke spontaneous interactions, highlighting confusions and illustrating belief systems, divided loyalties, and incongruencies between verbal and non-verbal levels of communication. It is especially useful with children since they seem to find this 'guessing game' easier than direct questions.

The above illustrations of circular questions lack the liveliness that is produced during a session. The questions are seldom asked in isolation and, with experience, a worker develops standard 'clusters' of questions designed to test particular hypotheses about the problems that arise most frequently. A useful way of broaching a difficult or sensitive area is to introduce it in terms of the worker's experience with other families, for example: 'In my experience of other families who have had this kind of problem, some have said that their extended families/friends/neighbours have been very supportive. Others have said they felt isolated and misunderstood. What has your experience been like, have you felt more supported or isolated?'

The reference to other families may do several things. It may make the family feel that they are not the only ones to go through this problem. It can emphasize the worker's experience in this area (workers without direct experience can make reference to their senior colleagues or to the literature on the particular problem). It might also help the family to define their experience, either by identifying with one of the descriptions suggested by the therapist or by prompting them to make their definition. Workers may find this kind of enquiry useful in many situations other than work with families. Theoretically, circular questioning is based on Bateson's idea (1979: 78–9), that information is revealed through differences. Here the practical application of this method is of prime concern. Readers wishing to investigate the theoretical basis more thoroughly should refer to Penn 1983, Tomm 1984a, 1984b, and 1985. It exploits the well-known tendency of individuals to be more willing to talk about other people's relationships than their own; hence it is sometimes referred to as 'gossiping in the presence of others'. The novelty of this investigative format serves to foil efforts by family members to control how they present themselves verbally. On the other hand, some families respond enthusiastically to this style of enquiry and are often enabled to make connections between events, behaviours, and beliefs that were hitherto thought to be unrelated.

Changing style

Therapists learning to ask triadic questions are presented with the problem of transgressing a basic rule of conversation, that is looking at the person(s) that we are talking about. A worker wanting to know about the relationship between two or more people will automatically orientate towards one of them, and ask a question. Triadic questioning requires a worker to break that social rule. To overcome this difficulty I have devised a way of developing a new reflex action, namely, *think, turn, ask*: Think of the information that you want to obtain, e.g. how does A relate to B? Turn to another person outside that relationship, e.g. C. Ask the question, e.g. C, how do you see the relationship between A and B?

Be naïve; slow down; persist; rephrase the question; practise; interrupt family members; use names/titles that indicate a relationship; use a family's language, phrases, and metaphors; follow a line of enquiry.

QUESTIONS MUST RELATE TO HYPOTHESES

Linking questions to a hypothesis creates a purposeful and coherent pattern and thus makes them more useful. If a worker has insufficient data prior to a session, circular questions can be used to elicit relevant systemic information to generate specific hypotheses. For example, after eliciting the presenting problem, questions such as: Who was the most keen to seek help? What was it that finally made them decide to ask for help? Why now? What is the opinion of the other family members towards help? If your agency is unable to help the family what will they do? If your agency is able to help them what will they be able to do? Such questions often reveal important information about family disagreements surrounding the problem, the event prompting the referral, and the transitional stage that is threatening the family's familiar transactional patterns. In the case of the Jones family (discussed in the previous chapter) there was sufficient information to formulate the hypotheses given.

EXERCISE 7.2

Consider the first hypothesis for the Jones family outlined in the previous chapter: the symptoms are functional in effecting a return to the grandparents' home.

Devise a series of questions related to the areas of family process that would be most perturbed by the transition of moving house. (This task would usually be begun in the pre-session discussion.) Use the genogram and the above question list as an aid. Then 1) state the area to be explored; 2) list the question(s); and 3) identify the person(s) you would ask the questions of.

SUGGESTIONS

Hypothesis 1. The symptoms were functional in returning them to the grandparents' home:

1) Area: separation/freedom from grandparents, school, friends, etc.

2) Questions:
   a) Who was most keen for Pat and her mother to move out (classification)?
   b) How was it decided that they should leave (sequential)? Who had the idea first? Who did they then talk to, what did they say? Was the decision amicable or was there a disagreement?
   c) Who misses living with grandparents the most, Pat or Mother (classification)? What do they do or say that makes people think that (action)? When they do that how do other people respond (sequential)?
   d) Who has given up the most friends, activities, etc. (classification)?
   e) Who has been most successul in making new friends (classification)?
   f) Did the problems begin before or after the move (diachronic)?
   g) If the problems persist (hypothetical), would it be more or less likely that Pat and her mother would return to the grandparents (classification)?
   h) Which grandparent do they think is missing them the most (classification)?
   i) When the problems occur who do they contact, what does

that person do or say, and do they take the advice or not (sequential)?

3) a) Questions would be asked to each in turn.
    b) Each would be asked if they agreed with the other.
    c) Hypothetical questions would be used to elicit opinions of absentees.

These are a small sample of the questions that could be asked. The verbal and non-verbal responses to these questions enable a therapist to elaborate each question, and weave question and response together into a discernible pattern that connects the symptom to the system.

EXAMPLE FROM THE SESSION

A series of direct questions has established that Miss Jones and Pat had lived at the grandparents' home since Pat was born. They have moved to their own home a few months ago. The mother's description of the problems included her worry that she and Pat were 'not getting on very well'. Pat would shout and scream if asked to do anything in the house and demand that her mother stay with her. The following transcript illustrates how the therapist starts to evaluate the first hypothesis using circular questioning.

THERAPIST. Miss Jones, who do you think Pat misses most from the 'old home'?
MOTHER. Her grandmother I think. They used to spend a lot of time together doing knitting and things, she was company for me mother.
THERAPIST. Pat who do you think your Mom misses the most, your grandmother or grandfather? [Reverse classification]
PAT. Both of them. [reluctance to give a difference is common]
THERAPIST. Yes, and which one do you think she misses most of all? [Persistence]
PAT. Well . . . I think me Gran.
THERAPIST. What does your Mom do that makes you think that? [Connects idea to behaviour]
PAT. I'm not sure what you mean.
THERAPIST. Well for instance, suppose that your Mom was worried about something and couldn't work out what to do [Hypothetical]

who would she be more likely to go and talk to, your Gran or Grandad? [Classification]

PAT. Oh, she always rings Gran if something goes wrong or if I'm upset.

THERAPIST. When your Mom rings your Gran what does your Gran say or do? [Sequential]

PAT. Well she used to come round and help . . . but now she doesn't so much because Grandad stopped her. He says we should be able to manage on our own now.

This type of interchange suggests that this particular hypothesis is worth pursuing and could be investigated in other areas and from different perspectives. If the therapist 'dries up' then a live supervisor may prompt the therapist with further questions such as: 'Was the relationship between the grandparents better before or after Pat and her mother moved out?' Additionally the grandparents may be invited to attend the next session. A therapist equipped with a method and store of questions is able to assume the leadership of a session. A therapist can track whatever issues a family raises in a circular manner that promotes the formulation and evaluation of systemic hypotheses. In the case example given, it was found that moving house had been a wrench for everyone concerned. Pat and her mother had shared a bedroom until the move but now each had her own. They agreed that the mother had been most keen on the move, then grandfather, then grandmother, and Pat last. The first hypothesis was evaluated as described above and thought to be useful.

Hypothesis 2 relating to the return of the father was rejected on the grounds that: a) Miss Jones and Pat had not seen the father for ten years; b) both spoke easily about this, giving no indication that there was any underlying distress about the subject; c) Miss Jones similarly convinced us verbally and non-verbally that she had no thought of reconciliation with the father.

Earlier in the session the supervisors behind the screen had heard Miss Jones say that she would like to have a permanent relationship with a man. The therapist had not pursued the statement at the time as she was following another line of enquiry. This earlier statement became more important to follow up as the second hypothesis was disconfirmed. The therapist was called out of the room for a time out to discuss how to evaluate this hypothesis.

EXERCISE 7.3

Develop questions that will help the therapist to pursue the hypothesis that the symptoms may be functional in regulating the development of a relationship between Miss Jones and a boyfriend.

SUGGESTIONS

These are revealed in the following annotated transcript.

Exploration of hypothesis 3

THERAPIST [to Mother]. What do you think your chances are of getting another relationship with a man going?

Hypothetical question projects past experience into future.

MOTHER. Not very good actually no.

THERAPIST [to Mother]. There's not much chance of that. What's happened to make you feel this?

Links feelings to specific events.

MOTHER. I wouldn't want to go through with the last [boyfriend]. . . . I wouldn't want to go through what I did with Terry, the way she behaved. I don't want to go through. . . . But if I did meet somebody, I'd try to make her more involved with us than the last one.

Shows connection between past experience and future decisions but the wish to try again.

THERAPIST [to Mother]. How strongly would you have to feel about someone to disregard Pat's behaviour?

Testing strength of feeling.

MOTHER. I don't think. . . . She'd come first. . . . You know. If she didn't like that person then I think that she'd seen something there what I don't see, and when she dislikes a person. . . .

Illustration of belief linked to feelings and behaviour. Mother gives Pat mystical power to make decisions about her relationships.

THERAPIST [*to Mother*]. So you would trust Pat's judgement rather than your own in those circumstances?

Comparison question confirms belief but avoids overt challenge to it.

MOTHER. Yes I would.

THERAPIST [*to Mother*]. If Terry and Pat had got along OK would you have ended the relationship with him?

Hypothetical question about past confirming current and future position.

MOTHER. No I don't think so. Me and Terry got on well together. I miss him.

Confirmed.

THERAPIST. I see. Pat, this is a very difficult question, and you may not be able to answer it, but what kind of a man would you like your Mom to have for a friend and perhaps to marry?

Question designed to provoke Pat to talk about difficult topic.

PAT [*clears her throat*]. I liked the one she was going out with before Terry.

Succeeds.

THERAPIST [*to Pat*]. How did you and Dennis get on together? [*Pat remains silent.*] You never played up with him . . . mmh.

Could have asked Mother.

Further confirmation.

The interview is beginning to show, at the level of behaviour and beliefs that this is an enmeshed relationship. Pat is being given the power to make decisions about her mother's relationships with men:

Behaviour: According to mother she ended the relationship due to Pat's behaviour.

Beliefs: 'If she didn't like that person then I think that she'd seen something there what I don't see.'

Note that in this model the therapist continues to elicit information about dysfunctional patterns but avoids making any overt challenge or negative connotation of them. This information is used to prompt further enquiry and confirmation, and at a later stage to provide a basis for an intervention.

At one point in the interview Pat begins to weep quietly. Enquiries about what topic had made her cry prompted her mother to relate the incident. Miss Jones and Terry were on the settee late one evening and Pat had come downstairs and attacked mother with a knife. As mother revealed this story Pat exploded into tears. The supervisors behind the screen hypothesized that as the therapist was making a relationship with Miss Jones the daughter's behaviour 'broke' it up. Punctuating this event from the point of view of the girl, we could say that she did not want this issue talked about; from the mother's perspective, that she gave a non-verbal message to her daughter 'do something to stop me from telling this'. Systemically this sequence was seen as following the same triangular pattern as with the boyfriend. Pat's behaviour was seen as regulating the development of the relationship between her mother and the therapist, in the same way as it had influenced the relationship with Terry. The therapist 'backed off' the particular issue that prompted the outburst and instead tracked along what was the usual sequence when Pat became upset. When Pat's crying had subsided the therapist returned to the subject that triggered the 'eruption'. The therapist pushes the family beyond their usual homeostatic threshold by continuing to discuss the incident. She continues to build a relationship with the mother despite Pat's implicit message to desist.

THERAPIST [to Mother]. You were telling me about a distressing incident that happened when Terry was there. What did Terry do in those circumstances?

Beginning a sequential investigation of problem area.

MOTHER. He . . . he didn't, he didn't do anything on the first few occasions when it happened, he said he wouldn't get involved in that way. It was up to us two to sort that out ourselves.

THERAPIST. Was there anything that he could have done that would have helped you?

MOTHER. W̦ell . . . on . . . on one
   of the times when it did happen
   and it was really bad, and er I
   did ask him to help me, I asked
   him to do something because I
   couldn't do anything.
THERAPIST. And how did he
   respond?
MOTHER. He talked to her, tried
   to talk to her, but she told him
   to shut up, to go away, go out,
   and if he doesn't go, I'll go.   Hypothesis confirmed.

The interview had been progressing for about 55 minutes. At this stage
we would take a long break of approximately 15–20 minutes in order to
decide the following:

1. a)   Which hypotheses were confirmed?
    b)   If a hypothesis was confirmed, what evidence do we have?
2. a)   What intervention shall we make in the family?
    b)   Whom shall we convene for the next session?
    c)   When shall the next appointment be?

It was thought that the hypotheses made in the pre-session discussion
were validated as plausible systemic explanations of the problems presented.

   If the problems persisted then it could result in a return to the previous
definitions of relationships: 1) Pat and her mother living with the grandparents; and 2) Miss Jones and Terry having a part-time relationship.

   The same symptom or problem may serve a different purpose for
the various people involved in the transitional stages. For the girl it
may mean a return to the grandparents while for the mother it may
provide a reason to end the relationship with her boyfriend that has,
apparently, nothing to do with the relationship itself ('Well, of course I
still want to go out with you but you can see the effect that it is having
on my daughter'). A similar exercise of punctuation can be performed
with each transitional stage.

   Practitioners attempting to change their current interviewing style
might find the following exercise useful. Analyse a tape (audio or
video) of how you interview at present. Identify your favourite or

standard questions or phrases and decide not to use them. For example, 'How do you feel about that?' is probably the most commonly asked question in dynamically orientated therapeutic sessions and probably the least asked question in a systemic interview. This is because although it may be useful to know about feelings, the answers tend to produce information about internal states rather than relationships. It may be necessary to outlaw some old favourites while concentrating on the development of new ones. In this way a worker's repertoire is expanded.

Summary

This chapter indicates that in order to evaluate systemic hypotheses, a worker needs to utilize systemic interviewing techniques. Circular questioning has been proposed as a useful method of eliciting systemic information in the verbal mode. Such questions enable a worker to gather information in terms of difference, pattern, and hence relationships. The pragmatic usefulness of these questions in generating and validating hypotheses has been illustrated through an annotated transcript of part of an interview. The reader is encouraged to experiment with this method of investigation and interviewing format from the position of lone therapist or the live supervisor. Techniques designed to assist workers to assimilate this method into their repertoire of skills have been suggested.

Family therapy is also well known for its use of action techniques in 'making patterns visible'. For those workers who prefer, or wish to sample, more physically active techniques of working, the next chapter is included.

8
Interviewing II

This chapter presents a sample from the group of skills known as action techniques. They transcend the verbal level to make patterns of family interaction more obvious and therefore amenable to change. A worker may choose to use an action mode for a variety of reasons:

1. Preference for a method which creates information through physical action.
2. Frustration with the failure of words to elicit interactional patterns.
3. A family is over- or under-talkative and so information is disguised or masked.

The techniques can be used as an alternative or an adjunct to complement or to enhance the verbal mode, or as a 'mixer' with it.

Papp describes the rationale for and the advantages of such techniques generally, by pointing out that they deprive couples and families of:

> 'their familiar verbal cues by changing the medium of expression from words to images, movements, space, and physical positioning. It penetrates the confusing morass of verbiage that often sidetracks both couple [or families] and therapist – the superficial details, irrelevant facts, and repetitious recountings – and reveals the ulterior level of the relationship.   (Papp 1983)

Such techniques create

'a living, moving picture in which complex relationships are condensed into simple, eloquent images uncensored by logic'
(1983:143).

Some therapists utilize these techniques routinely in assessment and the initiation of change. Others regard them as unconventional approaches to be resorted to when standard verbal methods have failed. The techniques outlined and illustrated here are enactment and sculpting.

Enactment

Enactment as defined by Minuchin and Fishman is the construction, by the therapist, of 'an interpersonal scenario in the session in which dysfunctional transactions among family members are played out' (1981: 79). This allows the therapist to observe, at close quarters, a family's interactional patterns sustaining and sustained by the problem. The ways in which verbal and non-verbal signals are used to regulate relationships within a family's acceptable range are revealed. The therapist can then move from the position of observer to that of change agent by intervening in the process by 'increasing its intensity, prolonging the time of transaction, involving other family members, [and] indicating alternative transactions' (1981: 79).

Minuchin and Fishman stress that families attempt to disguise (consciously or otherwise) their usual patterns of interaction by maintaining a verbal façade. When a therapist gets the family to show how they interact around a problematic issue in the session, 'He unleashes sequences beyond the family's control. The accustomed rules take over, and transactional components manifest themselves with an intensity similar to that manifested in these transactions outside of the therapy session' (1981: 78–9).

For an excellent and full literary description of this technique, see Minuchin and Fishman (1981: Chapter 7). (For a guided audiovisual demonstration it is possible to hire teaching videotapes from the Philadelphia Child Guidance Clinic or the Institute of Family Therapy (London). Addresses are given in Appendix I.

Enactment is described as a dance with three movements which might be summarized as:

1. Selection: The worker selects a particular problematic issue which the family have talked about or demonstrated.

2. Organization: The worker prompts and organizes the family to enact this problem in the session and withdraws to observe and to avoid triangulation.
3. Alternative: After sufficient observation the worker re-enters the scenario to propose alternative ways of dealing with the problem and asks the family to re-enact the scenario using this new strategy.

SELECTION AND ORGANIZATION

During the course of any session family members will present, verbally and non-verbally, knowingly or otherwise, many cues for the therapist to initiate enactments, such as:

a) Verbal cues.
    Whenever a person says something like 'I just don't know what he/she thinks about', 'I find it impossible to get through to her', 'We never talk about that kind of thing', this presents the opportunity for the therapist to stimulate a discussion enactment. 'Well why don't you ask him/her about that right now', 'OK, try discussing the problem with her now while I listen', 'Well why not give it a go right now, I'll help out if you get stuck'.
b) Non-verbal cues
    i) Whenever someone is looking puzzled, upset, sad, angry, happy, amused, the therapist should look at another person and direct them to ask a queston. 'Susie, can you find out from your Mum why she looks so sad?' 'I noticed your husband smile when you mentioned your mother, would you ask him what made him smile?' 'I don't seem able to explain to your son what "being upset" means, could you explain that to him for me please?'
    ii) Play and drawing can be a rich source of information about family process as well as a child's emotional state. Carpenter and Treacher (1982) suggest several ways of utilizing these activities in a family therapy session. 'Karen would you let Daddy help you to finish that lego building. Yes would you do that Mr Smith, I'd like to see how she handles advice.' 'Could you three children draw a picture of how you remember Mummy when she was alive?'
    iii) Children's misbehaviour during sessions provides an ideal

opportunity for a discipline enactment as the following exercise demonstrates.

EXERCISE 8.1

Selection and organization: Consider the following information and decide how you would arrange an enactment.

The family referred has a mother aged 33, father aged 32, and two children, a boy aged 8 and a girl aged 7. This is the first interview with the family. It is about twenty minutes into the session. The parents state that the behaviour of the two children is the problem. They are disruptive and disobedient. The mother indicates that she and her husband disagree and looks appealingly at the therapist who is male. The children soon leave their seats and go to play with the toys. Rapidly the noise level increases and it is difficult to continue a conversation. The seating positions are shown in *Figure 16*.

Figure 16 Initial seating positions

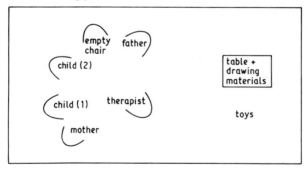

SUGGESTIONS

Sessions including children usually provide ample scope for choosing an enactment. A therapist can focus on some element of a child's disruptive behaviour, enquiring nature, drawing, or play.

THERAPIST. Is this the kind of behaviour that you meant when you said the children were disruptive?

FATHER. Yes exactly. We can never sit and talk, they always interrupt.

Comparing description of behaviour with event (beginning of hypothesis).

THERAPIST. I see what you mean. Fine, this is a good opportunity to see what happens. Would you [the parents] try to get them to play or draw quietly so that we can talk now?	Joins with parent and puts a positive label on this episode.

Open invitation for enactment to see who takes it up. |
MOTHER. We've tried a hundred times and it never works.	Blocking.
THERAPIST. Well one more time won't hurt, and I need to see what happens.	Persistence.
MOTHER. Oh all right then. [*Shouts*] Hey you lot pack it in will you.	Mother accommodates the therapist.
FATHER [*to Mother*]. Don't shout so loud. They're only kids after all.	Father quickly undermines mother and maintains problem.
MOTHER [*to Therapist*]. He [father] always takes their side.	Appeals to therapist for support.
THERAPIST. Talk to him about that because he needs to know what you think.	Therapist initiates another enactment.

The therapist, by responding in this way, avoids being triangulated, fuels the enactment, and maintains the intensity of the interaction. The family members are pushed past their usual homeostatic dead end which was manifested by mother complaining to an outsider and silent frustration between the parents.

Structural therapists tend to use enactment as a regular part of each session. Others may use it to highlight a particular issue in a dramatic and concrete way. Worker must pay careful attention to several factors about their own behaviour when they initiate an enactment.

Dealing with objections

Family members may initially express puzzlement or objections to requests for enactment. A worker must be encouraging without being dogmatic. If a person claims that an enactment would be too difficult then a therapist can offer to help out 'if you get stuck'. In the rare case of absolute refusal the reasons can be discussed and useful information gained before a different type of enactment is attempted.

Therapist posture

To initiate an enactment, workers must be very closely involved with the family members, and must make suggestions and give encouragement. When an enactment begins, however, therapists must distance themselves in some way so that they do not become triangulated. For instance a couple who have been asked to talk with each other may try to draw a worker back into the discussion either verbally or non-verbally. Methods of avoiding this trap include breaking eye contact, sitting back in your chair, or moving to a different part of the room. These non-verbal manoeuvres can be accompanied by statements as 'Carry on talking, I will listen.'

Sustaining

If an enactment begins to falter, encouragement should be offered to the person who has been given the task. A father has been asked to talk with his son about a problematic issue and the son does not respond to his father's overtures. A worker must avoid taking over the father's job of talking to his son, i.e. showing him 'how to do it'. Instead, direct any questions to the son *through* the father. For example, 'Ask your son what kind of things he would like to do with you'; 'Tell your son what it would mean to you if he spent some time with you'; 'Find out from your son what he thought had happened to you when you left home'.

A worker thus takes the position of 'coaching' rather than 'playing' for the family. Sluzki (1978) and Tomm and Wright (1979) provide specific guidelines that are particularly useful for workers attempting to promote family interaction.

Rewarding

Therapists should praise directly the person(s) to whom they gave the task. If the father in the above example succeeded in engaging his son in a conversation that seemed meaningful for them both, then congratulating the father implies praise to the son: 'You did that well, you helped your son to tell you something that was very difficult for him to say.'

If the therapist is persistently persuasive, family members can quickly adapt to this mode. Soon the therapist may only need to make a small gesture, such as a wave of the hand, to stimulate people to talk to one another. Enactments can be organized simply as part of a session or may become the focus of the whole session. Examples of the latter include Minuchin's family meal task (Hoffman 1981: 265–71) in which a family with an anorectic member attended the hospital and had a meal together under the observation of their therapist. The aim of the session was to establish how the family members dealt with the anorectic's refusal to eat. This practice was extended to facilitate the treatment of a family who lived a long way from the Charles Burns Clinic where their daughter was an in-patient. Both parents were accommodated for the weekend and participated in an intensive programme that included mealtimes, bedtimes, and playtimes. The whole weekend was devoted to an enactment of the family's difficulties.

ALTERNATIVES

An enactment reveals a problem's previously invisible structure, pattern, and rules. With this new information a therapist is better able to intervene by offering different and more functional patterns. Ideally the alternatives should be offered to the family immediately following the initial enactment.

EXERCISE 8.2
Stimulating an alternative transaction: Consider: 1) What alternative way of relating might be offered to the family described in Exercise 8.1? 2) How might you get the family to do this? 3) What part would you play in this scenario?

SUGGESTION

THERAPIST. You were right. This way doesn't seem to be working, does it?

MOTHER and FATHER [*together*]. No it doesn't. We're at our wits' end.

Confirming dysfunction by agreeing with parents.

THERAPIST. Well, OK, try something different. First can you decide between you what you would like the children to do for the next ten minutes while we talk. Then decide which of you will tell them. It's probably easier if you two sit together at that end of the room. I will talk to the children while you decide.	Takes opportunity in the flow of the session. Sets concrete task to move forward. Does not criticize failure. Alters spatial arrangement. Uses self to facilitate task.

The therapist sets the parents a discussion enactment and facilitates it by changing the seating positions and simultaneously engaging with the children to keep them out of the parents' discussion. This creates a boundary round and activates the parental subsystem. An alternative enactment would be to focus on the children playing together with reference to ways in which the parents can help them to develop co-operation, sharing, and negotiation. The therapist keeps an ear on the parents' discussion while asking the children to show him the toys they were playing with. He returns to the parents:

THERAPIST. Have you decided?	
MOTHER. Right. I've told him I want him to back me up instead of sniping at me from behind 'cos that makes me madder than what the kids are doing.	Appeals to therapist by hinting that husband is more the problem than the children.
THERAPIST. Does he agree with you?	Therapist hears but ignores and sticks to task completion.
MOTHER. I'm not sure, I think so.	
THERAPIST. Well check it out first before you do anything. Ask him now, because you don't want to get shot in the back.	Sticks to task, closes loophole by using mother's metaphor for lack of support and sabotage.
MOTHER [turns to father]. Will you do that then? Don't shoot me in the back, please [begins to laugh].	Mother extends metaphor and introduces humour to which father responds.

FATHER [*laughing*]. Right as
   long as you promise likewise.
   OK?
MOTHER. OK. Right, now let's
   get you two something to play
   with while we talk.

As the mother goes across to the children the therapist creates a boundary around the mother/children subsystem by going to sit beside the father to comment on how quickly the parents managed to come to an agreement compared to some other families and on how well the mother completes the task. The father spontaneously congratulates the mother when she rejoins them. This may be seen as the beginning of a change in the structure of the family. Discussion can then focus on consolidating what has just taken place and how the parents can continue to be supportive to one another. The children interrupt again, the therapist says nothing but indicates non-verbally that the parents should deal with it. To sustain the development of a new pattern this process will probably need to be reinforced in various ways. Sessions with the marital couple or the sibling subsystem may be useful at later stages in therapy. The duration of work will depend on the extent of the problem and its function in the family's wider social network.

The detailed enactment of this simple issue consumed most of the session. The parents express surprise that they have actually resolved something in the session and express doubts about its continuing. The therapist sets a homework task for the couple: some time every day when the children are not around, they are to have a discussion similar to the one that they had in the session. The next session will begin with the evaluation of this task.

It is a feature of a structural session to work persistently on the apparently small and ordinary events of a family's life. The family must be pushed beyond their usual threshold if a change, no matter how small, is to be made in the family's pattern during the session. The therapist then endeavours to consolidate the change by giving homework tasks on the same theme.

This example has focused on parent–child interactions, issues of discipline, and the drawing of boundaries – probably the problems that social workers encounter most frequently. However, enactment, play, and drawing are useful tools for eliciting information about the process within many subsystems.

The examples in the first part of this chapter show ways of going beyond the limitations of verbal descriptions. The structural school of therapy is rich in action-based techniques and it has only been possible to describe a few here. The reader is referred to the list of teaching resources on this approach (see References and Appendix I) for further investigation. The model demands that the therapist work mainly with the issues immediately available in the session. The cycle of work includes:

a) selection and enactment of a specific problem pattern in the session;
b) assessment of the dysfunctional structural aspects of the family revealed in the enactment;
c) initiation of change by restructuring these patterns during the session;
d) consolidation of change via homework tasks which give a focus for the next session.

In the process of gaining practical experience with these techniques a worker can expect to make mistakes and suffer occasional setbacks. If a task is not produced by the end of an interview then the period between sessions must be used to construct one. The evaluation of a task always produces information even when a family does not carry it out. Questions can be asked about who found it most difficult to carry out the task, what would have made it easier, and so on.

Sculpting

This technique uses action without words. It involves asking a family member to arrange the rest of the family into a tableau vivant that represents how he or she perceives family relationships in the past, present, or future, perhaps through a typical situation. Spatial proximity may be used to symbolize family members' perceptions of any of the relationships so far discussed. For example, emotional ties, power distribution, and transitional stages can all be portrayed in this way and thus be made overt. The purpose of sculpting is to bypass the verbal level. This overcomes the tendency of some families to talk too much, assists families who are inarticulate, and clarifies those patterns that remain elusive at the verbal level. It might be summed up in the aphorism, 'Action speaks louder than words.' The therapist acts as a director, helping the sculptor to mould the other family members into a tableau, with a minimum reliance on words. Once a sculptor has arranged other family members in a particular tableau he or she may insert him or herself into it. Participants are asked to hold the pose for a while and reflect on their particular position in relation to the others. The experience can then be utilized according to the theoretical orientation of the therapist and the feedback from the family. The technique can be used peripherally or as a central part of assessment and work. As with all the techniques described, the range of uses of a sculpt is determined by the experience and imagination of the user.

STEPS TO SCULPTING

1. Select someone to begin. Choose someone whom you think will be co-operative, but usually not the identified person.

2. Introduce the idea positively: a) as a planned procedure, or b) on cue from the family.

a)   'At this point what we do is to give families a chance to put their ideas into action. Sometimes it's difficult to put these ideas into words. It's called sculpting, or making statues. It makes it easier for people, especially the children, to show what it's like to be in their family. John, perhaps we can start with you.'

b)   At an opportune moment: For example, one person might say 'It's not that I'm trying to be difficult I just can't seem to find the words.' Then the therapist could answer, 'Yes, it is difficult, perhaps I can make it easier for you by using something called sculpting. . . . '

3. Give an example that is unlike their family: 'For instance, a family did it yesterday [this makes link with other families]. The father put the children sitting on top of their mother to show that he couldn't see his wife. What will yours be like, I wonder?'

4. Initiate movement. The therapist should not sit and expect the family to make the first move, but should go over to the person invited to begin and perhaps say 'What I want you to do, without using words,

is to shape the rest of your family into a scene that represents for you how they are with each other. You can use the whole room, you can have them standing or sitting.' Use a metaphor to describe the task that suits the family, for example 'putting people in their places', 'like a photographic pose of how the family looks to you', 'how all the bits and pieces fit together', 'a live family jigsaw'.

5. Support the sculptor(s), especially the first volunteer. Use guiding comments such as 'Is that clear?', 'Take a minute to think of something', 'Who will you start with?', 'Treat her like a waxwork dummy. Start with her head and work down. Who would she be looking at? Your son, OK, let's have him up now, children usually catch on very quickly. How would they look together?'.

6. Keep the family on the task. Talking should be discouraged with timely reminders – 'Don't tell me, show me'. Other family members who are inspired to give their version can be reminded that their turn will come.

7. Periodically ask the sculptor to stand back and assess the scene, make changes until it looks and feels right, then insert himself into the tableau.

8. On completion members are asked to hold their positions for a minute or so in silence. Ask the family to concentrate on where they are in relation to the others. How does it make them feel, think, and so on.

9. Obtain feedback. This may be done in a general and/or specific way. General feedback includes spontaneous thoughts and feelings prompted by being in a particular relational position. Specific feedback may be guided by the particular purpose of the sculpt: if the family were sculpting the changes that took place following the death of a grandmother, a separation, a new stepfather, etc., then the questions can be made more pertinent: 'Was it difficult to find a space?', 'Who moved aside to let you in?', 'Who took Grannie's place when she died?' (the dead/absent person can be included in the sculpt, played by a co-worker, a piece of furniture, an empty chair).

10. Moving on: the therapist may choose from several options depending on time available, the complexity of the information gained, and the emotional level in the session. It is not essential to insist that everybody has a turn if the purpose has been fulfilled. After tableaux

of 'how things are now', the focus may shift to a series of vignettes, 'how things might be better'. If children have sculpted their parents as they see them, the parents may then sculpt how they perceive the children. Families often find it intriguing when the children sculpt their view of the parents' relationship before the children were born.

Developmental sculpting may take the family through different stages, past, present, and future. These tableaux may be carried out in tandem with the construction of a genogram. Papp (1983), a notable exponent of sculpting, has developed it conceptually and practically by introducing movement into the technique. This extended version is called choreography and is used particularly with couples in therapy.

Sculpts can be a 'once off' exercise or be used to punctuate and highlight change during the process of therapy. Families who become familiar with the technique may prompt a sculpt spontaneously. Alternatively therapists may use a sculpt to illustrate a point they wish to make. Sculpting is not bound by time, location, or words. It is as flexible as the imagination of the participants. Powerful emotions may be aroused and these need to be handled sensitively. Sculpting has the advantages of being concrete, imaginative, useful, and fun. It can also be used as a training exercise with students or to facilitate a case discussion in a support group with colleagues, participants examining their own family, a family they are working with, or to emphasize a theoretical point under discussion.

The following brief example illustrates the use of all the techniques outlined so far in the evaluation of a hypothesis. A stepfamily was referred by a social services department, when the eldest daughter began to steal, stay out late, and so on. The family structure is shown in *Figure 17*. By the second session the therapist felt that he and the family were ready to attempt a sculpt. Verbal descriptions had been useful in preliminary explorations of the hypothesis which saw the 14-year-old girl as parental child to her two younger sisters. She had been dislodged from this position when her father moved in with a woman and her 7-year-old child. Loosely following the steps described above, the therapist enabled the stepmother to create the sculpt shown in *Figure 18*. This physical representation revealed the following perceptions. The mother, Shirley, thought that her own daughter had quickly been accepted into the family and was now part of the younger children's

Figure 17

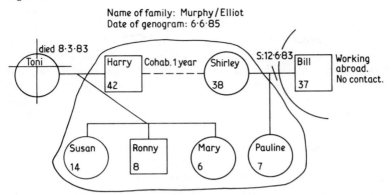

Name of family: Murphy/Elliot
Date of genogram: 6·6·85

subsystem which she placed in the corner of the room engaged in play. She positioned the teenage girl between herself and her cohabitee. It took less than ten minutes for her to assemble the sculpt. The therapist went on to explore this scenario using circular questioning, e.g. 'What would happen if you were to move towards Harry? Who do you think would be most pleased? . . . next most pleased?'

Figure 18 Drawing of sculpt

The daughter, Susan, began to talk more than previously and volunteered that she had felt like a 'spare part' since they had moved in with Shirley. Because Shirley never asked her to do anything, she felt that she wasn't trusted. Shirley responded by saying that when she and Harry had discussed living together he had requested that Susan have more freedom as she had been working so hard looking after him, herself, and her sisters since their mother had died. Shirley agreed to this and discouraged Susan from helping with the children or the housework. Susan experienced this as exclusion. Harry said that he had felt in the middle of the two women and had in fact concealed the issue of Susan's stealing for some time until it became too blatant to disguise. This secret had restored his closeness with Susan. A different story was beginning to emerge for all concerned.

The homeostatic function of the problem during this transition may be punctuated in several ways. The relationship between Harry and Susan had shifted from being symmetrical (co-parenting) to complementary (father–daughter), when father found a new wife. The relationship between Susan and Shirley began on a symmetrical note (rival partners for father and 'mothers' to the children). Harry, having divided loyalties, may be seen as simultaneously fuelling and being caught up in the conflict between his two rivalrous 'partners'. The problem covertly revived the previous relationship between father and daughter, creating a cross-generational coalition against Shirley. Revealing these processes during the session enabled the participants to gain a clearer understanding of their situation, notably the interlinking of their behaviours. Detriangulating the father from the women's relationship diminished competition and increased the degree of co-operation.

At this stage other members could have been asked to sculpt their version of the family. Instead, the therapist decided it would be more profitable to encourage Shirley and Susan to discuss openly and negotiate future arrangements leading to a new definition of their relationship. As it became clear that the two women could talk to each other without his help, Harry was given the task of taking the children to the play area while the discussion continued. The work begun during the interview was continued through 'homework' tasks that delineated the boundaries between the different subsystems in the newly formed stepfamily. The three techniques, circular questioning, sculpting, and enactment, were all useful in this session. What emerged clearly was the shifting relationship patterns during this unexpected transitional stage in the family life cycle.

Enactment and sculpting introduce an interesting and potentially useful dimension into the task of family interviews. Both techniques require a worker to take an active part in the process of enabling a family to portray the presenting problem in terms of relationships. Therapists must be aware not only of the family's non-verbal communication but also their own.

Summary of chapters on interviewing

These last two chapters illustrate the interviewing techniques needed to formulate and evaluate systemic hypotheses connecting the presenting problem with a transitional stage in the family's life. It is demonstrated that workers need to go beyond their own and the family's usual social conversational patterns, both verbally and non-verbally, to obtain this information. Circular questioning is suggested as an unusual and useful method on the verbal level. Enactment is demonstrated as a way of moving from words into action and thus establishing the connection between the two levels. Finally sculpting is illustrated as a way of bypassing the verbal channel completely, disarming the family of their 'Sunday best' verbal explanations, and using a physical tableau to represent the family relationships. It is shown how the three techniques may be used independently or together.

Techniques from psychodrama, art therapy, and hypnotherapy have also been found useful in defining the changing family relationships. It is surprising how often the very fact of asking families to discuss ways of renegotiating their usual relationship patterns prompts changes in these patterns. Assessment and change may, in some cases, be achieved simultaneously. This is not always the case, however, and it is common practice to construct a more formal intervention which is usually delivered to a family at the end of the interview. The aim of such deliberate interventions is to initiate, promote, and sustain change. The next chapter focuses on the construction and delivery of such interventions in family systems.

9
Intervening

This chapter defines and illustrates ways of intervening into those family patterns identified as problematic during the interviewing process. Interventions are considered in terms of process, timing, content, and delivery.

A therapeutic intervention may be broadly defined as any verbal or non-verbal communication from a therapist that has the potential for initiating a change in the family system. Requesting a family to come as a group, convening strategies, circular questions, enactments, sculpting, and other interviewing techniques, all have the potential to be intervention using this definition.

This chapter concentrates on those more formal interventions that a therapist prepares and delivers during or at the end of a session with the express purpose of inducing change.

Purpose of an intervention

Interventions may have several aims: a) to test the flexibility of a family system towards change and their attitude to therapy; b) to gather information through the completion (or otherwise) of tasks; c) to emphasize and continue the process, begun in the interview, of disrupting dysfunctional patterns of behaviour, beliefs, and systemic rules so that new, more functional patterns can develop. New patterns may be directly suggested by the therapist or may emerge spontaneously through an indirect intervention by the therapist.

CAUTION

Family therapy is renowned for creative and unusual interventions. Most family therapists would share the view that well-constructed, well-timed interventions are crucial to progress in family work. A note of caution is perhaps appropriate here. No intervention, no matter how imaginative, is an adequate substitute for gaining a thorough understanding of the problem through interview. Good interventions usually emerge from an interview in which a clear description of the problem has been gained in terms of behaviour and beliefs. Indeed it is likely that since no two families are identical, interventions which are not tailored to fit a particular family are doomed to fail.

Interventions as part of the therapeutic process

From a systemic perspective an intervention is part of a circular, or spiralling process as shown in *Figure 19*.

Figure 19 Circular process of systemic therapy

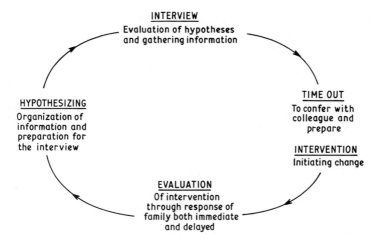

Systemic hypotheses must continually be modified on the basis of feedback from the family. A family's response must be regarded as part of the developing therapist–family system. An intervention which fails to trigger change can nevertheless be useful in obtaining information. For example, an apparently co-operative family was set the simple task of monitoring the number of times that one of the parents needed to intervene in fights between the children. The next session began with the exploration of this task. The father stated that the task had not been completed. Enquiry about this 'failure' revealed that the parents had been unable to agree as to when the children were fighting and needed assistance, and when they were merely disagreeing and should be left alone. This helped to clarify the aims of therapy and shape future tasks.

Timing of interventions

Timing depends on factors such as: model of therapy; experience of the therapist; the family's attitude to therapy; and agency imperatives.

MODEL OF THERAPY

An earlier piece of work (Burnham 1979) revealed significant differences between schools of family therapy with regard to the timing of interventions. Strategic/systemic therapists tend to follow the pattern outlined in Chapter 7. A session is spent gathering information in order to develop and evaluate hypotheses. Generally workers do not share their opinions with a family until the end of an interview. Interventions are constructed during time out and are often delivered in the form of an end-of-session message which reframes the problem and asks that the family carry out a task which is often indirect or paradoxical before the next session. Change is expected to occur mainly between sessions.

Structural therapists aim to revise relationships during the session and so tend to follow the format outlined in Chapter 8. Information is gathered and interventions are suggested during a session, perhaps several times during a single session. A family would usually be given an end-of-session task explicitly based on and continuing the work begun in the session. Discussions between co-workers are often held in the room with the family present.

THERAPIST EXPERIENCE

Most therapists (when possible) take time before intervening. Time out is used to consider the available options. Initial interventions can be used to facilitate engagement with families: 'It appears to me that you have been trying extremely hard to solve this problem, some families might well have given up before now. We'd like to consider what you've told us today very carefully and work out the best way to proceed', or 'I'm sure that if there was an easy answer to this problem you would have thought of it already'. This type of intervention can also be used to gain thinking time between sessions when possible interventions can be discussed with colleagues or derived from the literature. Tasks which require family members to monitor and record the problematic behaviours, thoughts, or feelings are extremely useful in 'buying time', gathering useful information, and providing a focus for the beginning of the next session.

THE FAMILY'S ATTITUDE TO THERAPY

This may be used as a guide to construct and time an intervention. For instance, if the family have been struggling with a problem for a long time, they may find it difficult to accept a solution offered by a therapist within five minutes. If the worker is seen as young and inexperienced (or old and fuddy-duddy) in relation to the family then the intervention must take this into account. If the family are action based and like to 'get going', then an early intervention might be offered, if only in the form of experimentation. If the family believe that one of its members is the problem, it would be unwise to challenge that view directly and risk a symmetrical battle early in the engagement phase. If the family are or have been involved with other helping agencies, this contact should be respected. It is usually unwise to adopt a 'superior' position to previous work.

AGENCY IMPERATIVES

Principles such as neutrality and non-interference may be irrelevant when the therapist is under an agency imperative to impose a solution such as removing a child to place of safety. In such situations it is still possible to reframe the parents' behaviour positively. For example, the parents could be commended for knowing when they were beyond their limit with the child and for doing the right thing by separating until a different solution could be found.

The components of an intervention

Most interventions have three basic components: a) acknowledging a family's distress and complimenting them on the efforts they have made to overcome the problem(s) so far; b) reframing the problem in terms of relationships within the family (or between the family and some other system) – this usually contrasts with the linear perspective of the family members; (c) suggesting a course of action.

ACKNOWLEDGING AND COMPLIMENTING

Acknowledging a family's distress helps to establish rapport and is best couched in terms that reflect a family's idiosyncratic language. Global statements, such as 'When something like this happens in a close family it is usually upsetting/distressing/puzzling/infuriating to everyone, even though each person shows it in a different way', ally with everyone but also introduces the idea of individual differences. Identifying individual resonses, such as 'When a child begins to "go off the rails" it often makes a mother feel that she hasn't given enough affection or makes a father think that he hasn't been firm/close enough', joins with each person and highlights what perhaps is a problematic complementary pattern. At this stage a worker is aiming to identify the problematic process without reference to its effectiveness. Compliments, such as 'I'm impressed with how you've persevered despite the setbacks you've experienced. Many families would have given up by now', while accepting a family's plight, stress qualities which are generally regarded, in British culture, as signs of strength of character during adversity.

REFRAMING

Central to most family therapy interventions is what Watzlawick, Weakland, and Fisch have called 'the gentle art of reframing':

> 'To reframe, then, means to change the conceptual and/or emotional setting or viewpoint in relation to which a situation is experienced and to place it in another frame which fits the "facts" of the same concrete situation equally well or even better, and thereby changes its entire meaning.'   (1974: 95)

The purpose of reframing is to change the meaning that an individual or family attaches to certain behaviours or interactions in such a way as to render the situation more amenable to behavioural and/or emotional change. For instance, Coppersmith (1981) illustrates the advantages of redefining some children's disturbances in terms of their normative developmental stage. Such redefinitions normalize a problem and place the solutions within the grasp of parents. It is important to avoid merely shifting a problem from one negative frame to another. Successful reframing usually emphasizes the potentially positive aspects of behaviour which is being viewed in a negative light. In the third session of family therapy a couple asked to examine the marital situation. A long catalogue of misfortune emerged including emotional, sexual, and medical difficulties. Throughout the session they expressed the view that there must be something fundamentally wrong with their relationship.

The therapist began the intervention by agreeing with the couple that their relationship had indeed been fraught with problems. However, experience indicated, the therapist said, that there must be a deep bond between them which held them together during difficulties which would have destroyed other less secure relationships. At the next session the couple reported that they now saw their marriage in a radically different light and they had already spent two enjoyable evenings out together.

This reframing repunctuated the couple's reality. Instead of viewing a poor marriage as the cause of their problems, the basic strength of their relationship was credited with enabling them to survive many crises. There was no attempt to minimize the difficulties; only to change the framework within which they were viewed and hence the meaning attached to the couple's distress.

Reframing is best couched in terms that are tuned to a family's belief system and expressive language. For example, after a chequered early life a 9-year-old boy, Saul, was placed with a warm, loving foster family who set about their task of 'compensatory love' with great enthusiasm. Not surprisingly the boy was somewhat overwhelmed by this affection and began to behave in ways that were variously described as 'ungrateful', 'rejecting', and 'evidence of his early deprivation'. The intervention began by accepting the claims that the boy behaved in the manner described. Puzzlement was expressed as to why he should 'reject all the love that the family wished to give'. Reframing this situation involved declaring that, in our opinion, children who have been 'moved from pillar to post' (the family's phrase) soon become very sensitive to the ways in which relationships might be spoiled. The therapist proposed that Saul rejected the loving advances of the family in order to avoid spoiling the close relationships that already existed in the family. It was precisely because this was such a loving family that he was being very careful to avoid depriving any other family member of their share of love until he was sure it was safe to do so. Contrary to what common sense might suggest, our experience indicated that the better the family the longer the integration of a new member might take.

This reframe successfully avoided blaming either the family or Saul. Their 'failure' was seen as a consequence of being a good family. His 'rejection' was framed as consideration for the family. This different view enabled family members to alter their attempted solution which had been to flood him with affection.

There are many ways of reframing a situation. A reframe should be regarded as a different perspective rather than the 'truth'. The aim of reframing is to shift the family's current view, but not necessarily to make them accept the therapist's opinion. Therapists must not idealize their own perspective; they thus avoid entering into a battle with the family over which is the 'correct' view. A reframe may usefully be prefaced by a statement that allows workers to alter their position at a later date. For example, 'in our/my experience it is often the case that', or 'I wondered about your situation for some time and then the idea occurred to me that'. If a family strongly disagrees with a therapist's view, it is better to adopt a one-down position rather than enter into an argument about its validity. For example, 'Well that's the idea that occurred to me today, perhaps everyone can think about that before we meet next time.'

SUGGESTING A COURSE OF ACTION

New perceptions introduced by reframing may promote behavioural change through their effect upon a family's belief system. However, most family therapists augment these perceptions with a prescription aimed at altering the repeated behavioural patterns in which the symptoms are embedded.

Classification of interventions

Whether it is possible to classify the type of intervention suitable for a particular family or problem is part of the larger debate about matching family therapy models to particular family types. No satisfactory answer has yet emerged. The intention here is to offer one way of classifying interventions and indications as to how to use them. One of the clearest and most helpful classifications of interventions is in Papp (1983: 29–35). She uses terms coined by Rorhbaugh *et al.* (1977) to divide interventions into two basic types. Direct interventions are those which the therapist intends the family to follow (compliance based). Indirect or paradoxical interventions are those which the therapist intends the family to defy (defiance based). Choice may be based on: 1) status of the problem in terms of duration, chronicity, and systemic function; 2) family attitude to professional help in general and the worker's agency in particular; 3) therapist preference.

DIRECT INTERVENTIONS

Interpretation, explanation, advice, and behavioural programmes or tasks are direct interventions which openly attempt to change the family rules and patterns of interaction. They include commenting on family procᵉss, providing information and feedback, and promoting and clarifying communication as well as establishing age-appropriate tasks, instructing parents how to handle their children, negotiating subsystem adaptation to a new developmental stage. Therapist intention is that the family should follow the task or advice given. Therapists using a direct approach must display considerable ingenuity in introducing the intervention and motivating families to follow their directions. The literature of structural family therapy (e.g. Minuchin 1974, Minuchin and Fishman 1981) and behavioural family therapy (e.g. Douglas 1979, 1981) offers many examples of direct interventions.

The illustration in Exercise 9.1 shows how an intervention is arrived at. It is not recommended that the content be copied wholesale.

EXERCISE 9.1
Read the following summary from the first part of an interview and complete the exercises given at the end.

The therapist in this case was a 25-year-old female social work student on her first family therapy placement. The author supervised from behind a one-way screen. The family had been referred by their GP. The following information was gained during the first interview.

The presenting problem was the refusal of a 4-year-old boy to use his potty. This was becoming worrying since he would retain his faeces for several days and when he did pass a motion in his pants he experienced considerable pain and his anus would bleed; he would become more reluctant to pass a motion and so would experience more pain and bleeding the next time, and so on. The GP's examination excluded physical causes or solutions. A health visitor had advised the mother about diet and behaviour modification but initial improvement had not been sustained. His refusal to use the potty was matched by his refusal to eat the foods that would ease his motions. The boy had never been toilet trained. The 3-year-old daughter was said to be copying him and was beginning to disobey her parents. The mother was English and the father Pakistani. Father had lived in England since he was 4 years old. Mrs Singh had had polio as a child and even now her mobility was considerably impaired. There had been some doubt that she would be able to have children or be able to cope with them if she did. The mother was not able to take the children out as often as she wanted, but had managed to enrol them in a local playgroup. Mr Singh had worked at a local car factory until recently, when he had been made redundant. He said he was confident of getting a job with an uncle who owned a wholesale textile company.

Two issues seemed to have prompted the mother to go to the GP for help at this particular point in time. First, she was keen for her son to go to playgroup as she believed it was important for him to meet other children. She was worried that if he was still soiling his pants he would not be accepted by the other children. Second, the father, who was spending more time at home now that he was unemployed, became annoyed at the boy for not using his potty and had smacked and shouted at him. The parents seemed to have a good relationship but disagreed over this issue.

The symptom did not at this stage seem to be serving a function in the marital relationship. The couple felt that their transcultural marriage had been accepted by both families and was seen as good. The parents were perceived as generally competent and keen to be good parents. The children were both extremely attractive and well cared for, and went freely to both parents during the session. They readily answered questions posed by the therapist.

In the first intervention, the couple were complimented on how well the children behaved during the session and thanked for their co-operation. They were asked to monitor the problem separately before the next session and not to discuss their observations until then. No advice was offered at this stage, on the grounds that we preferred to consider what they had told us very carefully before making any suggestions.

By the second interview, both parents had made their separate observations and had complied with the therapist's request not to discuss it. This was taken as a further indication of the couple's suitability for a direct intervention. Twenty-five minutes into the session, we asked the parents to take the children to the reception area and leave them there. We said that we usually give parents an opportunity to discuss issued related to adults without their children present. Separation between parents and young children is thus enacted under the therapist's observation.

The family enacted what might have been a typical scenario for them at home around the potty. The mother looked a little apprehensive about taking the boy out, the boy seemed to sense this and began to resist, the sister followed suit, the father became authoritative and tried to insist. A mini-battle ensued in which the parents failed to get the children to leave the room and ended up disagreeing with each other.

Please complete the following exercises:

1. Punctuate the summary from the perspective of each family member.
2. Repunctuate the situation in a different way from any of the family members.
3. Suggest ways of directly intervening in the situation.
4. Say how you might frame the intervention to the family.

SUGGESTIONS
1. In the family's punctuations the reader might recognize a complementary interpersonal pattern. The mother probably sees herself as having to protect her son from her overstrict husband who in turn feels that he needs to be strict to compensate for his wife's overprotectiveness.

The children are frightened that Daddy will make them do things and so run to Mummy. When Mummy obliges by protecting the children this infuriates the father who feels more justified in his view that his wife is too soft. Her husband's fury convinces the mother that she was right to protect the children from his harshness. From each punctuation the behaviour of the individuals makes sense. They see that they must behave in the way they do because of the way in which they see the other people behave.

2. In the therapist's alternative punctuation, the current systemic process is that the parents shape one another's responses into a complementary pattern of hard/soft approaches to the problem with the children. The children arouse father's wrath by calling on mother's protectiveness and vice versa. This process is likely to be repeated around many issues to do with the children.

The family is at a transitional stage where the parents are expecting the children to make more contact with the outside world, at playgroup in the first instance. This transition has been made more difficult by two factors. First, the mother's physical disability has disengaged her, and therefore the children, from outside contacts, thereby fostering an enmeshed relationship between her and the children. Simultaneously the father is at home more of the time because of unemployment, and so the parents' differences with regard to the rearing of the children are being highlighted through increased contact.

3. and 4. The intervention actually delivered in this case was:

'We would like to congratulate both parents on the successful job that they have made of bringing up their two children so far. We see how well Mrs Singh has overcome her own disability and shown that she is determined to be like any other mother. You have tackled and overcome the difficulties that can beset a marriage between two people from different cultures. You have two children who would be the envy of many parents. The children are attractive, well mannered, and obviously play well together. They are a credit to you both as their parents.

We think that you have done the right thing to come for help before things get any worse. You, Mrs Singh are extremely sensitive to your children's needs and understand them very well. You realize that they need to be with other children and experience other adults who are as understanding as you. So to prepare them for the playgroup we propose that you should arrange mealtimes and potty times as they will be at playgroup. If the children complain when you are firm, then you will know that you are helping to prepare them to be with less sensitive adults.'

A behaviour chart was established using the parents' observations to establish a reward system. The rationale for this intervention was to:

a) join with the parents first by: i) commenting on their achievements in overcoming previous difficulties with the children despite a physical disability; ii) praising the children by giving credit to the *parents*; iii) defining their coming to therapy as evidence of their astuteness, not their failure.

b) prepare the ground for the intervention by: i) suggesting that things may get worse as a way to increase motivation to follow directives; ii) reframing the problem as one of getting to the next developmental stage and giving mother the credit for already recognizing and initiating it; iii) anticipating and redefining the children's protests as evidence that the mother is being good to them rather than vice versa.

c) intervene directly by: i) avoiding directly commenting on what the parents were doing wrong; but ii) giving direct advice on how to handle the presenting problem.

Over a period of four sessions the problems of toilet training was resolved. The boy went to playgroup and became increasingly independent and confident. At two-year follow-up the situation had remained satisfactory.

The fact that this intervention was successful is not the issue here. All therapists must expect to take time, make mistakes, and correct them before intervening. The above is a relatively simple case in which direct intervention was used. The therapist and supervisor tackled the problem by putting it in a developmental framework, motivating the family to follow their directives, and giving clear instructions on how to solve the problem. The solution was offered in a way that fitted into the parents' belief system of remaining good and sensitive parents. The problems presented to social workers and other professionals who use a family therapy approach are often more complex.

Direct approaches offer a wide range of intervention skills. These techniques gradually increase the intensity of the challenge needed to restructure dysfunctional patterns and motivate families to change. Pursuing a direct approach requires the therapist to maintain an affiliation with the family while simultaneously challenging them to change patterns which are often strongly entrenched. An alternative to increasing the strength of a direct challenge is to approach the problem with indirect or paradoxical interventions.

INDIRECT (PARADOXICAL) INTERVENTIONS

This group of interventions is usually associated with the models of therapy described in Chapter 4 as strategic or systemic. Cade (1984), in a succinct yet comprehensive overview, defines paradoxical techniques as 'those interventions in which the therapist apparently promotes the worsening of problems rather than their removal'. Emphasis must be on the word 'apparently', since a therapist using a paradoxical intervention is anticipating that the family will actually resolve the problematic sequence by defying the therapist's injunction to persevere in keeping it.

Paradoxical interventions are increasingly being used to change those homeostatic patterns of behaviour and beliefs that seem to be particularly rigid or entrenched and are thought not to be modifiable by direct, logical means.

Systemic rigidity may be indicated at the referral stage where, for example, a particular family has been involved in a series of failed therapies and is difficult to convene. Evidence may emerge during the initial session in the form of unco-operativeness, evasiveness, denial, or outright rejection of a worker's requests or suggestions. It may only emerge after several sessions, when a therapist becomes aware that an overtly co-operative family has covertly undermined therapeutic endeavours. Sooner or later a worker becomes aware of a therapeutic deadlock in which the more the therapist tries to help the family change, the more the family stays the same. The family's message to the therapist, manifested in a variety of overt or covert ways, says 'help us, but don't ask us to change'. Expressed simplistically it sometimes seems that, paradoxically, the only way that the therapist can help the family to be different is by requesting that they stay the same.

Simply asking people to continue to have problems merely appears crude and cynical. To be effective, a paradoxical intervention must highlight the function that the problem(s) perform(s), but in such a way that the symptoms are abandoned and replaced by alternative, non-symptomatic solutions. In family therapy a paradoxical intervention must:

a) reframe the problem as part of an interactional process which has a positive function in the family relationship patterns and the rules governing them. This rationale should be plausible and should be based on information from the interview, but be unexpected and unacceptable. This increases the likelihood that the family will defy the prescription. Reversing a validated hypothesis is a useful way of providing such a rationale. It is best to assign the motive to the 'unconscious' in order to avoid immediate disqualification by the family members.

b) prescribe the continuation of the process and rules by asking the family members to continue behaving, thinking, and feeling as they are.

c) point to some future event that would indicate that the problem is no longer necessary for the system.

d) recommend that the family restrain themselves from pursuing this event prematurely, that is advise them not to abandon the problem until a different solution has been found.

For example, a family were referred because of the depressed behaviour of the second eldest child, a 14-year-old boy. His symptoms were the most recent in a long line of problems manifested by the children since the marital relationship entered a transitional stage initiated by the father's decision to spend more time at home. The validated hypothesis was that the children's problems kept the mother attached to the children and distant from the father, thus driving the couple apart. The family seemed locked in a vicious circle in which the children were worried that they would lose their relationship with their mother, the mother felt overburdened with responsibility, and the father became increasingly jealous of the children. The intervention made the following points:

a) The children had decided, unconsciously, to have problems, with the common aim of helping their parents to unite by giving them a focus for their renewed relationship (reversal of the hypothesis).

b) The children should therefore continue to sacrifice their own independence and happiness until they were certain that their parents no longer needed their help (prescription of the problematic process).

c) When it is clear to the children that the parents' relationship is secure then they will be able to give up their problems (future event).

As anticipated this reframe fitted the situation but was unacceptable to every member of the family. The children ceased their problematic behaviour now that it was defined as helping rather than hindering the parents from getting together. Both parents resented the idea that they needed the children's assistance in their marriage and began to draw appropriate boundaries around their marital activities.

In situations where it is impossible for a therapist to prescribe continuation of the actual behaviour, for example suicide attempts, violence, incest, or robbery, it is often as effective to commend the intention underlying the behaviour. One could say for example that two people who constantly abuse one another have decided to fight continually, thus sacrificing the opportunity to have a close relationship, so that other members of their family can appear to be saints. Therefore they should continue to find other ways of not enjoying each other until they are convinced that the other members of their family do not need them to perform this task.

EXERCISE 9.2

Imagine you are in time out and consider the case of the single mother Miss Jones and her daughter Pat, discussed in Chapters 6 and 7. (See summary in Chapter 7.) The most important hypothesis was that the daughter's problems were functional in regulating the relationship between the mother and her boyfriend. This situation was thought not to be amenable to a direct intervention, on account of information implying that: a) the enmeshed relationship between mother and daughter that had existed for many years seemed to be ultra-sensitive to intrusion from outsiders; b) a relationship 'rule' seemed to dictate that the mother should accept her daughter's 'command' to exclude the boyfriend; c) the daughter had already rejected the help offered by the referrer: this indicated that direct intervention would be unsuccessful; d) attempts by the therapist to establish rapport with the daughter during the interview had failed.

Given the above information, complete the following steps to construct a paradoxical intervention.

1. Punctuate the situation from each person's perspective in order to connect the participants' behaviours into a circular process.
2. Reframe the problematic behaviours to give them a positive function in maintaining the stability of the family system.
3. Prescribe the continuation of the current interactional process. Its cessation should be linked to some future systemic event that will render the problem unnecessary.

SUGGESTIONS
1. State linear negative punctuations, e.g. the girl is controlling; the mother is overprotective.
2. Redefine these behaviours as positive, e.g. controlling as helpful concern; overprotection as sensitivity.
3. Prescribe the problematic process using a rationale that connects these redefinitions to the maintenance of family stability or balance around the particular transitional stage: the problematic behaviour is designed to ensure that no one in the family ever gets hurt again by having an emotional relationship. So for the time being everyone should continue to behave as they do for the emotional safety/stability of the family
4. Point the family in the direction of change but restrain them from immediate change. Say, for example, at some time in the future perhaps everyone will be able to contemplate new relationships but it would be premature/dangerous at this time. Building an intervention in this way allows the family 'game' (process) to be described without specific criticism of anyone.

The intervention made in this case was follows:

'Your family, Miss Jones, you and Pat, have undergone many changes in the last few years and must have many memories of these changes. We are very impressed that through all of this you and Pat have remained so close. We see Pat as a sensitive and intelligent girl who recognizes at an unconscious level that after a period of change you two both need some time to pause before you are able to think about the possibility of becoming a complete family. And so we have the idea that Pat behaves in this way not for herself but because you both need more time to adjust. We think that the danger of coming into therapy is that even talking about these sorts of changes may be going too fast for you. We usually see families weekly but we feel that this would be going too quickly for you and so we are not going to see you for three weeks. This may still be rather quick for you and so if Pat feels that we are going too fast we want her to let us know. We want her to interrupt, to be upset during the sessions, and we know that you, Miss Jones, will have to be very patient over this. During the time between now and the next session we expect that Pat will continue to be difficult and possibly to make scenes and we want you, Miss Jones, to manage the situation exactly as you have been doing without making any changes.'

The following session was scheduled for three weeks' time with Miss Jones and Pat. It was decided not to include the grandparents at this stage since when it was suggested Miss Jones stated that she would prefer to sort this out on her own. As this seemed to be a sign of independence from her family of origin her decision was accepted.

The immediate response of the family to the intervention should be noted and taken into account for the next interview. Mistakes can be rectified and new directions can be taken. In this case, the mother looked reflective and relieved. Pat looked puzzled. The therapist felt that a good connection had been made with Mother, sufficient to make her come back even though Pat might protest. But the team were concerned that although Pat's behaviour had been positively reframed, the mother's had not been sufficiently so. A suggested improvement was 'and through all these changes your primary preoccupation has been the welfare of your daughter. So it is evident that you both act for the benefit of the other.'

By the following session, the situation had improved considerably. Mother and daughter were looking more relaxed, and Pat was responding more readily to questions. They reported giving more time to their own separate interests and enjoying doing so. When Mother mentioned the possibility of a boyfriend the mood changed again and similar patterns were observed to those in the first session.

When a positive change is seen following a paradoxical intervention, further changes are often stimulated if a therapist remains cautious and gives a restraining intervention which, while recognizing the improvement, casts doubt on its continuation. The following restraining message was given:

'My colleagues are surprised that things have eased so quickly and feel we need to remind you that in our experience making a new life together takes time. It may be that the present improved situation is only temporary, and that lasting improvement will take longer. You are not yet ready for changes, it is much too soon for each of you to be thinking of having too much enjoyment when you are apart. It may be some time before you are ready for this and we want you to go slowly.'

Paradoxically, in response to this intervention, as anticipated, they continued to individuate and pursue their own interests. The team considered that second-order change could not be evaluated until the issue of Mother and a boyfriend had been tested. Obviously the therapist had no control over when or if the mother chose to have a boyfriend. A long gap of seven months was allowed before the next appointment to allow for development and further changes. At this next interview the problem of therapeutic impasse was considered in terms of Cronen and Pearce's multiple levels of context (Cronen, Johnson, and Lannaman 1982; Cronen and Pearce 1985). This issue is illustrated in the next chapter on therapeutic impasse and failure.

Summary

This chapter has defined and illustrated ways of intervening in family systems. Direct and paradoxical strategies to initiate and maintain the process of change in family systems have been examined. It is proposed that interventions should be regarded as part of a circular process in the therapist-plus-family system. Exercises have been included to help readers to take the first basic steps towards creating their own interventions. The next chapter examines the much neglected area of impasse and failure.

10
Failure

Mistakes, errors, impasse, and failure are ingredients in the development of any model of working. Yet it is only recently that authors, such as Jenkins, Hildebrand, and Lask (1982), Treacher and Carpenter (1982), Carpenter *et al.* (1983), Papp (1983), Coleman (1984), and Manor (1984), have written about the subject of failure in detail. If it were not for these pioneers in failure a novice might think that family therapy experts always succeed. This chapter offers some guidelines for dealing with difficulty, impasse, and failure. As Jenkins, Hildebrand, and Lask state, the consequence of persistent failure by a therapist is at least discouragement and perhaps eventually profound disillusionment and burn-out.

The word failure sounds final and should only be used after all other possible descriptions have been exhausted. True failure is rarely experienced; there are many situations that merely seem like it.

EXERCISE 10.1
Taking the idea of failing seriously, consider what steps a family therapist must take to fail completely.

SUGGESTIONS (inspired by Watzlawick 1983)
To fail completely, workers must:

1. Set unrealistic goals which no therapist could attain.
2. Propose a Utopian view of life that can be reached only through therapy.

3. Hold themselves responsible for everything that happens in a family's life.
4. Retain a particular hypothesis even though it is contradicted by every shred of information.
5. Avoid sharing difficulties with colleagues and maintain an air of competence at all times.
6. Always side with the scapegoat in a family, even though he or she does not appreciate this.
7. Persist in the view that the family system is the source of all problems and ignore all other systems such as school, neighbourhood, biology, finance, and accommodation.
8. Expect fundamental and lasting change to occur by the second session.
9. Assume that all cultures have the same family structures and make no attempt to learn about different cultural patterns.
10. Broadcast to their colleagues that they have found the answer to all the agency's problems in *family therapy* and that they are now *family therapists*. Bore them at every opportunity with the virtues of family therapy, not forgetting to tell them how pathetic their antiquated method of working is: e.g. 'Oh, you're not *still* doing I.T. are you?'

A worker who faithfully follows these ten fundamental principles (plus personal idiosyncratic variations) may become a truly proficient failure. However, it is not as easy as it looks, and just when you seem to have failure in your grasp, something happens to foil your carefully laid plans. Those who want to adopt a more realistic view should read on.

Success and failure

Any concept of failure must correlate with a concept of success. If a worker's concept of success is measured by goals which are nebulous, Utopian, or rigid, then the chances of failure are greatly increased. Similarly if difficulties, confusion, errors, or impasses are negatively connoted as failures rather than positively reframed as therapeutic challenges or lessons, then this may lead to premature resignation by the worker.

DEFINITION OF SUCCESS

Success must be defined in terms of clear goals, such as who in the family must show change, and how soon this change might be expected to take place.

Goals set for the termination of therapy must be attainable and recognizable. Vague or Utopian goals, such as being happy, feeling closer, or getting on better, need to be supported by concrete goals defined by the family members. Improvement in the presenting problem is the most likely goal to establish congruence between a family's wishes and a therapist's aims. A change in the nature of a family system is desirable but a therapist may need to settle for partial success. For example, after five sessions of therapy a family stated that the problem they first presented, the behaviour of their 14-year-old son, had much improved. The therapist thought that a marital problem had not been tackled. Despite various attempts by the therapist to motivate the couple to continue therapy, both parents were adamant in their decision to cease. These wishes were respected. A pessimistic therapist might see this as partial failure while an optimistic therapist sees a partial success.

A therapist must have a flexible view of family structure since, as Lewis *et al.* (1976) stress, there is 'no single thread' indicating healthy functioning in a family. Competence must be considered along many dimensions. Contemporary therapists must accept that keeping the family together is not necessarily the aim of family therapy. It may be more appropriate to help a family separate in the best way possible. Regarding transcultural issues, Lau (1984) advises that western therapists will maximize their chances of success with families of other races by becoming familiar with the cultural and religious differences in their family structures, rules, rituals, and methods of handling life cycle transitions.

Who needs to change for success to be registered? A family with six children were initially seen after the attempted suicide of the eldest daughter. After seven sessions, this girl was much improved; she went back to school, and confessed to being in the happiest phase of her life. As therapy drew to a close, the second daughter stopped eating and was eventually admitted to hospital for anorexia. As she became more independent, and her eating ceased to be an issue, another child manifested behavioural problems, and so on. Most workers are familiar with this kind of process in which as soon as one problem is solved, it is replaced by another. Should this be counted as two successes and another problem, or as failure? More realistically it might be defined as an impasse, or a further move in the therapeutic game between therapist and family. A new hypothesis was made which linked the symptoms in the children with the wish to maintain the relationship with professionals.

When is the success of therapy evaluated? A family who appear to have changed during the course of therapy may be re-referred for a similar problem in six months' time. A family who drop out of therapy with no apparent changes may, at six-month follow-up, show significant signs of improvement and attribute this to the therapist. Family systems change at different rates and so the time of evaluation must allow for those families who change after therapy has ended. For example, a family had been given a paradoxical intervention which positively connoted the poor relationship between a mother and her stepdaughter: the therapist said that he was sure that they would be able to get on with each other when they felt that a decent time had elapsed since the death of the girl's mother, who had died four years previously. It was stated that this might possibly take another five years or so and that they must be patient. The therapist recommended that they continue to fight and argue to show how much they both honoured the memory of the dead mother. The father was given the task of making sure that the two women fought regularly. The family dropped out of therapy. Follow-up, ten months later, revealed that the threesome were getting on much better and the fighting had virtually ceased. The family reported that they had not been able to face the prospect of another five years' fighting and decided that four years was a 'decent enough time'.

These guidelines about success in terms of goals, people, and time enable us to approach a better definition of failure. Failure occurs when minimal, feasible goals set at the beginning of therapy have not been achieved within a realistic time, despite the best efforts of the therapist.

RECOGNIZING FAILURE

There are various signs that a therapy is on the road to failure. Do you find yourself doing any of the following:

1) working harder and harder without achieving any change at all?
2) dreading family sessions, the phenomenon that Treacher and Carpenter (1982) refer to as 'Oh no. Not the Smiths again!'

3) conducting sessions consisting of pleasant but aimless chat?
4) arguing with a particular family member?
5) devising increasingly elaborate interventions with decreasing amounts of change and degree of conviction?

Such signs indicate a therapist is at an impasse. What then can be done to overcome this stage? Jenkins, Hildebrand, and Lask (1982) elaborate on the error of totally blaming either a therapist or a family for failure. This only increases the despondency of the therapist or decreases the motivation of the family. Analysis of an impasse must be systemic, punctuating the therapeutic system from each aspect. For our present purposes the therapeutic system is divided into: therapist factors; therapist context; family factors; and family context. Some potential problems are identified and various solutions are offered.

THERAPIST FACTORS

Inadequate record keeping

Family therapy sessions are notoriously difficult to record owing to the number of people involved, the emphasis on process rather than content, and the amount of information on the non-verbal level. No recording at all can lead to aimless and repetitive interviews. An interview structured around evaluating hypotheses aids recording. It is perfectly acceptable for the worker or live supervisor to take notes during a session. The family tree is an excellent information-storage system. An intervention should always be kept verbatim. Video or audiotape recording a session is ideal. The family might be asked to keep written records of problems and so on.

Problems of skills

No worker ever reaches a stage of perfection. Therapists increase their skills repertoire as the complexity of their work increases. Some early problems are:

Lack of technique: A worker must continue to read, attend workshops and courses, and rehearse relevant techniques preferably in a support group. A common mistake is to use the correct technique but the wrong language. Families usually have a way of describing events that fits with their belief system. Therapists who question or intervene in ways that persistently clash with this language are not likely to be influential. If a particular problem cannot wait for the worker to develop the necessary skills then referral to another worker, or another agency, might be appropriate. Alternatively, it is possible, using the method of live supervision, to develop skills while being guided by a more competent worker.

Timing and pacing.   Successful application of techniques requires sensitivity to the speed at which a family is able to accommodate to an outsider. Some families adapt quickly and accept intensive questioning and direct interventions relatively soon in the therapeutic process. Other more reserved families only treat interventions seriously if the worker proceeds more slowly. A therapist should look for clues about the tempo which a family adopts in the early stages of work. They should observe the pace at which a family speak and behave, and the language they use. For example, a therapist interviewing a family whose members look anxious, talk quietly, and use expressions such as 'we talked for ages before we decided to ask for help', would be unwise to adopt a rapid pace of working. The interval between sessions is also an important factor to consider. If therapy is failing, a longer gap between sessions can help both therapist and family. Palazzoli (1980) discusses the theoretical basis for and pragmatic advantages of a long interval between sessions.

Proximity to family.   As with the issue of tempo, a therapist must aim to assess the degree of proximity needed to adapt to a family. A worker will find that using a close, empathic style does not work in every case. Minuchin and Fishman (1981: Chapter 3) point out that it is necessary for the therapist to develop the ability to relate to families from a position of closeness, distance, or a median point. Family members give many clues about the distance they will tolerate.

Neutrality.   This indicates a worker's ability to side with everyone and therefore with no one in particular. At any point a therapist will be more aligned with one part of a family than another, e.g. while talking with one person(s) about another, or seeing an individual during the course of therapy. For various reasons, workers may find that they lose their overall neutrality and collude with a particular point of view (punctuation). Neutrality can be regained by repunctuation (see Chapter 3). For example a worker may find that he or she has been persistently siding with a 'scapegoated' child. Repunctuation involves a worker considering such questions as: What is the child doing that makes the parents behave in the way that they do?

Therapists' views will stem from their position and experiences in their family of origin and procreation, as well as in other important relationships. In identifying why a therapy is 'stuck' these issues must be included as possible reasons. An obvious example is when younger therapists side with the younger members of a family and collude with their opinions and actions, thus alienating the parents.

Interventions may not be succeeding because of the family's view of the worker: he or she is the wrong age, gender, class, or colour, and has the wrong professional identity and so on. It is generally more effective to 'advertise rather than conceal' such undeniable differences (Watzlawick, Weakland, and Fisch 1974:124–26). For example workers may adopt a one-down, complementary position to a parent who is much older than themselves by saying: 'I know that it's usual for young people like myself to disregard the opinions of the older generation but I think that a lot of the traditional values make sense.' In this way the older person may then be more able to accept the opinions of the younger generation, including the therapist. Other differences may be dealt with in a similar fashion. Many advocates of co-working emphasize the importance of having a male/female team to retain a balanced perspective. This is important but other differences based on age, class, or religion require equal consideration. A worker's personal value system may be radically incongruent with a family's and thus make repunctuation difficult. If repunctuation would contravene a worker's personal code, then it might be best to refer the family to a different worker.

THERAPIST CONTEXT

Issues of therapist context are dealt with in detail in Part 3. Brief reference is made here to some of the important factors.

Supervision

A lone therapist may have a supervisor who is not knowledgeable about or sympathetic towards a family therapy approach. Efforts may then be directed towards establishing contact with a consultant from a different team or from outside the agency. Agency managers must be reassured that they would still be in control of overall case management according to agency policy. Ideally contact should be established between outside consultant and line manager.

Live supervision can run into problems if difficulties are not discussed as they arise. Even a successful working relationship encounters difficulties relating to a particular family or type of problem over which the members of the team disagree. These differences are best regarded as new punctuations and should be made overt and discussed. For instance, the team of which I am a part was at an impasse with a particular problem. This persisted until we were able to discuss and resolve a difference relating to the different perspectives of two team members on a religious issue.

Conflict with agency colleagues

Unsympathetic, unsupportive agency colleagues can sometimes be a problem particularly for beginning therapists. Conflict can often be minimized by avoiding a competitive stance towards other styles of working. Seeking the views of colleagues practising a different model of working helps to diminish any impression of aloofness or superiority and may give some useful ideas. Adopt a humble and helpful approach.

Problems in the wider professional network

An impasse in therapy may be due to a lack of liaison between different agencies involved with a particular family. Health visitors, general practitioners, social workers, and teachers are just a few of the professionals whom any family will meet at some stage in its life cycle. If these agencies pursue radically different policies then the family may become the victim of conflicting advice and find it more difficult to change. Such difficulties may be resolved by simple but effective information-sharing and agreement on the respective roles of the professionals. For example when working with a family in which the eldest boy was refusing to go to school we were clearly not making any headway. This impasse was not overcome until we discovered that while we were reframing his behaviour as understandable in terms of the family system, the general practitioner's receptionist was regularly giving the parents a sick note to present to the school. In more serious situations inter-agency contact needs to be regular and may take the form of network meetings as advocated by the Rochdale NSPCC Special Unit (Davies *et al.* 1985) and Dimmock and Dungworth (1985).

Palazzoli *et al.* (1980b) discuss cases where a family's involvement with another professional may be threatened if therapy succeeds. Take for example a family in which the mother relied not on her husband but on a male social worker for guidance and support; the family was referred 'to enable [it] to be more independent'. Initial attempts met with failure. Lack of success in family therapy was seen as being functional in maintaining the relationship between the family and the other professional. This hypothesis led to an intervention that positively connoted the relationship between the mother and social worker, and prescribed its indefinite continuation. It was further recommended that she always turn to the social worker for help and thus protect her husband from having to make any important decisions in the family. Soon after this intervention, the family began to take more responsibility for itself.

A systemic view gradually enables the worker to see the interconnectedness between different systems and perhaps to recognize that problems may be between a family and some other professional system rather than internal to the family.

FAMILY FACTORS

Resistance and lack of motivation are often pejorative terms applied to those families who apparently defy a therapist's best efforts to change them. As systemic analysis has become more sophisticated the error of such descriptions has become clearer. These words are now more correctly seen as describing a relationship between family and therapist rather than a characteristic of the family.

The first step in overcoming 'resistance' is to follow statements such as 'This family is resistant', or 'But they aren't motivated', with the question 'To what or whom is the family resistant?' The characteristic can then be understood as part of a pattern between the family and someone or something else. This opens up more possibilities for increasing motivation or decreasing resistance. This subject has been written about extensively (Palazzoli *et al.* 1978, Anderson and Stewart 1983, Papp 1983, de Shazer 1984, Cade 1985). Here it is only possible to illustrate a few of the more important issues. Methods of anticipating and dealing with some of these issues at the stage of referral and convening were discussed in Chapter 7. This section considers such problems as they emerge during therapy.

At least part of all resistance by family members is resistance to the intrusion of a worker. This must be regarded as natural and indeed desirable. The opposite case, a family who immediately revealed their every secret to a stranger, would be regarded as not a little unusual and uninhibited. 'The family refuse to be helped' or 'They deny the real problem' are statements frequently made by frustrated therapists. At this stage it is important that they take time to hypothesize about potential reasons for non-compliance rather than persist with the current strategies.

Disagreement over the causes of the problem

Reluctance to change might reflect a basic split in the family, or between the family and professionals, about the cause of the problem. Common disagreements revolve around such issues as: is the problem organic or social? is the problem school- or family-based? is the child intellectually impaired? is the mother too soft or the father too strict? Questioning designed to elicit differences is a priority before further change-orientated interventions are attempted.

It is generally unwise to take a firm position when such disagreements occur unless you have the backing of those professionals who make decisions about causality. Maintain a neutral stance in the debate. If options other than family therapy have not been previously examined, then it may be necessary to consider them before proceeding. If the resultant tests prove negative then family members can continue family therapy, reassured that the worker took their worries seriously. If the results are inconclusive and a family remains sceptical, then an 'as if' technique can be adopted (Treacher and Carpenter 1982). This involves accepting a family's doubts and offering to proceed 'as if' the problem is something that the family can solve. This can be offered within the framework of the therapist's certainty that such a caring and concerned family would wish to try everything before accepting that the situation is unchangeable. Alternatively, work with the family can continue under the title of family 'meetings' rather than 'therapy'.

Disagreement about the goals of therapy

A family might agree about the nature of the problem, but their respective aims about desired outcome might be quite different. For example, a mother and her 15-year-old daughter left the family home after the daughter had disclosed that her father had made sexual advances towards her. The mother and daughter agreed that they wanted help with sorting out their lives after the recent traumatic revelation by the daughter. Careful questioning revealed that the mother's goal was to get the family back together, whereas the daughter's aim was to build a life separate from her father. Progress could not be made until the options had been examined and goals had been clarified.

Disadvantages of change

An outside observer may perceive a family's problems as unbearable yet the family may have covert reasons for keeping things as they are. Recently the author interviewed a family in which the father had failed to respond to what was generally regarded as an effective anxiety management programme. As examination of previous therapy showed that several attempts had been made to help the individual family members. In the first family interview the question was posed: 'What would be the disadvantage for each person in the family if the father was to become more confident?' After the initial astonishment that usually greets this question, his wife said 'Well I suppose that if he became more independent then he may decide to leave me.' Systemic functions of the husband's problem began to be revealed. Sometimes after an initial problem has been resolved another emerges. For example, after three sessions, the relationship between a 14-year-old girl and her mother improved after years of estrangement. The family re-referred themselves four months later reporting that the 10-year-old son was glue sniffing and needed to be watched 'every minute of the day' by his mother. Enquiry showed that one effect of the improving relationship between mother and daughter had been to displace the boy from his mother's affections. His response might be seen as a homeostatic move in the transition prompted by therapy.

Habitual clients and difficulties in termination

Some families are termed 'needy', 'inadequate', or 'habitual clients'. They are often familiar with agency practice and priorities. Whenever termination is suggested the family invariably present another problem in a way that ensures that the worker must respond. A repetitive sequence develops in which the more the worker tries to help the family to become independent, the more dependent on the worker the family seems to become. Workers begin to doubt whether second-order change will ever occur. In such cases it is useful to define the relationship clearly as assistance not therapy. Help should be offered without an expectation of change. A worker may say:

'I have discussed my work with some colleagues and they say that I have been unrealistic to keep raising your hopes about changing. In an agency there are about 10 per cent of all cases that do not change and probably your family is one. They have advised me to stop trying to help you to be more independent and instead support you. I will come to visit you regularly whether you ask me to or not, whether you have a problem or not.'

This strategy removes 'having to have a problem' from the family–therapist relationship and can lead to a decrease in the intensity and frequency in the presentation of difficulties.

The 'illusion of alternatives' (Watzlawick 1978) gives families an element of control over termination, for example,

'Now that things are going better perhaps I should see you less often. My colleagues say that I should continue to see you at least every two months. I thought that you were strong enough for it to be three months. After discussion we decided that perhaps your family are the best judges of when it should be.'

The family is given the choice between an interval of two months or three months. This 'choice' is within the framework 'there will be an increase' which is chosen by the therapist. Whichever option the family chooses the time interval between sessions is lengthened.

Families who are sent for therapy

A worker's attempts to help may be resisted, overtly or covertly, because a family have been sent for therapy by another agency, for example, or under some legal threat. Therapy may still be possible as long as these reasons are made overt and clear. A family attending our clinic showed extreme reluctance to be engaged during the first session. They gave little information no matter how hard the therapist tried. Eventually they were asked whose idea it had been to seek help. The parents replied that a social worker had decided to discontinue care proceedings on the condition that the family attended therapy. The referral letter had said that the family was motivated to seek help. Work with the family was able to proceed when the threat had been brought into the open, and it was made clear that they would not be seen unless this was their choice. In serious situations a therapist may openly ally with the referrer and state that unless the family co-operate then they will support the move for the children to be removed or not returned to the family (see Chapter 5 pp.89 – 91).

FAMILY CONTEXT

The error of viewing an individual as the exclusive focus of therapeutic attention must not be replaced by the error of seeing the family as the sole source of dysfunction. Any person is a member of several systems simultaneously. For example a 10-year-old boy may be described as a child, son, brother, friend, patient, pupil, choirboy, scout, grand-child, and so on. The different systems to which these descriptions refer are connected and influence one another through the person concerned. If work with a family is failing, then examination of a family's extended network including kinship, friends, and neighbours is recommended by most family therapists. Spark (1974) and Guerin and Guerin (1976) recommend convening members of the extended family as a routine procedure. Sluzki (1978) advocates convening additional people when therapy has become deadlocked. Family members may be asked 'Who outside your immediate family is most concerned (influential) with the current problem?' If this person(s) cannot be convened then their contribution can be examined by asking each member of the family questions such as 'If [the absent member] were here, what would they say about your family coming for therapy?', or 'Who does she think is most responsible for the problem?' All the questions asked of those present in a session can be asked of an important but absent member.

A final example may tie together many of the points made in this section. It refers to the case of the single mother and 10-year-old daughter presented throughout Part II of this book. The temper tantrums and physical attacks had ceased, so a fourth session was planned with a gap of five months to establish whether change had been maintained. While Pat had been away on holiday, her mother had by chance re-established a relationship with Harry, an ex-boyfriend. Pat and he seemed to be getting on well. The therapist examined the impact of this news of a change in a neutral fashion. The therapist asked questions such as 'If you and Harry should decide to make a go of it [mother's words] then whose opinion between yourself, Pat and your parents would be most influential in making the final decision?' Mother replied that it would be Pat first, her parents (Pat's grandparents) second, and herself last. We concluded that the rule seemed largely unchanged: Pat was still being given the power of veto over her mother's relationships.

Pat, who after the first session had become more open and talkative, resumed her silence during this interview, and persisted in answering 'I don't know' or 'I'm not sure' to any question asked. At this stage the therapist took a break and the team forced themselves to answer the following questions:

1. Was the idea that Miss Jones should not give Pat the final decision based on a value judgement rather than a sound theoretical principle?
2. How might our questions be maintaining instead of challenging the current rule?
3. What was there about the therapist system (worker plus supervisors plus agency context) that might be rendering our interventions impotent?

In order to answer the first question, we decided to ask another one: Did Miss Jones want a) only a father for Pat or b) also a partner for herself? If the answer was a) then Pat could make the decision since it would be 'her' relationship that was at stake. If the answer was b) then she could not make the decision, since she could not know what was the right relationship for someone else.

The second and third questions were tackled using Pearce and Cronen's concept of multiple levels of context (introduced in Chapter 1). The presentation of the therapeutic system in *Figure 20* shows that the questions asked by any worker arise from the context of the non-verbal

Figure 20 Multiple levels of context: an analysis of therapeutic impasse

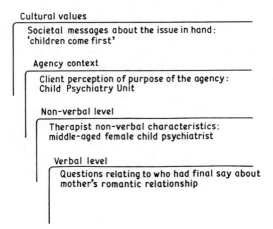

information of the worker, which arises from the context of the client's perception of the agency's purpose, which arises from the context of contemporary cultural mores. As time passes it is easy for a worker to forget the various ways in which clients may interpret these levels of context and therefore give different meanings to the worker's actions.

The therapist's questions were intended to introduce the idea that the couple could not continue to control each other's lives, but may have been having the reverse effect. Although our team's emphasis was on a family approach, the name of the agency, and the title, age, and gender of the therapist, set within the context of contemporary cultural mores, gave the questions a different meaning from that intended. These levels of context and the interplay between them often go unnoticed. After a period of working for a particular agency professionals may forget the messages that are implicitly communicated to their clients by their personal information (such as: gender, age, accent, and professional title) as well as the name and function of their agency. Clients 'hypothesize' about what professionals think and do, just as professionals hypothesize about their clients. For example, a parent's decision not to attend a family meeting may be based on an assumption that professionals will blame them for the problem with their child. This impression may be formed through previous experience of therapy and/or prevailing 'popular' opinion about who is held responsible when there are difficulties between parents and children. In this particular case the therapist had not given direct advice in order to avoid becoming yet another person taking responsibility for their decisions. Instead she had examined the basic question: who would have most say between Pat and her mother in the 'choice of a partner' for Miss Jones, in a variety of ways over many issues. For example: '(to Pat) How will you know when your mother is ready to make a firm commitment to another person?; (to mother) 'When Pat is a teenager do you think that she will give you the responsibility of choosing her boyfriends?' The therapist attempted to maintain a neutral tone of voice so as not to convey an opinion. The intention was to elicit answers that would highlight the difficulties created when the major responsibility for choosing a partner is delegated to another who cannot be in possession of the information necessary to make that choice. This would emphasize the importance of mother and Pat choosing their own partners and friends rather than delegating such responsibility. These questions seemed to be having the opposite effect to that intended. The more we asked who would have the final say, the more the mother answered that Pat would have the final say; the more that the mother answered Pat, the more we asked who will have the final say?

During our team discussion it became clearer that we had become blind to the multiple levels of context which qualified these questions. The therapist's neutrality effectively meant that the family had to hypothesize about her opinions. The available 'clues' were that the therapist was female, late middle age (a grandmother 'figure'), and a child psychiatrist working in a clinic for children. Current 'popular' opinion consistently impressed upon the parents that they must always put the interests of their children first. We hypothesized that given these layers of context Miss Jones presumed that in the therapist's opinion Pat's views should be paramount and therefore interpreted the questions as a test: are you still giving Pat the final say?

This analysis led us to make an intervention which enumerated a variety of ways in which other families in similar situations had solved this particular dilemma. The neutral tone of the message conveyed that we had no particular bias about which was the 'correct' solution. Pat's reluctance to communicate her opinion about her mother's relationships was positively reframed as a message to her mother 'it must be your own choice'. Therapy continued and was marked by an increasing individuation between mother and daughter and the establishment of other intimate and enduring relationships. The rule of the relationship: 'Other people are a better judge of who is good for me than myself' changed.

This impasse had been overcome not by gathering even more information about the family, as is often useful, but by examining the multiple levels of context in which a therapist operates. The influence of these levels can be forgotten and overlooked through familiarity with one's working context.

Summary

This chapter has considered the subject of failure as an important issue in working with families. It is often through mistakes that important breakthroughs are made. Difficulty, impasse, or outright failure can be positively reframed as a therapeutic challenge; this avoids a futile blaming stance. Punctuation of the therapeutic system from the aspect of each of the important elements makes a systemic analysis of an impasse possible. This often facilitates the formulation of another hypothesis, if not for the family in question then for future practice.

Part III examines how practitioners in non-clinical settings have been able to apply in their own work the concepts and skills of the kind outlined in this book.

PART III
Agency context

Introduction to Part III

Therapy is never practised in a vacuum. Workers must always consider their agency context when applying any models of working, especially when that model introduces a substantial difference into the agency's habitual mode of practice. In 1975 Jay Haley argued that it was a fundamental error to adopt a family therapy approach in an agency that used other models of working. He proposed exclusivity in the form of separate family therapy agencies. By 1982 over 300 private institutions of family therapy had emerged in the USA. In the UK, however, private practice has not mushroomed to the same extent.

In 1985 there had been significant contributions from both sides of the Atlantic describing the practice of family therapy in public institutions: Bentovim, Gorell Barnes, and Cooklin (1982); Treacher and Carpenter (1984); Berger and Jurkovic (1984) and Campbell and Draper (1985). In the foreword to Berger and Jurkovic, Haley states that the book addresses a major issue in the therapy field: 'what to do about the social systems that impinge on the family-oriented therapist' (Berger and Jurkovic 1984: ix). The past decade has thus seen a movement away from exclusivity in favour of the use of family therapy in public sector agencies. Within the public sector there exists a heterogeneous collection of agencies. Some are more able to adopt an openly therapeutic role where the practitioners may legitimately call themselves therapists. Other agencies perform multiple functions and therapy is accorded low priority.

Part III of this book examines how some practitioners in social services offices and probation departments have used a family therapy approach although their agency's first task was not one of therapy. This study pays particular attention to the three phases of getting started, surviving, and developing. Case examples are used to illustrate issues of application.

The teams involved in this study were the social services departments of Newcastle upon Tyne, Cleveland, and Birmingham, and a divorce conciliation team in Birmingham. These particular agencies were chosen on account of personal contacts via training courses; their selection is not based on research criteria. Information was gathered through audiotaped semi-structured interviews, questionnaires, and case studies submitted by the participants. The author selected and edited information from a rich source of material submitted by participants.

11

Integrating family therapy into a social work agency

Often, when adopting a new approach, practitioners will be keen to apply novel techniques in their work without considering the concomitant effects on their work setting. The introduction of a new idea or different way of working into an agency can be viewed systemically as triggering a series of transitional stages in that agency system. Successful integration depends only partly on an individual worker's enthusiasm to read about, rehearse, and implement techniques. Agency traditions are explicitly or implicitly challenged in many areas of the working context. Relationships between staff members may undergo redefinitions based on differing attitudes towards a new way of working. Existing alliances may be broken and new ones formed. Coalitions can develop that lead to secrecy and destructive rivalries. These factors need to be considered and dealt with carefully if newly learnt skills and proposals for changing working practice are to have a reasonable chance of being adopted by an agency. Strategies for introducing clients, colleagues, and management to a new approach are vital for its survival and development.

Held (1982), analysing this process from the perspective of a family therapist arriving in an agency, advises against being seen as a 'new broom' and thereby creating antagonism and resentment in established staff members. This chapter considers the position of practitioners attempting to integrate a systemic approach into the agency they work in. Although specific agencies are considered the lessons are generally applicable.

Beginning

SUPPORT GROUPS

The importance of gaining the support of a co-worker cannot be over-emphasized. A colleague from the same office is ideal, but occasionally a worker from another office can be recruited. All contributors stressed the importance of a support group in getting started. The most common features of these groups were as follows.

Membership

Numbers ranged from four to eight, usually working in pairs. In the first instance, recruitment was often due to a particular individual's enthusiasm and credibility. It was important not to make general, extravagant claims about the method but to directly engage people perceived as interested in trying new ways of working. The criterion for membership was keenness to learn; entry was not restricted to qualified staff. Groups were initially closed so as to encourage the development of trust and confidence, and facilitate honesty about personal and professional inadequacies. The divorce conciliation team were already a task-centred team, responsible for preparing reports for the civil cases in a section of the city. All groups eventually required members to practise as well as express interest. In several cases it was thought to be an advantage to have a member of management as part of the group.

Purpose

Groups met regularly, usually weekly, and focused on issues of theory, practice, role play, and case discussions. Contributors stressed that the enthusiasm which flourished in the formation of these groups needed to be channelled constructively. The Newcastle group drew up a list of aims that could realistically be achieved in the first and second years. These objectives included: the allocation of time for joint family work; the purchase of technical equipment necessary to record interviews (audio in one year – video in five); permission for some members to embark on formal family therapy training at the local polytechnic; and referral of families to the group in a planned way. All groups went through a 'purist' phase, adhering to a particular method until its skills were mastered.

Benefits

Members commented on the relief experienced by sharing responsibility for difficult family work and the inspiration derived from the pooling of different talents. Groups tended to be task centred. Concepts were grasped through regular discussion. Skills were rehearsed and mastered through role play. Groups found it helpful to tack back and forth between discussing a particular article and implementing its proposals. Successes and failures were discussed in detail in order to learn from the experiences of others. Role play centring on micro skills practice, such as how to introduce an enactment or sculpting, or improve circular questioning, was regarded as especially useful. Each person was required to take a turn at being a role play therapist. The fact that the groups were initially closed enabled participants to expose and try to overcome their weaknesses in a supportive environment. Once participants began to tape record interviews, selected passages portraying difficulties could be used to focus discussion on specific problems. The ability of extrovert members to introduce new techniques in their work with families very quickly was complemented by the talent of others to translate theories into practical methods. Encouragement to experiment, take risks, and overcome difficulties was another feature common to the groups.

Suggestions arising from case discussions could be relayed to a family, thus giving workers what Gorell Barnes (1984: 119) has called a 'long distance team'. Workers report that these team messages introduce a novel slant to their work which is appreciated by themselves and the families. A practitioner without a live supervisor is thus able to employ the kind of strategic messages suggestd by Cade (1980) and Papp (1980, 1983). For example, workers can take messages from the group that explicitly or implicitly criticize the worker rather than the family for lack of progress in therapy. Families often respond by increasing their efforts to change and so 'rescuing' the worker from the group. Similarly, issues which, for various reasons, remain stubbornly covert in a family can be highlighted through a 'therapeutic debate' (Papp 1983). This involves reporting to a family that the reasons for and solutions to their problem were debated (with their permission) by the group. After discussion half of the members thought x while the other half thought y. The worker may adopt a neutral position on each point of view, facilitate discussion between family members, and undertake to represent the family's response to the group. Groups stressed that they could not have maintained the momentum for the family therapy approach had they remained as isolated individual practitioners.

It seems clear that the participants in these groups were able to begin practising family therapy due to collegial support and encouragement. There is every reason to suppose that others could benefit from similar groups. Careful consideration was given to the introduction of this approach to the agencies' clientele.

CLIENTS

The issues relating to clients have been considered in detail throughout this book. The points worth repeating here are: avoid blame; stress strengths; and develop routines which clients can see that the workers believe in; Contributors stressed that time spent on the mechanics of convening the first family session was well worth while. Attention to small details, such as invitation letters, finding a room and time, and learning how to operate technical equipment, was associated with well-conducted, worthwhile sessions. All contributors managed to find a suitable room after a period of time, though home visits continued to form a part of the work.

Finding an 'appropriate' family with whom to start was tackled in several ways. Some gave up the idea that there was such a thing and proceeded to work with the next new case referred. The Newcastle group did a lot of work with elderly clients and their families.

The Birmingham group, in consultation with the author, devised a split service that functioned as follows. The group of four involved in family therapy worked in pairs, allocating one afternoon each week to seeing families. They called this the family clinic, and it was held in the area office. If a family therapy worker was on duty when a client who seemed suitable for family therapy (mainly those with children's problems) came to the office the worker did not switch roles by attempting to persuade the family to accept him or her as a family therapist. Instead, the duty officer took the details of the problem, then informed the client that there was a specialist service available within the office for this kind of problem. They were given the name of one of the other family therapists and the telephone number. This cross-referral system meant that when a family rang the family therapy service the relationship was already defined. This effectively avoided the problem created if a duty officer attempted to persuade a family to accept family therapy. It switched the emphasis of motivation to the family. The number of families who were effectively engaged increased after implementation of this policy.

Some practitioners decided to remain in their more familiar role as social workers or probation officers but to change their method of working. The divorce court welfare officers are an example. Families referred for court reports were invited to go to the office for a meeting at which the divorced couple and their children would be present. Telephone queries and opposition to this method were met with polite and firm reassurances that this was how they worked. Initial reservations on the part of workers and families have been overcome with practice and this form of the practice is now common for these and other divorce welfare officers (see Guise 1983; Howard and Shepherd 1983; Shepherd, Howard, and Tonkinson 1984).

Adopting the title 'family therapist' may well hinder rather than facilitate the introduction of a new approach. When in doubt about this, it may well be politic to change the way you work rather than your job description. Viaro (1980) describes this approach, whereby therapy is carried out under the name of assessment, family meetings, feedback sessions, etc., as 'smuggling family therapy through'. The process may be better described as adopting a systemic approach to the agency task. The work emerging from these groups has to be considered within the context of their agencies. Their success or failure depended to a large extent on the way in which they related to those colleagues and management who were not members.

Surviving

The establishment of such innovative groups may be received in a variety of ways. People whose response requires special consideration include: other colleagues in the agency; administrative staff; and the wider professional network. Encouragement and praises were often accompanied by criticism and caution. Groups eventually found it most fruitful to consider all responses as part of an interactional process in a systemic framework. Workers must always remember that their behaviour could be prompting negative feedback from colleagues and management. Held comments astutely on this process when she says: 'Therapists must begin to perceive themselves as members of the systems in which they work and so as potential contributors to the ''resistances'' that may emerge' (1982: 40). With this thought in mind the reader might like to attempt the following exercise.

EXERCISE 11.1
Answer the following questions: What issues would most perturb your colleagues or management if family therapy were introduced into your agency setting? Who would be most likely to object to its introduction? How could these objections be overcome?

SUGGESTIONS
These and other such worries should be taken seriously: live supervision usurping existing supervisory roles; agency function and priority, being ignored; waste of time from two people working on one case.

Useful principles are: *observe* and *listen* for comments about family therapy; avoid immediate confrontation; prepare answers carefully; *consider* such problems systemically – ask yourselves what are we doing that makes them behave in this way?; *respond* in a way that shows you have taken their position seriously.

The following were the most common problems experienced by the groups and some of the solutions they found.

HOW TO RELATE TO COLLEAGUES: AVOID RAMPANT ENTHUSIASM

Constant enumerations of the virtues of family therapy began to be met with glazed looks from colleagues. Other practitioners in an agency may feel that the family therapy enthusiasts are disqualifying all other methods of working; then destructive rivalries may be formed. If appreciation of other models is shown, however, mutual respect may follow. Rather than evangelizing, some practitioners thought it better to wait until colleagues asked about the group's activities and then display a willingness to be helpful.

When a certain group had become established, its members found it useful to offer an occasional 'open day' for those colleagues who wanted help with a particular case but did not want to join the group permanently. This type of consultation became a regular feature in their office. It showed that family therapy was a useful resource for the agency as a whole and invalidated accusations of élitism.

In general, therefore, initiators are advised to adopt a complementary position on other approaches. This can be expressed by emphasizing the value of the traditional skills of other workers, making modest claims for a family approach, and being helpful to colleagues rather than adopting a 'missionary position' on family therapy. For example, when a colleague asks for your opinion, avoid implying in a superior fashion that 'family therapy can be used with all cases'. Offer advice based on systemic principles, giving practical suggestions on how to solve the immediate problem. For instance you might say, 'It can be helpful to get the family together before working with the boy on his own so that your individual work goes more smoothly', or 'In a case like this it can be useful if you adopt a one-down position to the authoritarian father and say that you are surprised that he is not more angry. Not many fathers would have stood by their sons in these circumstances.' If colleagues find this sort of advice helpful, then they may well become more interested in a systemic approach.

ADMINISTRATIVE STAFF

Asking families to come to the office instead of seeing them at home can be a considerable departure from traditional practice. The divorce conciliation (Birmingham) group wisely recognized that it might perturb the administrative staff who had not so far been required to register at the office families in the midst of divorce. In discussion, receptionists expressed anxieties about how couples would behave in the waiting room. Would they fight? Would there be crying children? If so, what should they do? These natural anxieties were overcome by explaining the new procedures, formalizing appointment times, devising new registration forms so that a reassuring routine was established, ensuring that the worker was available before the interview in cases of some emergency in reception, and showing receptionists the facilities and some work in progress. This approach was most successful and receptionists are now a useful source of information on such matters as how the family relate to one another while they are in the waiting area.

HOW TO RELATE TO MANAGEMENT

All contributors had taken definite steps to consider, inform, and engage their line managers while establishing their groups. Doubts and criticisms should be considered and positively reframed as natural caution, which is not an insurmountable barrier but can be useful in helping a group to reformulate ideas and restructure their practice. One group (Birmingham Social Services Department) anticipated criticisms that family therapy was a peripheral luxury, suitable only for those clients who were motivated. They demonstrated their approach through a role play at an area meeting; it was well received. Subsequently their plans were documented and submitted to management. A concrete proposal was made for a project on the use of a family therapy approach to tackle the problem of requests for reception into care. These proposals included details about: the amount of time needed as a percentage of the working week; review dates; an outline of the method couched in terms compatible with the agency ethos (for example, it was emphasized that the model was short term and focused on the resolution of problems). The area management team sanctioned the project. In retrospect the group felt it had been essential to base the projects in terms of agency priorities and within management rules.

Newcastle workers submitted regular progress reports that reached senior management. Eventually a working party was set up to consider the practice of family therapy within the department. This led, in time, to other progressive developments such as the release of staff for formal training, the allocation of a specialist post in family therapy, and the renting of premises and equipment solely for the practice of family therapy. Interestingly, the protagonists of family therapy chose not to assign a title such as family therapy 'centre' or 'institute' to the premises. They opted to use its ordinary street address, thus maintaining their non-pretentious profile in the eyes of both colleagues and clients.

Management were convinced by a combination of factors including persistent enthusiasm, judicious confrontation, realistic claims for what family therapy could do for the department, concrete proposals for implementation, and evidence that the approach worked. The process took five years of effort. It was evident that this kind of progress could only have been achieved in such a relatively short space of time by contributors investing a considerable amount of energy and personal time. A spirit of openness and collaboration had avoided some of the pitfalls created by secret coalitions.

The term 'live supervision' may, justifiably, make a manager worry that his or her position is going to be usurped by members of a group who may not even be on the department's staff. Permission should always be obtained and reassurances given that decisions in terms of agency policy and accountability will remain within the line management structure. Assurances should be given that live supervision will take place within a framework which has been agreed in general case supervision. Some practitioners use the term 'live consultation' to distinguish it from management supervision. In instances where a manager is part of the group then some issues can be dealt with more directly.

WIDER PROFESSIONAL NETWORK

The reverberations of the above changes were felt and responded to by the wider professional network of which the agencies are a part. The divorce conciliation team took time to explain to the courts and solicitors the reasons for their departure from the traditional investigative approach. Magistrates soon favoured the new approach. Gradually, fewer supervision orders were needed as parents were enabled to reach agreement regarding children's custody and access in a non-adversarial way. The systemic approach was seen as playing an important part in this trend.

Solicitors and barristers have been less quick to appreciate the benefits of a non-adversarial approach. The legal system is essentially based upon the principle that a solicitor represents the interests of one party who is in dispute with another. This aim contrasts with a systemic approach that seeks to facilitate agreement between the parties by direct negotiation rather than through a court-room battle. This team felt that their relationship with solicitors was improving (indeed they received referrals from some) but much work remained to be done in this area.

Similarly the responses of other practitioners in a professional network (such as health visitors, general practitioners, nursery nurses, residential workers, and educational welfare officers), whose work influences and is influenced by a family therapy group, must be considered if the practice is to survive. Not all professionals will, or indeed should, embrace a family therapy approach as eagerly as group

members. Timing and pacing are as important with other professionals as with families. The contribution of other professional groups
must be valued.

Development

The chapter has looked at how to initiate and consolidate the practice
of family therapy in agencies whose function is not designated as 'therapeutic'. It goes on to consider the progression of the different groups'
practice.

TRAINING

Most groups were initially self-trained, relying on literature, role play,
examination of audiotapes, and regular workshops organized by local
branches of the Association for Family Therapy. Significant progress
occurred when members attended formal training courses organized
by a local polytechnic or centres of family therapy training. Cleveland
emphasized that for many practitioners the formality of these courses
added a vital ingredient to their undoubted enthusiasm and natural
talent. They became able to express ideas more clearly and initiate
change in family systems in a more organized and effective way. Most
of those attending formal training courses initially felt deskilled but
they always appreciated the final benefits. Systemic feedback to colleagues was usually most effective.

Groups often organized introductory courses for beginners and
'brought in' outside expertise on particular problematic issues. Groups
also arranged for outside consultants to examine and comment on
their work. Line managers were always consulted and invited to participate in training exercises. Inclusion of management increased the
likelihood that new methods would be implemented.

NEW MEMBERS OF THE GROUP

Groups which survived tended to attract interested colleagues. Applications for membership were dealt with in a variety of ways. Birmingham Social Services Department engaged new members when people
left. Newcomers were eased into the group via a one-month planned
induction programme which included specified reading and observing

an experienced worker. Then they worked initially with a colleague of similar experience. Novices expressed their appreciation of this procedure.

The group adopted the motto 'organize or be organized' and took advantage of a departmental reorganization to ensure that all members of the duty team were also family therapy practitioners.

'Expelling' members was a more difficult but necessary task, in the case of those who never began to practise and had no other good reason for being part of the group. Cleveland and Newcastle developed a more fluid concept of the group's purpose. Founding members acted as consultants for colleagues on request from them and their manager.

FACILITIES

Most groups achieved their objective of obtaining videotape equipment within five years. One group had not set itself this aim and still relied on audiotaping, or did without tape altogether. Newcastle Social Services had actually rented adequate premises to utilize the videotape to its full potential. Responsibility for organizing this resource was delegated to the specialist family therapy group who in turn made it an open resource, offering a consultation service to colleagues across the city. The divorce conciliation team likewise operated a flexible, non-élitist policy.

An account of the progress of all these groups charts their efforts to replicate the standards of practice and facilities of the better-known centres for family therapy. Certainly all contributors acknowledged a debt to these centres for the initial stimulation and formal training opportunities provided. However, breaks from orthodoxy were required for these groups to fulfil their potential in their own context.

BEYOND ORTHODOXY

In general, adopting family therapy was in itself a distinct departure from orthodox practices in the helping professions. Family therapy has since developed its own orthodoxies represented by the various schools of practice. All groups went through a 'purist' phase during which their work was based almost exclusively on a particular model of family therapy. The clarity and rigour of those models espoused by Haley, Minuchin, the Milan group, and MRI was popular with all groups. One worker interviewed expressed the opinion of others when she said 'The confidence of having a clear model spreads into other areas of your work. It's a philosophy, not just a technique, and the family is just one system that we work with.' However, contributors eventually discovered that in order to build on initial (perhaps isolated) successes they needed to depart from the orthodoxy of family therapy. It was clear from their accounts that even successful variations in their chosen model were initially seen as evidence that they were 'not doing it properly'. Jenkins (1985) describes this phenomenon as orthodoxy becoming the tyrant rather than the servant of practice.

At the simplest level, overcoming orthodoxy meant workers introducing a new family therapy method into their work, learning its techniques, and thus broadening their therapeutic repertoire. Others brought in skills from other therapeutic models that could be used within a systemic framework. For example the techniques from psychodrama of doubling and role reversal were found to be especially useful in helping those families who had difficulty in expressing their opinions or feelings.

Changing recommended procedures was also useful. One group which had experienced difficulty in engaging families began to offer first appointments with a time gap of two weeks. Families felt they were being offered a special service and this increased their motivation to attend. But this was not appropriate for families in crisis: 'In this agency it seems that if we give a long time gap then we lose the impetus inherent in a crisis. We often achieve more change if the family are in crisis.' The initial feeling of being deskilled by a different model began to disappear once the workers realized that their previous skills could still be used within a systemic framework. While groups were going through a purist phase members frequently felt 'chastised' if they went outside the constraints of the model. One worker reported becoming frustrated by this, even though at a different level she appreciated the benefits accruing from an initial strict adherence to one model. She said that working in a tightly organized group made her feel that she was losing her individuality. Her innovative work was done 'in private' and was not at first shared with colleagues. Eventually she became so discontented that she brought her dilemma to the group. Two positive results of this were that the group took time to look at their own interactions, and sanctioned breaking with orthodoxy as a way of introducing original ideas. Essentially the groups moved between what Bateson

(1973) calls 'strict' and 'loose' thinking, that is between rigour and imagination. Bateson regards this as the essence of scientific advancement.

Both the Cleveland and Newcastle groups, having achieved their long-term aim of adequate premises complete with two rooms connected by a videotape link-up, came to regard this accommodation as a 'greenhouse' in which new ideas and skills were produced and cultivated. These ideas were then 'hardened off' in many different areas of their individual and joint work. The groups realized that although it was essential to learn the techniques of experts and use the technical equipment to develop such skills, the systemic approach was applicable to many other large areas of their work. Once they became aware of this, they could allow themselves to be innovative in ways that had not been possible for their original teachers. As Byng-Hall remarked 'the best therapy is done in your own agency, with your own clients, with your own colleagues and at your own pace' (1984).

Summary

The successful integration of a family therapy approach into an agency requires consideration of the agency's functions and its place within the professional community. This chapter has proposed that doubts and criticisms on the part of clients, colleagues, and hierarchy can be anticipated and are best regarded systemically as a natural homeostatic response in a transitional stage. They should not be seen as malevolent sabotage. Strategies for beginning, surviving, and developing have been offered from the experiences of groups who have overcome the typical difficulties of beginners. The following chapter looks at the work of these groups through specific case studies.

12
Applications of family therapy in social work practice

This chapter presents two quite different case vignettes illustrating contributors' use of a family therapy approach in their agencies. Important issues are highlighted including convening, impasse, and the use of different methods, as well as relating to colleagues, management, and other professionals. The material for this chapter was contributed by the practitioners named. It has been edited by the author.

Case study 1: Cleveland Social Services (North Division) (Sue Richardson (S.R.))

Issues affecting family work in a social services department are illustrated in the following case example (see *Figure 21*).

Following Allan's removal into care some months previously, Peter began presenting as beyond the control of his parent: he began to truant, steal, and bully his siblings.

COMPLEXITY AND CHRONICITY

This case could be seen as 'unsuitable' for family therapy. Family problems were long-standing and Mrs Nelson had established a relationship of dependence on social workers over a period of six years. Her family of origin were notorious as habitual clients of social services and were difficult to work with in any constructive fashion. Various workers had enthusiastically embarked on establishing a helping relationship with the family only to end up feeling drained and disillusioned. A repetitive

Figure 21

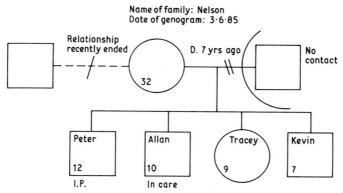

Name of family: Nelson
Date of genogram: 3·6·85

Relationship recently ended

32

D. 7 yrs ago

No contact

Peter
12
I.P.

Allan
10
In care

Tracey
9

Kevin
7

pattern was established whereby the more time, workers and energy that were allocated to the family, the more time, workers and energy were demanded by the family.

MAKING A DIFFERENCE

A case conference invited S.R. as an exponent of family therapy to help formulate a therapeutic strategy for this family. S.R. was then on a post-qualifying course in family therapy which involved the students' line managers. Among other advantages this involvement seemed likely to increase the commitment of management to the strategies employed in a systems-based approach to this family.

It was immediately recognized that the solutions previously attempted by the various helping agencies needed to be taken into consideration. To change the repetitive pattern of the Nelson family's response, it was considered important to alter the organization's pattern of response. Accordingly, the case conference decided not to offer residential care as a solution for Peter, thus attempting to avoid starting a 'revolving door' sequence in which the referral of Tracy and Kevin might follow.

RELATING TO COLLEAGUES

It is important not to appear to be disabling the work of colleagues. The existing worker was included in the initial session and contracted to liaise with Allan's residential unit, allowing S.R. to be responsible for work within the family.

'My role was defined from the start as a co-worker without taking over administrative responsibility for the case. I adopted a one-down position and my colleague was used as a helpful source of information about the family system. In my enthusiasm, however, I made the mistake of undervaluing my colleague's experience and local knowledge. This affected the work with the family since I was without important knowledge of how some of the other systems were operating until problems arose.'

The introduction of a family therapy approach perturbed the homeostatic balance of the prevailing family–professional relationships. The extent to which some members of the professional network had become enmeshed in the family system was not evident at the outset. For instance, one worker functioned as a go-between, passing on messages from the family to S.R. when they could not attend sessions. Engagement was successfully achieved only after this professional was detriangulated, as a result of a rule with the family that messages would only be received directly. Other similar experiences in subsequent cases led to greater attention being paid to gathering information about homeostatic alliances between professionals and family members. Clarification of professional roles and tasks is essential in such cases. In this particular case some professionals became allies and actively promoted the strategies advocated by S.R. Others maintained their usual practice, visiting frequently and undermining a family therapy approach. Attempting to overcome such actions by ignoring or discouraging them was, S.R. concludes, a systemic error. Those interventions which addressed the homeostatic process between family and professionals had the most beneficial results for the family.

WORKING WITH THE FAMILY

S.R. insisted on seeing the family at an Intermediate Treatment Centre. Sessions were tape recorded and the live supervisor sat in the room. 'I felt it was important to use a neutral venue, rather than the family home, to help in re-defining and structuring the work.' The emphasis in early sessions was on joining and problem exploration. Mrs Nelson's feelings of being overwhelmed were acknowledged.

THERAPIST. What have you tried to get Peter to do as he is told in the home?	Eliciting attempted solutions to problem.
MRS NELSON. I don't do anything. I just let him out for the sake of peace. He sits and stares at me and makes me feel awful so that I give in.	'Peace at any price.'
THERAPIST. I am very struck by how depressed and awful you feel.	Avoids asking 'how do you feel?' and plays a hunch: 'anticipatory empathy'.
MRS NELSON [eyes filling with tears]. I'm on tablets from the doctor – depression. I've been feeling bad.	

Mrs Nelson resisted the therapist's attempts to define Peter's 'not doing as he is told' in specific behavioural terms. She predicted that therapy would not work and could not/would not choose a focus.

The initial intervention began by a statement of respect for the efforts of the family. It continued by stating that to offer direct advice, at this stage, was not appropriate since the problems were long-standing and difficult. The worker expressed the need for time to think carefully about the family's difficult and complex situation.

Sometimes it is obvious that direct advice would be premature and would only be rejected; or a worker feels unable, within the time and information available, to construct an intervention. On such occasions the above message is usually acceptable and gives the therapist time to organize the information gained into systemic hypotheses or an intervention that fits a family's particular situation.

The worker's initial triadic hypotheses were:

1. Within the family: An enmeshed relationship between Mrs Nelson and the children in which Mrs Nelson was recruiting Peter to help her perform her parental tasks.
2. Between the family and professionals: Peter's problems were designed to ensure that Mrs Nelson was needed and to maintain the connection with outside help and support for the family.

The first session was followed by a frustrating period in which the family expressed dislike of the I.T. Centre and missed appointments. The family was twice reconvened via home visits – one with the educational social worker. Transport was provided for two further appointments (an example of the effort often needed to convene and engage difficult families).

'The work, however, did not really progress until I switched the venue to the family home on the understanding that furniture was rearranged and the live supervisor and tape recorder came too. This is not our usual practice but was helpful in this case. I learned that the important thing was not to be perfect but to keep thinking systemically.'

FOURTH SESSION

Structural interventions such as enactment and focusing were used to good effect in the early stages. Peter had stolen £10 from his mother during the past week. Mrs Nelson showed difficulty in being specific about the consequences of such misbehaviour and admitted to being inconsistent by 'giving in too easily'. She protested that 'he won't talk to anybody'. Such statements indicated an inappropriate hierarchy, with Peter in charge and Mrs Nelson disqualified as a parent. Mrs Nelson was therefore given instructions by the therapist which ignored her disqualification of herself.

THERAPIST. It's really important that you should talk to Peter now because I can see you're really determined to succeed and make a go of it. You've made such a good start but we've a sneaky feeling that something will happen to pull you down again, that Peter will find a way of getting round you and you will find it hard to stick to your word. It's important for you to tell Peter exactly what you want of him and what you expect him to do. Even if he doesn't talk, you can still tell him.

Peter was then moved to sit next to his mother, facing her, and the therapist repeated the instructions: 'Tell him exactly what you want of him over the next two weeks and exactly what you're going to do to make sure he does what he's supposed to.'

Allan, who was brought to these sessions from residential care, appeared to be observing this interaction intently and had to be prevented from interrupting while his mother spoke to Peter. Allan's seating position was moved further away from his mother. The therapist's persistence paid dividends and Mrs Nelson eventually made clear demands of Peter. Punishments and rewards were also discussed. Peter was then moved back to join the sibling subsystem. This demarcation of generational boundaries was further clarified when all four children were asked to occupy themselves together for the remainder of the session. The therapists congratulated Mrs Nelson on her achievements and created with her a list of expectations for the children in the coming weeks. This was pinned to the kitchen wall. This direct, task-centred family therapy was continued with some progress.

SUBSEQUENT SESSION

The atmosphere was more relaxed, the children running into the room and presenting as enthusiastic on arrival. Mrs Nelson was more talkative and less depressed. She began by reporting an improvement in Peter's behaviour which she linked with the previous session:

MRS NELSON. Things have been different since last week.

THERAPIST. How do you mean, different? Do you mean better?

MRS NELSON. Yes. I think it's because we were going to come here again and Peter didn't want anything said about him.
    Mother tries to give credit for the change to 'threat' of therapy.

THERAPIST. I'm interested to hear about these improvements. It must definitely be something you've done between you.
    Therapist defines change as coming from the family.

MRS NELSON. I dunno. The day before yesterday he said, 'Do you think I've been good Mam since I went to that meeting?' I haven't had to speak to him at all this week, he's been very good. I haven't had to tell him to do anything, he's just done it.
    Resists accepting praise for changes. Expands upon the improvements.

He seems to be a lot better
towards Tracy as well.

THERAPIST. Has he been more   Explores the concrete
helpful in the house? What   manifestations of change.
kind of things has he done?

MRS NELSON. I've hardly had to
do anything. Yesterday I went
shopping and when I came
back he'd done all the kitchen,
all the tops and everything.

The therapist responded by expressing pleasure but restraining the
family from changing too quickly.

NEXT SESSION

Mrs Nelson reported that Peter had been to school every day that
week. She attributed this change to a visit from the education social
worker. The therapist challenged this view by reframing Peter's
improvement as complementary to Mrs Nelson's behaviour, thus
establishing her in a parental executive function.

THERAPIST. It sounds to me like you've put your foot down. I get the
impression that you're standing up to Peter.

MRS NELSON. I've found out that upsetting myself all the time is not
doing any good. . . . I was just counting the bottles of pills I've got in
the kitchen the other day. I must have fourteen or fifteen bottles of pills
for nerves and one thing and another. I'm not taking anything now.

Mrs Nelson also reported that Peter and his siblings were going to bed
on time at her insistence and this had helped her to feel more competent. She related this change to the intervention made in session three.
She said 'I feel I'm the boss of the house now. Like you said, ''who's the
strongest between me and him''. Sometimes I used to think he was, but
now, he's starting to alter a little bit – not much like, but he is.'
    This family had begun to improve. Mrs Nelson, encouraged by the
therapist, began to take credit and therefore responsibility for the
changes. The inappropriate hierarchy of the family was effectively
restructured . This is often the point at which a therapist can begin to
think about withdrawing. In this case the initial improvements were

not sustained, however. In a subsequent session deterioration had set in. Mrs Nelson said:

> 'I feel as though I want Peter away from me because he's not going to change. As for you coming here, it's not going to work. I've been having social workers for near on eight years now and things have got worse. I know you're here to help me but Peter's all right for a fortnight and naughty for a fortnight. That's the way it's been going on all the time.'

Some workers prefer to continue with a direct, compliance-based approach, increasing the intensity in the ways described by Minuchin and Fishman (1981). It was decided by the support group that S.R. should seek a consultation with members of the post-qualifying course in order to obtain an alternative perspective. The family agreed to such a discussion taking place. This 'long-distance team' saw a repetitive pattern developing in the family–therapist system whereby the harder the therapist pushed the family to change, the more resolutely they stayed the same. The recommendation of the course was to repunctuate this sequence by asking the therapist to introduce a new move into this 'game without end'. Information gained in earlier sessions supported a hypothesis that Mrs Nelson felt antagonistic towards her family of origin and was determined to be more successful than them. Reversing this hypothesis provided a positive connotation of this family's failure to sustain change, making it evidence of loyalty to the extended family's tradition of failure and dependency. This rationale enabled the workers to reverse their usual position, stop pushing for change, and paradoxically prescribe the family's negative responses to therapy.

THERAPIST. I've often thought about what you said about your family, that you want to be different from them and you've worked very hard to be different.	Uses information from previous sessions related to belief system.
MRS NELSON. Oh I am, yes.	
THERAPIST. At the same time, I wonder. Although you're different in one way,	Introduces doubt and prepares the positive rationale for a paradoxical intervention.

underneath it's hard to be
different from your own family.
It's very hard to reject your own
family, even though you think
'I don't want to be like them,
I'm not like that'.

MRS NELSON. It's not that I
don't like my family, I do. It's
just, I've had a rough
upbringing. All the family's
been in trouble, every one of
them, even the lasses, you
know what I mean and I think
I've had that much of it, my
brother's been in prison and
my sister's on the game – you
know, and I think, well, I've
been trying to bring these up
different and all I can see in
these is my brothers, and it
hurts, because Allan's away
and Peter's heading the same
way.

Emphasizes the self-fulfilling
prophecy dictated by family of
origin.

THERAPIST. Yes, I know you feel
that, but at the same time,
underneath, although you
might not be aware of it,
people do feel bad about being
different from their own
families. When you say you
feel a failure in some ways,
although obviously you won't
realize it, maybe without
knowing it, you feel a lot more
comfortable being a failure
because it means you're not
different from your family.

She must remain a failure in
order not to be disloyal to her
family of origin.

MRS NELSON. Well I think I'm
the only one who's stood by

She begins to rebel at this
unacceptable rationale.

my kids. The others never
stood by their kids.

THERAPIST. But what I'm saying   The message is reinforced.
to you is: can you really
expect to be successful when
you consider the problems
you've got and what you've
been through in your own
life? Maybe change is
expecting a bit too much. Are
we expecting too much or
you, are you expecting too
much of yourself? It is what
you're used to, having all
these problems and I know it's
not comfortable in one way to
feel a failure but maybe in
some way you need to feel
that.

MRS NELSON. I think I've seen
that many problems in my
own family, like you said, I
think that's why sometimes I
can just shove it to one side.
Like the £10. I was mad just
for that day, then back to
normal, why cry over it?

This paradoxical intervention was typed out in detail (see Appendix V)
and a copy given to Mrs Nelson to study. It concluded that since it was
important that nothing should change, family therapy should end. It
was further recommended that the educational social worker and educational psychologist, the professionals who had been involved previously, should become reinvolved. Future visits by S.R. would be for
the non-specific purpose of monitoring the family's situation.

   Where unusual forms of interventions are used, particularly in a
statutory case, it is important to have regard to the existing systems of
accountability. Also the number of other systems involved increases,
e.g. residential workers for Allan who also visited the home.

Figure 22 Family and professional network

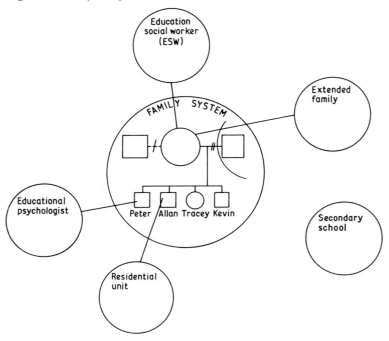

ROLE OF MANAGEMENT

This family graphically illustrates the essential role of management support in underpinning therapy. At the crucial point, the introduction of a strategic approach in the work, Mrs Nelson appeared before an education subcommittee regarding Peter's non-attendance at school; her explanation was that S.R. had been encouraging Peter to continue to misbehave and disobey his mother. This was endorsed by the educational social worker who endeavoured to provide an explanation of paradox to the committee. Although S.R. had been careful not to suggest that Peter should fail to attend school, the explanation contained sufficient truth to cause a potentially serious difficulty. Questions were asked by the elected representatives, including the Chairman of Social Services Committee, via the Director, and the chain of line management. Seniors dealt with this situation swiftly and competently, taking on the responsibility for providing the members with information while leaving S.R. free to continue work with the family. 'What proved invaluable was an existing commitment to systemic work developed by the District Director over a period of time, whose response was that of an ally.'

CARE OUTCOME

Peter's symptoms diminished as Mrs Nelson exerted more control in 'defiance' of the therapist's predictions that this could only result in disloyalty to her family of origin. Shortly after the end of the sessions Allan was returned home successfully. Three years later the family remains together, free of major problems. The social services department, however, remains part of the family system. Professionals who have perceived and defined a family as incompetent are often the most difficult people in the network to convince that change has taken place. This is a different order of problem which must be taken into account in the definition of 'success'. For a family to become independent from professionals and for professionals to relinquish control of families it is necessary that what constitutes sufficient change is clearly defined. Only in this way can both systems know when that stage has been reached.

SUMMARY

This vignette endeavours to demonstrate that family therapy may be used effectively with the kind of chronic problems that are common in a social work agency with statutory responsibilities. Adapting to less than 'ideal' circumstances, the workers introduced a 'difference that made a difference' into the family's usual 'attempted solution' by altering the agency's usual response of reception into care. The clear definition of professional roles was shown to be crucial to the successful engagement and therapy of a complex family and professional network.

Structural and strategic techniques were used to good effect in initiating change and overcoming impasse. Management support was vital for the worker's unusual initiative; this case illustrates the hazards to be negotiated by other workers and the need to retain the support of colleagues when introducing new methods of working. Finally it raises an interesting systemic question of the degree of difference sufficient to convince workers in an agency to relinquish control in their relationship with a family.

Case study 2: Birmingham divorce court welfare (Sheila Davies (S.D.))

Divorce may be described as an unexpected transitional stage in a family life cycle. The remit of divorce court welfare officers is to prepare a report for the divorce court in respect of families where the parents are in dispute about custody of or access to the children. Referrals come mainly from the divorce court and magistrates domestic court. A small proportion (between 5 and 10 per cent) are self-referrals or referrals from other agencies or from solicitors' pre-court hearings. Traditionally this service is organized on an investigative basis with an individual officer interviewing each of the 'contestants' in their homes to assess their suitability in terms of parenting ability and material standards. An officer is then expected to reach a conclusion as to which is the better parent to have custody of the children, what access the non-custodial parent should have, and so on. Essentially this process conforms to an adversarial model, which, as Francis points out:

> 'is at odds with one of the implicit assumptions of conciliation – that decisions relating to children are the responsibility of their parents. The legal process can allow those involved to collude in making various counter-assumptions: that after separation, one parent needs to be identified as better than the other; that parents themselves are incapable of making appropriate decisions about their children; that outside ''experts'' are capable of seeking out the ''correct'' decisions; and that divorce and separation somehow confer an automatic right on society to put one's abilities as parents under the microscope.'
> (Francis *et al.* 1983)

Guise (1982) credits the pioneering work of such independent services as the Bristol Family Court's Conciliation Scheme in initiating a shift towards a process based on conciliation. Subsequent work by the probation service has extended this concept by including children in conjoint interviews with both parents. Guise proceeds by stating emphatically that 'We believe it is essential to have the children present; in their absence there is the hazard of them becoming merely prizes to be bargained for' (Guise 1983: 58). The emphasis is on enabling separating couples to resolve residual marital issues so that they can remain effective parents. Specific family therapy techniques are found to be particularly useful in this work. However, for the purpose of clarity the Birmingham group have found it more useful to think of their work as a systemic approach to divorce conciliation since family therapy might give the impression that they are trying actively to reunite the family.

The last chapter outlined the basic procedures involved in convening the separating family; further details can be found in the works of Guise (1983), Howard and Shepherd (1983), Shepherd, Howard, and Tonkinson (1984) and Robinson and Parkinson (1985). The following case example presents some of the practical issues involved in its application.

ENDING OF MARRIAGE CEREMONY

Friedman (1980) points out that divorce is an increasingly important nodal point in the life cycle of families. He mentions that several religious groups (the Jewish tradition began 1,500 years ago) have experimented with the creation of a divorce ceremony as a 'rite of passage' through this stage. The next vignette has been included because it represents, to the best of my knowledge, an original contribution to techniques designed to help professionals clarify relationship issues. The account emphasizes two important points: first, that an approach which is seeded and nurtured in the 'greenhouse' can be useful in the least ideal situations; second, that originality often stems from an imaginative and inspired break from orthodoxy. Most of the expected stages in the life cycle are commissioned by rites of passage designed to facilitate the process by clearly dissolving old definitions and initiating new ones. A concept familiar to those involved in work with divorcing or divorced couples is the 'non-emotional divorce'. This suggests that, despite a physical and/or legal divorce, one or both partners (and almost certainly the children) harbour the hope that the family will be reunited; persisting failure to agree over custody and access may well perform the function of keeping these hopes alive. Divorce, like other unexpected stages, does not have the benefit of an established ritual. A legal declaration may not be adequate to end the emotional connections between a couple. This example shows how such a ritual was 'invented'.

Figure 23

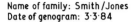

Name of family: Smith/Jones
Date of genogram: 3·3·84

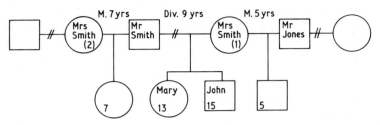

THE PROBLEM

The couple were divorced and both had remarried. There had always been problems over arrangements for Mr Smith's access to the children. The latest dispute occurred when the former Mrs Smith (now Mrs Jones) said that her daughter Mary did not want to spend her two-week holiday with Mr Smith (her father). Mr Smith travelled from Derby to Birmingham and demanded that Mary should go with him. Mrs Jones had sent Mary to friends. An argument took place and Mr Smith left very angrily threatening to smash the home up.

THE REFERRAL

Mr Smith contacted his solicitor who suggested attendance at In Court Conciliation in Birmingham where the children lived. At the court proceedings Sheila Davis (S.D.) was the conciliation officer on duty. The 'contestants' were referred to her by the judge.

THE INTERVIEW

Twenty minutes later she interviewed the couple in the Court Chambers. The room was large, carpeted, and curtained, with a large desk on which was a leather blotting paper desk set. The officer positioned three chairs in a small circle away from the desk.

The couple remained in deadlock about the issue of Mary going to visit her father. The worker hypothesized that Mrs Jones was afraid she would lose Mary to the new Mrs Smith, as she had lost her husband to her. At one period there was a long silence during which both looked extremely sad. Mr Smith broke the silence, saying to Mrs Jones 'Does this room remind you of anywhere?' She did not answer but looked sad. He said 'The Registry Office where we got married.' She responded with the *non sequitur* 'When do you want to see John?' Access arrangements were then made for John to visit Mr Smith at half term but no progress was made on the access arrangements for Mary.

Gradually the worker developed a hypothesis based on the verbal and non-verbal clues evident in the session: 'I felt very strongly that this couple, even though they had both remarried and produced other children, had not let go of their marriage' (non-emotional divorce). The following description is in the worker's own words:

'I stood up, and asked Mr Smith and Mrs Jones to stand, said to them both "You may think I am stupid because of what I am about to do." I then took both of their hands in mine and held them at my side, I looked at both of them and said "All special events in our lives have some form of ceremony: weddings; christening; twenty-first birthday; graduation; and following death, a funeral and a period of mourning; but when a marriage ends, nothing; sometimes anger, hurt, pain, sadness, hatred, all mixed together but no ending ceremony." I had brought their hands up to my waist height with me still holding them. I then said I would like them to look at each other and Mrs Jones to say the following: "Goodbye to you Fred as my husband and hello to you in your relationship as just father to our children. I will remember the good things of our previous relationship and I wish you well." And the same to be said by Mr Smith to Mrs Jones.

During this part of the ceremony, I am bringing their hands together, but at first making sure my hand is between them (as in the one potato, two potato hand game). When the first person starts the sentence I remove both my hands and put one on each shoulder of the couple, giving them strength; they are holding hands.

When both of them had finished they were still holding hands. I left the room. When I returned a few minutes later they were both sitting down looking shy. Mr Smith was the first to speak. He said how moving he had found the experience. Mrs Jones then said how right I was about ceremonies for everything, except divorce. She then laughed and said the only ceremony they had was when she threw Mr Smith's case out of the front door when he said he was leaving. Mrs Jones said to her ex-husband, "When you collect John at half term Mary will also be ready to go with you, if that is OK by you." This was a spontaneous comment by Mrs Jones, I had not mentioned access.'

The interview and ceremony took about thirty-five minutes. It was the first time S.D. had met this couple. Another interview was offered for further conciliation but was not required as access was operating successfully.

POST-SESSION ANALYSIS

S.D.'s hypothesis regarding the problem over access was that Mrs Jones was afraid that Mary was growing up and would want to live with her father and stepmother; therefore she would lose not only her husband to the other woman, but also her daughter – a very serious fear.

Mr Smith was a big man, a coal miner, and his only form of retaliation was aggression. Observations of the couple indicated that there was a lot of sadness around the ending of the marriage.

Mr Smith gave S.D. the cue for the ceremony when he said how much the room reminded him of the Registry Office when the couple were married. The couple were helped to redefine their relationship as Mother and Father, not Husband and Wife.

DISCUSSION

This ritual was introduced to the other members of the team and is used regularly though not routinely. It can be described as an amalgam of sculpting, enactment, and ceremony. Imaginative readers will recognize other situations where such a 'service' might be useful, for example when a child is stillborn, when an old person is leaving home to take up residence elsewhere, or when a family find a traditional ceremony is not congruent with their personal belief system.

PROCEDURE AND HINTS FOR PRACTITIONERS

The following summarizes the guidelines to practitioners offered by S.D. (See also those already offered for action techniques.)

1.   Listen for verbal statements and observe non-verbal signals that represent clues about the emotions surrounding the 'unexpected'

transition, such as the sadness when the Registry Office was mentioned.

2. Choose words syntonic for the client, and which you feel comfortable with.

3. Be aware of the tactile sensation as you take the couple's hands and move them closer. Listen to the tone of their voices when they make their statements. Be sensitive to the responses when you place your hand on the couple's shoulders.

4. You should feel comfortable during the experience. It can be a very emotional event for everyone and you will need to be prepared to experience strong emotions. 'Don't be afraid to share tears with them.'

5. Timing is extremely important and you must be guided by intuition. Sometimes it will feel right in the first interview or it may be appropriate to wait until a later session.

6. A ritual will not be appropriate in all cases. If a ceremony does not achieve a clear definition, it nevertheless reveals a great deal to both the worker and the couple. For instance it may show distinctly which parent is having most difficulty (or the way in which each member of the couple is experiencing difficulty) in emotionally relinquishing the marital relationship. The episode itself may have the effect of sowing seeds for future work with the couple.

7. A cautionary note: Workers should be alert to the possibility of a couple wishing to reconcile their marriage after the ceremony. In this event a worker should adopt a cautionary stance and the couple should be seriously warned that it really may be premature. If a couple are persistent in their wish to reconcile, then counselling should be offered. Only a small proportion of those who considered remarrying actually did so.

SUMMARY

This case demonstrates the contributor's contention that the principles of a systemic approach can be useful in day-to-day practice without the advantages of the technical hardware. It also perhaps illustrates paradoxically that the security gained by having a clear method enables workers to break the rules of the method and be innovative.

Summary

Important points and comments have been summarized at the end of each chapter throughout this book. This chapter therefore will emphasize some of the most important steps in the applications of family therapy.

Important steps in taking a systemic approach seriously

A coherent systemic framework has been presented for the practice of family therapy. This framework can help practitioners to gain a useful perspective of interlocking interactional patterns which co-evolve over time. It proposes that these patterns are maintained by both the beliefs and behaviours, in a recursive fashion, of those involved in their co-evolution. It explains how problems are likely to arise and be maintained during nodal transitional stages in the development of a family system. It suggests ways in which practitioners can trigger changes by intervening at various levels of a system so that a family can overcome the problem and continue on its developmental course. The potential advantages of such an approach are more likely to be realized if practitioners are mindful of the following points.

(1) Remember that the theoretical schema put forward by a systemic approach to family therapy is not proposed as the 'true' or complete explanation of all human dilemmas. Nor does it pretend to be a panacea for all the problems facing the helping professions. For example, Bruce, writing about his work with the chronically 'disturbed and

disrupted' families of children in a secure unit, reminds us that 'To expect such families to engage in formal family therapy without first going through a phase of helping them to feel secure within the Centre is like giving a starving child a lecture on vitamins' (1982: 509). Bruce points out the wisdom of expanding the view of a problem situation to include the family, the centre staff, and any other professionals involved.

(2) Maintain the skills that have sustained your practice to date. Introduce new concepts and skills in the order and at a pace that best suits you. Inevitably practitioners experience some discomfort or the feeling of being deskilled when using novel techniques, especially when they are competent in another model of working. Too sudden or dramatic a change in their style may also be alarming for clients and colleagues.

(3) Choose a model, concept, or skill and master it before proceeding to another. This method promotes the process of 'learning to learn' and may help to avoid the confusion inherent in the tendency to hop from one model to another. Those for whom it is important to be eclectic may find it is more fruitful to be able to choose from a repertoire of techniques in which they develop competence rather than selecting from a wide range of skills with which they are only superficially acquainted.

(4) Create, maintain, and value co-operative relationships in your work setting. Avoid alienating your colleagues through the overuse of family therapy terms that may be more appropriate in a different agency. Explain systemic concepts in the language of your own work setting and in ways that highlight its potential for your agency.

(5) When there are problems with integrating this approach into your agency it is important to include in a systemic analysis your own beliefs and behaviour. The situation indicated by the oft heard statement: 'I can't do family therapy because my colleagues/management/clients won't let me' can be repunctuated by practitioners asking themselves the following questions:

a)   'What am I doing that prompts my colleagues/management/clients to behave/think in this way?'
b)   'How can I behave differently so that colleagues/management/clients can allow integration to progress?

c) 'How is it functional (useful) to me for integration not to proceed smoothly?'

d) 'What are the triadic relationships involved in this particular impasse?'

The answers to these questions can help create a different perspective on your dilemma and open up more useful avenues of action.

(6) Work hard on creating viable co-working relationships. Joint activities often aid the development of such a relationship. For example, simultaneously reading the same articles and books, and attending workshops together will help a mutual understanding of concepts and skills, leading to more effective teamwork.

(7) Initially, at least, work with systems within your comprehension. Applying systemic thinking to a wide range of systems may be an aesthetically attractive proposition but can be pragmatically immobilizing if attempted too soon. Concepts such as transitional stages, interactional sequences, and punctuation can be used to analyse whatever system is under consideration. For those practitioners not regularly working with families it might be a good starting point to complete a family tree with an individual, plot the transitional stages that have taken place in a staff group, or analyse the interactional sequences between themselves and the client they consider they are helping the least.

(8) Gradually include systems other than the family in your thinking. As you become competent at recognizing and describing interactional patterns, positively reframing, and initiating change with family systems you may then gain sufficient confidence to work with other systems in this way. For example, you could look at how the interaction within a school and between that school and a family helps to maintain a child's non-attendance, or you could analyse the emergence of problems in a home for the elderly in terms of transitions in the staff group.

(9) Evaluate what you do. Kniskern and Gurman (1980) surveyed family and marital therapy outcome studies and concluded that the approach was demonstrating encouraging results. It is important that the criteria used for evaluation is, in part if not completely, aimed at eliciting information on how useful the approach is in achieving agency

goals. Assistance in constructing outcome studies may be obtained by contacting the Association for Family Therapy (research sub-committee) (see Appendix I)

(10) Make constructive challenges to traditional views. About twenty-five years ago family theory and therapy challenged the view that human problems were either primarily a manifestation of a person's intra-psychic disposition or the result of 'faulty' learning. A family approach came to be regarded by many as one of the most exciting theoretical and practical innovations to appear in the sphere of the helping professions for some considerable time.

In many therapeutic and academic centres the once-novel approach of family therapy has become a traditional method of working, produc-ing conventions and orthodox practices that are necessary for ideas and skills to be clearly and effectively disseminated. However, the con-tinued evolution and usefulness of a family/systemic approach also depends on innovative practitioners working in agencies outside the clinical/academic system.

There is evidence that this is happening. In 1977 Sue Walrond-Skinner, an acute observer of and participant in the family therapy field, wrote a paper describing the indications and contra-indications for family therapy (1981b). Writing as a practitioner in an exclusively therapeutic agency she contra-indicated many of the severe problems faced by those working in generic health and social services agencies. Yet, practitioners working in non-exclusive agencies (and therefore with less choice about what type of problem they work with) have since begun to develop applications of a family/systemic approach that were not thought possible by pioneers such as Walrond-Skinner. There-fore, although practitioners should not regard a family/systemic approach as a panacea for all problems, there may be areas of develop-ment not yet explored.

The above points are not an exhaustive list of important issues. They can be regarded as useful guidelines to becoming a practitioner who has the conceptual and practical abilities to work with the various interlocking systems of which practitioners and their clients are a part. It is important that these steps continue to be elaborated in ways that are most relevant for the reader in working with his or her colleagues for their clients in their agencies.

Appendix I: Training resources in family therapy

There is a growing number of opportunities for professionals who wish to become familiar with a family therapy approach and also for those who want to proceed to formal training. The following is a list of organizations that offer training opportunities at various levels.

The Association for Family Therapy

This is a national association with the aims of promoting the scientific study, practice, research, and teaching of family therapy. The Association has regions and branches throughout the country which bring together people from all professional disciplines who are concerned with the care or treatment of families. Many branches offer a varied programme of workshops and courses for practitioners (including non-members) at different levels of interest and experience. Details about your nearest branch can be obtained from: Mrs Pauline Jenkins, Administrative Secretary, 6, Heol Seddon, Danescourt, Llandaff, Cardiff CF5 2QX.

Training institutions

The following organizations offer a variety of clinical and training services:

The Scottish Institute of Human Relations (Ltd)
56, Albany Street, Edinburgh EH3 3QR. Tel. 031 556 6454.

Royal Edinburgh Infirmary
Dr J. Evans. Young People's Unit, Lauriston Place, Edinburgh, EH3 9YW.

Newcastle-upon-Tyne Polytechnic
Ruth Reay, Faculty of Community and Social Studies, Northumberland Buildings, Northumberland Road, Newcastle-upon-Tyne NE1 8ST.

The Charles Burns Clinic
Mrs Christine Neal (Secretary), Centre for Postgraduate Psychiatry, Family Therapy Programme, Queensbridge Road, Moseley, Birmingham B13 8QD. Tel. 021 449 4481.

The Child and Family Service (Shropshire)
Course Tutors (Family Therapy), The Monklands, Abbey Foregate, Shrewsbury, Shropshire. Tel. 254561.

The Tavistock Clinic
Training Secretary (Family Therapy), Department for Children and Parents, 120, Belsize Lane, London NW3 5BA.

The Institute of Family Therapy (London) (Ltd)
Training Secretary, 43, New Cavendish Street, London W1. Tel. 01 935 1651.

The Family Institute (Cardiff)
105, Cathedral Road, Cardiff CF1 9PH. Tel. 26584/28747.

Kensington Consultation Centre (London)
The Administrator, 9, Hayes Court, Camberwell New Road, London SE5 0TQ. Tel 01 708 0899.

The Maudsley Hospital
Dr Justin Schlicht, Family Therapy Course Director, Psychotherapy Unit, The Maudsley Hospital, Denmark Hill, London SE5 8AZ. Tel. 01 703 6333.

The Marriage and Family Institute (Dublin)
The Administrator, 6, North Frederick Street, Dublin 1. Tel. 725034.

University of Birmingham
Extra Mural Department, Winterbourne, Edgbaston Park Road, Edgbaston, Birmingham. Tel. 021 472 1301.

University of Kent at Canterbury
The Organizing Secretary, Social Work, Health Service and AITU Courses, The School of Continuing Education, Rutherford College, The Univerity, Canterbury, Kent CT2 7NX Tel. 0227 66822.

Training tapes (audio and video)

The following institutions hire tapes of clinical material edited and narrated for teaching purposes:

Institute of Family Therapy (London)
Address above

Philadelphia Child Guidance Clinic
Two Children's Centre, 34th Street and Civic Center Boulevard, Philadelpha, PA 19104, USA. Tel. (215) 243 2722.

Mental Research Institue
Offer audiotapes of their conference series 1979–85. INFOMEDIX, c/o MRI Conference Series Listing, 12800 Garden Grove Blvd., Suite F, Garden Grove, California 92643, USA.

Appendix II: Invitation/ appointment letters

Letter to convene a family system

The following is the letter which is used routinely to invite families for their first interview at our Family Clinic.

Agency name
and address

Dear . . . .

We have heard from . . . [referrer's name] . . . about the difficulties that your family is having at the present time and we have been asked to give our opinion.

We find it most helpful if we see the whole family, for the first interview at least. So if you have other children, or anyone else living with your family, could they also come along and join in the discussion.

We can offer your family an appointment on [date] at [time] at the Charles Burns Clinic.

Would you please return the enclosed postcard within one week. If we do not hear from you by then, we shall assume that you do not want the appointment and we shall offer it to another family on the waiting list.

Yours Sincerely,
[Therapist's name]

This letter is periodically amended when our experience suggests that changes in our procedures are necessary.

Letter to convene a family and professional system

When we are aware that another professional is closely involved with a family either in a voluntary or statutory capacity our usual procedure is to invite that professional to at least the first interview. The letter to the family contains a paragraph stating that:

> We understand that . . . . is closely involved with your family and so have invited them to attend this first interview.

The letter to the professional states that:

> Dear . . . .
>   Re: the . . . . Family
> We understand that you [and perhaps the department] have been involved with the above family for some time. We have offered the . . . . family an appointment on [date] at [time] at the Charles Burns Clinic. It would be most helpful if you could attend at that time also to participate in the discussion with the family. The family are aware that you have been invited to attend the interview.

Non-routine letters

Inevitably there are new, unusual, or different situations which require a letter to be constructed according to the nature of the request, the family set up, or legal situation. For example, our work with sexually-abused children and their families involves situations where one or both parents has no access to the child(ren), due to bail conditions or imprisonment. Our initial convening procedures include letters to Prison Governors and the courts in order to establish a therapeutic regime at the earliest possible opportunity.

Appendix III: Pre-session questionnaires

Each first appointment letter from the Family Clinic includes two forms. Form I is standard to the clinic as a whole. Form II gathers 'Additional Information for The Family Clinic'.

Form I

requests factual information about:
The name, address, dates of birth, and school of the identified patient and other children in the family. Names, dates of birth, and occupations of both parents, plus the date of marriage.

Form II

ADDITIONAL INFORMATION FOR THE FAMILY CLINIC

1. If you have anybody living in your home apart from those mentioned on the other sheet, please list them below.

Name   *age*   *Relationship to Family*

2. Has anybody recently left your home?
    If yes, please specify:

3. Has anyone recently come to live in your home?
    If yes, please specify:

4.   Have there been any deaths in your family recently?
     If yes, please specify:

5.   Please give a brief description of your present problem(s).

6.   Are you receiving help for this or any other problem from anyone
     else?

Who wrote this account?

When families return these two forms they often provide valuable
information about the family composition and indicate transitional
stages in the family's life cycle (expected and unexpected). This data is
most useful in the hypothesizing stage of the pre-session preparation.
Agencies may wish to develop forms to gather information which is
more pertinent to their particular task and function.

Appendix IV: Videotape consent form

Agency name and address

THE FAMILY CLINIC – VIDEOTAPE CONSENT FORM

During our considerable experience in the Family Clinic, the team have found that the use of videotaped recordings is an invaluable aid in our work with families. It is also sometimes useful in our training programme.

Please read the following paragraphs and, if you are in agreement, sign where indicated.

1. We consent to videotapes being made of these sessions and to these tapes being used to aid the team's work with our family.

Dated .... *Signed* ....
....
....
....

2. We consent to the excerpts from these recordings, or descriptions of them, being used by the Charles Burns Clinic staff for the purposes of research and/or teaching.

We understand that the Charles Burns Clinic staff will edit out from these recordings, or from descriptions of the recordings, as much identifying information as is possible.

Dated .... *Signed* ....
....
....
....

On behalf of the Charles Burns Clinic, I undertake that, in respect of videotapes made with the above family, every effort will be made to ensure professional confidentiality and that any use of videotapes, or descriptions of videotapes, will be for professional purposes only and in the interests of improving professional standards through research or training programmes. Every effort will be made to protect the anonymity of all those involved in the sessions.

Dated .... *Signed* ....
Member of the Charles Burns Clinic

The above is the videotape consent form currently used in the Family Clinic at The Charles Burns Clinic (Birmingham). As with all our procedural documents it has been produced through a process of trial and error. Earlier versions were directly based on the form used at the Family Institute (Cardiff). This version differs from the earlier form in several respects, most notably in that it explicitly offers families a choice between the uses to which the taped material will be used: option 1 alone, or 1 and 2.

Note Readers should be careful to adapt this form to their particular agency and its purpose.

When using tapes for teaching purposes our standard introduction includes the statement that:

'Our agreement with families permits us to use tapes for teaching to professional audiences. If anyone in the audience knows this family in a non-professional capacity would they please indicate this as they would not be allowed to participate in the viewing or discussion of the taped material.'

The Institute of Family Therapy (London) uses a written version of the above which has to be signed by each member of any audience which views taped material.

Appendix V: Verbatim letter from case description in Chapter 12

S.R. (the family therapist) had in a previous session asked Mrs Nelson to describe 'All the things I would do if Peter wasn't a problem'. Mrs Nelson listed many activities including: 'Develop hobbies; Join a slimming club; Do things with my own and other people's children, like before; Get dressed up and look good; Go out in the evening; Get closer to my boyfriend [she had recently ended this relationship]; Settle down with him or someone else; Have Allan [the child in care] home; Do without social workers and be a ''happy go lucky person'' like before.'

S.R.'s letter was as follows:

Dear Mrs Nelson,

    I have spent a lot of time thinking very carefully about your situation and consulting with colleagues who are experts. Together we have come to the following conclusions which we feel are important enough to write down for you to study and remember.

    We are very touched by how much affection there is between yourself and the children and how protective you are to one another in your family. We are amazed at how you struggle against the odds with Peter and go on seeking advice from social workers and others although it has never worked. We are quite moved that you are prepared to go on trying and failing all the time. We think that this is likely to go on indefinitely and that you will always need help from at least one social worker and as many other people as possible for as long as we can see.

We think that Peter has got the idea in his mind that you cannot cope with everyday things in life. He imagines that you are frightened you will fail and become just like other people in your own family. We think that, although he does not realize it, by behaving the way he does, Peter is trying to protect you from failure and get you the help he thinks you need from other people. We think you are quite capable of managing without help but Peter doesn't. Although we see you as a capable person, Peter knows you better than we do. He has information that we don't and so we think it is important for him to carry on behaving the way he does because he understands you better. He has sacrificed his relationship with you in order to help you and so we think it is important for him to continue in the same way for the time being.

Another worry we think Peter may have is about your boyfriend. We have an idea that Peter thinks it is too soon for you to be thinking of getting serious with anyone again and that you can't cope with friendships. We have noticed the way he plays up to protect you from getting too involved with Ronny and we think he should continue to do this for the time being so that you don't have to run the risk of another failed relationship.

We are very struck by what a lively and imaginative person you are. You have a lot of talents to choose from if you wanted a life of your own. I enclose a list of all the things you mentioned in our last discussion to show you what we mean. I hope you will not be too upset by being reminded that you cannot put any of them into practice because of your problems with Peter. You may be tempted to try but please remember that what Peter is doing is to help you and you should avoid everything else for the moment.

We think that you should go on getting as much advice as possible and should listen to whatever other people have told you. I intend to ask Mrs Marshall [educational psychologist] to start visiting you again since you cannot be expected to manage on your own. I will also tell Mrs Bradley [educational welfare officer] to visit as often as possible when Peter is off school.

We think it is vital that nothing should change for the time being until Peter is convinced that you can cope. It would be wrong for us to continue our sessions to try to get things to change. However, because I have enjoyed seeing you, I would like to pop in, in a month's time, just to say hello to you and the family.

Yours sincerely, [S.R.]

References

Ackerman, N.W. (1958) *The Psychodynamics of Family Life*. New York: Basic Books.
—— (1966) *Treating the Troubled Family*. New York: Basic Books.
—— Adams, R. and Hill, G. (1983) The Labour of Hercules. Some Good Reasons Why Social Workers Should not Try to be Different and Practise Family Therapy. *Journal of Family Therapy* 5:71–80.
Ainley, M. (1984) Family Therapy in Probation Practice. In A. Treacher and J. Carpenter (eds) *Using Family Therapy*. Oxford: Blackwell.
Anderson, C.M. and Stewart, S. (1983) *Mastering Resistance: A Practical Guide to Family Therapy*. New York: Guildford Press.

Barker, P. (1981) *Basic Family Therapy*. London: Granada.
Bateson, G. (1971) A Systems Approach Evaluation of Family Therapy. *International Journal of Psychiatry* 9: 242–44.
—— (1973) *Steps to an Ecology of Mind*. St Albans: Paladin.
—— (1979) *Mind and Nature: A Necessary Unity*. London: Fontana.
Bateson, G., Jackson, D.D., Haley, J., and Weakland, J. (1956) Towards a Theory of Schizophrenia. *Behavioral Science* 1: 251–54.
Beels, C. and Ferber, A. (1969) Family Therapy: A View. *Family Process* 8: 2.
Bell, J.E. (1967) Family Group Therapy – A Treatment Method for Children. In G.D. Erickson and T.P. Hogan (eds) (1972), *Family Therapy – An Introduction to Theory and Technique*. Monterey, Calif.: Brooks/Cole.

Bentovim, A. (1979) Theories of Family Interaction and Techniques of Intervention. *Journal of Family Therapy* 1: 4.

Bentovim, A., Gorell Barnes, G., and Cooklin, A. (1982) (eds) *Complementary Frameworks of Therapy and Practice* vol. 2. Academic Press/ Grune & Stratton

Berger, M., Jurkovic, G.J., and Associates (1984) *Practising Family Therapy in Diverse Settings*. San Francisco: Jossey-Bass.

Breunlin, D. and Cade, B.W. (1981) Intervening in Family Systems with Observer Messages. *Journal of Marital and Family Therapy* 7: 453–60.

Bruce, T. (1982) Family Work in a Secure Unit. In A. Bentovim, G. Gorell Barnes, and A. Cooklin (eds) *Family Therapy: Complementary Frameworks in Theory and Practice*. London: Academic Press.

Burnham, J.B. (1979) *Minuchin and Milan: A Comparison of the Theory and Practice of Salvador Minuchin's Structural Therapy and the Milan Version of Strategic Therapy*. (Dissertation submitted at the Family Institute, Cardiff (in press).

Burnham, J.B. and Harris, Q. (1985) Therapy, Supervision, Consultation Different Levels of System. In D. Campbell and R. Draper (eds) *Applications of Systemic Family Therapy: The Milan Approach*. London: Academic Press.

Byng-Hall, J. (1980) The Symptom Bearer as Marital Distance Regulator: clinical implications. *Family Process* 19: 355–65.

—— (1984) Personal communication.

Cade, B.W. (1980) Resolving Therapeutic Deadlocks Using a Contrived Team Conflict. *International Journal of Family Therapy* 2: 253–62.

—— (1984) Paradoxical Techniques in Therapy. *Journal of Child Psychology and Psychiatry* 25: 509–16.

—— (1985) Unpredictability and Change: A Holographic Metaphor. In G. Weeks (ed.) *Promoting Change through Paradoxical Therapy*. Homewood, Ill.: Dow Jones-Irwin.

Cade, B.W. and Seligman, P.M. (1982) Teaching a Strategic Approach. In R. Whiffen and J. Byng-Hall (eds) *Family Therapy Supervision: Recent Developments in Practice*. London: Academic Press.

Campbell, D. and Draper, R. (eds) (1985) *Applications of Systemic Family Therapy: the Milan Approach*. London: Academic Press.

Carpenter, J. and Treacher, A. (1982) Structural Family Therapy in Context: Working with Child Focused Problems. *Journal of Family Therapy* 4: 15–34.

—— (1983) On the Neglected Arts of Convening and Engaging Families and Their Wider Systems. *Journal of Family Therapy* 5: 337–58.

Carpenter, J., Treacher, A., Jenkins, H., and O'Reilly, P. (1983) 'Oh No! Not the Smiths Again!' An Exploration of How to Identify and Overcome 'Stuckness' in Family Therapy. Part II. Stuckness in the Therapeutic and Supervisory Systems. *Journal of Family Therapy* 5: 81–96.

Carter, E.A. and McGoldrick, M. (1980) *The Family Life Cycle*. London and New York: Gardner Press.

Coleman, S.B. (ed.) (1984) *Failures in Family Therapy*. New York: Guildford Press.

Cooklin (1979). Personal communication.

Coppersmith, E.I. (1981) 'Developmental' Reframing: He's not Bad, He's not Mad, He's Just Young! *Journal of Strategic and Systemic Therapies* 1: 1–11.

Cronen, V., Johnson, K.M., and Lannaman, J.W. (1982) Paradoxes, Double Binds and Reflexive Loops: An Alternative Theoretical Perspective. *Family Process* 21:91–112.

Cronen, V. and Pearce, B.W. (1985) Toward an Explanation of How the Milan Method Works: An Invitation to a Systemic Epistemology and the Evolution of Family Systems. In D. Campbell and R. Draper, *Applications of Systemic Family Therapy: The Milan Approach*. London: Grune Stratton.

Dale, P., Davies, M., Morrison, T., and Waters, J. (1986) *Dangerous Families – Assessment and Treatment of Child Abuse*. London: Tavistock Publications.

Dale, P., Morrison, T., Davies, M., Noyes, P., and Roberts, W. (1985) A Family Therapy Approach to Child Abuse: Countering Resistance. *Journal of Family Therapy* 5: 117–44.

Dare, C. (1979) Psychoanalysis and Systems in Family Therapy. *Journal of Family Therapy* 1: 137–53.

Davies, M., Waters, J., Dale, P., Morrison, T., and Roberts, W. (1985) *Promoting Change with Child Abuse Families – Protection Before Therapy*. Rochdale: Rochdale Child Abuse Training Committee.

de Shazer, S. (1982) *Patterns of Brief Family Therapy: An Ecosystemic Approach*. New York: Guildford Press.

—— (1984) The Death of Resistance. *Family Process* 23: 11–17.

Dimmock, B. and Dungworth, D. (1983) Creating Manoeuvrability for Family Systems Therapists in Social Services Departments. *Journal of Family Therapy* 5: 53–69.

—— (1985) Beyond the Family: Using Network Meetings with Statutory Child Care Cases. *Journal of Family Therapy* 7: 45–68.

Douglas, J. (1979) Behavioural Work with Families. *Journal of Family Therapy* 1: 371–83.

—— (1981) Behavioural Family Therapy and the Influence of a Systems Framework. *Journal of Family Therapy* 3: 327–39.

Dungworth, D. and Reimers, S. (1984) Family Therapy in Social Services Departments. In A. Treacher and J. Carpenter (1984) (eds) *Using Family Therapy*. Oxford: Blackwell.

Erikson, E.H. (1979) *Identity and the Life Cycle*. New York: W.W. Norton.

Fisch, R., Weakland, J.H., and Segal, L. (1982) *The Tactics of Change: Doing Therapy Briefly*. London and San Francisco, Calif.: Jossey-Bass.

Foley, V.D. (1974) *An Introduction to Family Therapy*. New York: Grune Stratton.

Francis, P., *et al.* (1983) Mightier than the Sword? *Social Work Today* 14: 17.

Friedman, E.H. (1980) Systems and Ceremonies: A Family View of Rites of Passage. In E.A. Carter and M. McGoldrick (eds) *The Family Life Cycle: A Framework for Family Therapy*. New York: Gardner Press.

Furniss, T. (1983) Family Process in the Treatment of Intrafamilial Child Sexual Abuse. *Journal of Family Therapy* 5: 263–78.

Gillman, M. (1983) A Framework for Introducing Family Therapy into a Social Services Area Team. A dissertation submitted to the Charles Burns Clinic, Family Therapy Training Programme.

Gorell Barnes, G. (1980) Family Therapy in Social Work Settings: A Survey by Questionnaire, 1976–78. *Journal of Family Therapy* 2: 357–78.

—— (1984) *Working with Families*. British Association for Social Work. London: Macmillan Education.

Grunebaum, H. and Chasin, R. (1982) Thinking like a Family Therapist: A Mode for Integrating the Theories and Methods of Family Therapy. *Journal of Marital and Family Therapy*.

Guerin, P. (1976) Family Therapy: The First Twenty-Five Years. In P. Guerin (ed.) *Family Therapy: Theory and Practice*. New York: Gardner Press.

Guerin, P. and Guerin, K. (1976) Theoretical Aspects and Clinical Relevance of the Multigenerational Model of Family Therapy. In P.J. Guerin (ed.) *Family Therapy: Theory and Practice*. New York: Gardner Press.

Guise, J. (1983) Conciliation: Current Practice and Future Implications for the Probation Service. *Probation Journal* 30: 2.

Haley, J. (1963) *Strategies of Psychotherapy*. New York: Grune Stratton.
—— (1973) *Uncommon Therapy: The Psychiatric Techniques of Milton H. Erickson, M.D.* New York: W.W. Norton.
—— (1975) Why a Mental Health Clinic Should Avoid Family Therapy. *Journal of Marriage and Family Couselling* 1: 3–13.
—— (1976) *Problem Solving Therapy*. New York and London: Harper Colophon.
—— (1980) *Leaving Home*. New York: McGraw-Hill.
—— (1984) *Ordeal Therapy*. San Francisco, Calif.: Jossey-Bass.

Hartman, A. (1979)*Finding Families: An Ecological Approach to Family Assessment in Adoption*. London: Sage.

Held, B. (1982) Entering a Mental Health System: A Strategic-Systemic Approach. *Journal of Strategic and Systemic Therapies* 1: 40–50.

Herr, J.J. and Weakland, J.H. (1979) *Counselling Elders and Their Families: Practical Techniques for Applied Gerontology*. New York: Springer.

Hildebrand, J., Jenkins, J., Carter, D., and Lask, B. (1980) The Introduction of a Full Family Orientation in a Child Psychiatric In-Patient Unit. *Journal of Family Therapy* 3: 139–52.

Hoffman, L. (1981) *Foundations of Family Therapy*. New York: Basic Books.

Howard, J. and Shepherd, G. (1983) Conciliation – New Beginnings? *Journal of the National Association of Probation Officers*, September: 87–92.

Hudson, P. (1980) Different Strokes for Different Folks: A Comparative Examination of Behavioural, Structural and Paradoxical Method in Family Therapy. *Journal of Family Therapy* 2: 2.

Iveson, C., Sharps, P., and Whiffen, R. (1979) A Family Therapy

Workshop: A Review of a Two Year Experiment in a Social Services Department. *Journal of Family Therapy* 1: 397–408.

Jackson, D.D. (1967) The Eternal Triangle: An interview with Don D. Jackson. In J. Haley and L. Hoffman (eds) *Techniques of Family Therapy*. New York: Basic Books.

Jenkins, H. (1985) Orthodoxy in Family Therapy Practice as Servant or Tyrant. *Journal of Family Therapy* 7: 19–30.

Jenkins, J., Hildebrand, J., and Lask, B. (1982) Failure: An Exploration and Survival Kit. *Journal of Family Therapy* 4: 307–20.

Jordan, W. (1972) *The Social Worker in Family Situations*. London and Boston: Routledge & Kegan Paul.

Kingston, P. and Smith, D. (1983) Preparation for Live Consultation and Live Supervision when Working without a One-Way Screen. *Journal of Family Therapy* 5: 219–33.

Kniskern, D. and Gurman, A. (1980) Clinical Implications of Recent Research in Family Therapy. In L. Wolberg and M. Aronson (eds) *Group and Family Therapy*. New York: Brunner Mazel.

Kramer, Sebastian (1981) Personal communication.

Lau, A. (1984) Transcultural Issues in Family Therapy. *Journal of Family Therapy* 6: 91–112.

Lederer, W.J. and Jackson, D.D. (1968) *The Mirages of Marriage*. New York: Norton.

Lewis, J.P., Beaver, R., Gossett, J.T., and Phillips, V.A. (1976) *No Single Thread: Psychological Health in Family Systems*. New York: Brunner Mazel.

Lindsey, D. (1979) Working with Rage and Anger – the Establishment of a Therapeutic Setting in the Homes of Multi-problem Families. *Journal of Family Therapy* 1: 117–25.

McGoldrick, M., Pearce, J.K., and Giordano, J. (1982) *Ethnicity and Family Therapy*. New York: Guildford Press.

Madanes, C. and Haley, J. (1977) Dimensions of Family Therapy. *Journal of Nervous and Mental Disease* 165: 2.

Manor, O. (ed.) (1984) *Family Work in Action: A Handbook for Social Workers*. London and New York: Tavistock Publications.

Minuchin, S. (1974) *Families and Family Therapy*. London: Tavistock Publications.

Minuchin, S. and Fishman, C. (1981) *Family Therapy Techniques*. Cambridge, Mass.: Harvard University Press.

Minuchin, S., Rosman, B.L., and Baker, L. (1978) *Psychosomatic Families: Anorexia Nervosa in Context*. Cambridge, Mass.: Harvard University Press.

Minuchin, S., Montalvo, B., Guerney, B.G., Rosman, B.L., and Schumer, H. (1967) *Families of the Slums: An Exploration of Their Structure and Treatment*. New York: Basic Books.

Napier, A.Y. (1978) (with Whitaker, C.A.) *The Family Crucible*. Cambridge, Mass.: Harvard University Press.

O'Brien, C. (1984) Personal communication.

O'Hagan, K. (1984) Family Crisis Intervention in Social Services. *Journal of Family Therapy* 6: 149–81.

Palazzoli, M.S. (1980) Why a Long Interval between Sessions. In M. Andolfi and I. Zwarling (eds) *Dimensions of Family Therapy*. New York: Guildford Press.

—— (1983) The Emergence of a Comprehensive Systems Approach. *Journal of Family Therapy* 5: 165–77.

—— (1984) Behind the Scenes of the Organisation: Some Guidelines for the Expert in Human Relations. *Journal of Family Therapy* 6: 299–308.

Palazzoli, M.S. and Prata, G. (1982) Snares in Family Therapy. *Journal of Marital and Family Therapy* 8: 443–50.

Palazzoli, M.S., Cecchin, G., Prata, G., and Boscolo, L. (1978) *Paradox and Counterparadox*. New York: Jason Aronson.

—— (1980a) Hypothesizing – Circularity – Neutrality: Three Guidelines for the Conductor of the Session. *Family Process* 19: 3–12.

—— (1980b) The Problem of the Referring Person. Family Process. *Journal of Marital and Family Therapy* 6: 3–9.

Papp, P. (1980) The Greek Chorus and Other Techniques of Paradoxical Therapy. *Family Process* 19: 45–57.

—— (1983) *The Process of Change*. New York: Guildford Press.

Papp, P., Silverstein, O., and Carter, E. (1973) Family Sculpting in Preventive Work with Well Families. *Family Process* 12: 197–212.

Penn, P. (1983) Circular Questioning. *Family Process* 21: 267–80.

Pincus, A. and Minahan, A. (1973) *Social Work Practice. Model and Method*. Itasca, Ill.: Peacock.

Pottle, S. (1984) Developing a Network-Orientated Service for Elderly People and Their Carers. In A. Treacher and J. Carpenter (eds) *Using Family Therapy*. Oxford: Blackwell.

Reder, P. (1983) Disorganised Families and the Helping Professions: 'Who's in Charge of What?' *Journal of Family Therapy* 5: 23–36.

Reiss, D. (1971) Varieties of Consensual Experience: A Theory for Relating Family Interaction to Individual Thinking. *Family Process* 10: 1–28.

—— (1981) *The Family's Construction of Reality*. Cambridge, Mass., and London: Harvard University Press.

Ritterman, M. (1977) Paradigmatic Classification of Family Therapy Theories. *Family Process* 16: 1.

Robinson, M. and Parkinson, L. A Family Systems Approach to Conciliation in Separation and Divorce. *Journal of Family Therapy* 7, 4: 357–77.

Rohrbaugh, M., Tennen, H., Press, S., White, L., Raskin, P., and Pickering, M. (1977) Paradoxical Strategies in Psychotherapy. Paper presented at the American Psychological Association, San Francisco, Calif.

Satir, V. (1964) *Conjoint Family Therapy*. Palo Alto, Calif.: Science and Behaviour Books.

Scott, R.D. and Starr, I. (1981) A 24-Hour Family-Orientated Psychiatric and Crisis Service. *Journal of Family Therapy* 3: 177–86.

Shepherd, G., Howard, J., and Tonkinson, J. (1984) Conciliation: Taking it Seriously. *Journal of the National Association of Probation Officers*, March 1984: 21–4.

Skynner, R. (1976) *One Flesh: Separate Persons*. London: Constable.

Sluzki, C. (1978) Marital Therapy from a Systems Theory Perspective. In T. Paolino and B. McCrady (eds) *Marriage and Marital Therapy*. New York: Brunner Mazel.

Smith, D. and Kingston, P. (1980) Live Supervision without a One-Way Screen. *Journal of Family Therapy* 2: 379–87.

Spark, E. (1974) Grandparents and Intergenerational Family Therapy. *Family Process* 13: 225–37.

Specht, H. and Vickery, A. (eds) (1977) *Integrating Social Work Methods*. National Institute Social Services Library, No. 31. London: George Allen & Unwin.

Speed, B. (1984) Family Therapy: An Update. *Association for Child Psychology and Psychiatry Newsletter* 6: 2–14.

Speed, B., Seligman, P., Kingston, P., and Cade, B. (1982) A Team Approach to Therapy. *Journal of Family Therapy* 4: 271–84.

Speer, D.C. (1970) Family Systems: Morphostasis and Morphogenesis or 'Is Homeostasis Enough?' *Family Process* 9: 3.

Stanton, M.D. and Todd, T.C. (1981) Engaging 'Resistant' Families in Treatment. *Family Process* 20: 261–93.

Teismann, M.W. (1980) Convening Strategies in Family Therapy. *Family Process* 19: 393–400.

Tomm, K. (1982) The Milan Approach to Family Therapy: A Tentative Report. In Freeman, D. *et al.* (eds) *Treating Families with Special Needs*. Ottawa: Canadian Association of Social Workers.

—— (1984a) One Perspective on the Milan Systemic Approach. Part I: Overview of Development, Theory and Practice. *Journal of Marital and Family Therapy*, April 1984.

—— (1984b) One Perspective on the Milan Systemic Approach. Part II: Description of Session Format, Interviewing Style and Interventions. *Journal of Marital and Family Therapy*, July 1984.

—— (1984c) Personal communication.

—— (1985) Circular Questioning. In D. Campbell and R. Draper (eds) *Applications of Systemic Family Therapy: The Milan Approach*. London: Academic Press.

Tomm, K.M. and Wright, L.M. (1979) Training in Family Therapy: Perceptual, Conceptual and Executive Skills. *Family Process* 18: 227–50.

Treacher, A. and Carpenter, J. (1982) 'Oh No! Not the Smiths Again!' An Exploration of How to Identify and Overcome 'Stuckness' in Family Therapy. Part I: Stuckness Involving the Contextual and Technical Aspects of Therapy. *Journal of Family Therapy* 4: 285–306.

—— (eds) (1984) *Using Family Therapy*. Oxford: Blackwell.

Viaro, M. (1980) Case Report: Smuggling Family Therapy Through. *Family Process* 19: 35–44.

Von Bertalanffy, L. (1968) *General System Theory*. New York and London: Penguin.

Walrond-Skinner, S. (1976) *Family Therapy: The Treatment of Natural Systems*. London and Boston: Routledge & Kegan Paul.

—— (1981a) Introduction to S. Walrond-Skinner (ed.) *Developments in Family Therapy: Theories and Applications since 1948*. London: Routledge & Kegan Paul.

—— (1981b) Indications and Contra-Indications for the Use of Family Therapy. In S. Walrond-Skinner (ed.) *Developments in Family Therapy: Theories and Applications since 1948*. London: Routledge & Kegan Paul.

Watzlawick, P. (1978) *The Language of Change: Elements of Therapeutic Communication*. New York: Basic Books.

Watzlawick, P. (1983) *The Situation is Hopeless but not Serious: The Pursuit of Unhappiness*. New York: Norton.

Watzlawick, P. and Beavin, J. (1977) Some Formal Aspects of Communication. In P. Watzlawick and J. Weakland, *The Interactional View: Studies at the Mental Research Unit 1965–74*. New York: W.W. Norton.

Watzlawick, P., Beavin, J., and Jackson, D.D. (1967) *Pragmatics of Human Communication: A Study of Interactional Patterns Pathologies and Paradoxes*. New York: W.W. Norton.

Watzlawick, P., Weakland, J., and Fisch, R. (1974) *Change: Principles of Problem Formation and Problem Resolution*. New York: Norton.

Whitaker, C. (1976) The Hindrance of Theory in Clinical Work. In P.J. Guerin (Jr) (ed.) *Family Therapy: Theory and Practice*. New York: Gardner Press.

—— (1984) Proceedings of a two day conference with Carl Whitaker. Organized by The Institute of Family Therapy (London).

Name index

Subject index